WHAT NOW

WHAT NOW

Everyday Endurance and Social Intensity
in an Australian Aboriginal Community

Cameo Dalley

berghahn
NEW YORK • OXFORD
www.berghahnbooks.com

First published in 2021 by
Berghahn Books
www.berghahnbooks.com

© 2021, 2024 Cameo Dalley
First paperback edition published in 2024

All rights reserved. Except for the quotation of short passages
for the purposes of criticism and review, no part of this book
may be reproduced in any form or by any means, electronic or
mechanical, including photocopying, recording, or any information
storage and retrieval system now known or to be invented,
without written permission of the publisher.

Library of Congress Cataloging-in-Publication Data

Names: Dalley, Cameo, author.
Title: What Now : Everyday Endurance and Social Intensity in an Australian Aboriginal Community / Cameo Dalley.
Other titles: Everyday Endurance and Social Intensity in an Australian Aboriginal Community
Description: New York : Berghahn Books, 2021. | Includes bibliographical references and index.
Identifiers: LCCN 2020017518 (print) | LCCN 2020017519 (ebook) | ISBN 9781789208856 (hardback) | ISBN 9781789208863 (ebook)
Subjects: LCSH: Aboriginal Australians—Australia—Mornington Island (Qld.) | Mornington Island (Qld.)—Ethnic relations.
Classification: LCC GN667.Q4 D34 2020 (print) | LCC GN667.Q4 (ebook) | DDC 305.899/150943—dc23
LC record available at https://lccn.loc.gov/2020017518
LC ebook record available at https://lccn.loc.gov/2020017519

British Library Cataloguing in Publication Data

A catalogue record for this book is available from the British Library

ISBN 978-1-78920-885-6 hardback
ISBN 978-1-80539-717-5 paperback
ISBN 978-1-80539-904-9 epub
ISBN 978-1-78920-886-3 web pdf

https://doi.org/10.3167/9781789208856

Contents

List of Illustrations	vi
Acknowledgements	viii
Notes on Text	xi
List of Abbreviations	xiii
Introduction A Return	1
Chapter 1 Locating the State	22
Chapter 2 Whitefellas and Blackfellas	52
Chapter 3 Contemporary Aboriginal Family	89
Chapter 4 Alcohol Management and Violence	126
Chapter 5 Connections to Land and Sea	164
Conclusion Many Returns	205
Appendix Residential Survey 2010	211
References	213
Index	231

Illustrations

Figures

0.1.	Aboriginal children with school teacher Lucy at the Mornington Island Mission, 1936.	6
1.1.	Aboriginal children and Aboriginal mission staff at the Mornington Island Mission, 1936.	26
1.2.	Reverend Wilson leads a church service at the Mornington Island Mission, 1936.	27
2.1.	Gate and fencing on the northern side of the hospital compound.	63
2.2.	Example of Queensland Police Service House.	65
3.1.	Genealogy showing the relationship between a man and his de facto partner (in grey) identified in a 'straight' subsection relationship.	101
3.2.	Genealogy showing the relationship between a teenage couple (marked in grey) described as 'too close'.	102
3.3.	Houses of the Middle families, February 2010.	109
3.4.	Genealogy showing the distributions of residences for the Middle families in February 2010. Two couples, Tom and Jean and Sue and Ian, are used as exemplars and focal points to describe interactions within the broader extended network.	110
4.1.	Lelka Murrin Tavern licensing and rules, March 2008.	135
4.2.	Plan of the Pub grounds, March 2008.	137
4.3.	Front entrance to the Pub (entrance door on left) with notice board listing those 'barred off'. Note the security camera at top right, pointed towards the exit gate.	148

5.1.	Map showing the area of sea claimed (inside the continuous line) and granted (inside the dotted line) during the Wellesley Sea Claim.	168
5.2.	Genealogy showing the derivation of country from a classificatory grandfather.	173
5.3.	Genealogy showing relationships surrounding an Aboriginal man (in grey).	174
5.4.	Genealogy showing the transmission of country affiliations among a close group of kin. Those in grey were born in places other than traditional Kaiadilt country.	177
5.5.	Genealogy showing the ways in which Ian, Sue (marked in grey) and their children derived country affiliation.	179
5.6.	Cyril Moon talks to the Wellesley Islands Rangers about country, September 2007.	183
5.7.	Genealogy of a typical day out bush, identifying which kin shared cooking fires.	185
5.8.	Children cooking and eating mud shells that they had helped to collect during a trip out bush, June 2009.	187
5.9.	Plaque on Bentinck Island commemorating the establishment of Stage One Outstation at Main Base, *Nyinyilki*.	199

Table

4.1.	Reasons for off-Island mobility, based on author observations.	153

Acknowledgements

Research for this book commenced and drew to a close during a period of notable change in the development of policy guiding the lives of remote-living Aboriginal people in Australia. During this time, I was very fortunate to spend over eighteen months living on Mornington Island. Over the last fifteen years the Aboriginal residents of Mornington Island have allowed me into their lives and the most intimate of family moments, entrusting me with their memories, experiences and hopes for the future. I sincerely hope that this book is a fitting testament to the spirit of that shared experience.

On Mornington Island, particular thanks to Trisha Evans and Sean Linden, Katrina Watt and Kevin Scholes, and Bradley Wilson, and all of their children and extended families. More often than not it was these families waiting for me at the airstrip when I arrived and it was they who were the last ones frenetically waving me off as my plane departed. Thanks also to Sasha Binjari, Lawrence Burke and Jane Wilson, Mrs Mary Cameron (dec.), Mrs Annie Chong, Karen Chong, Maxwell Gabori and Linda Jingles, Sarah Isaacs, Aaron Kelly and Kym Roughsey, Jade Linden, Delma Loogatha and Tommy Wilson, Dirk Loogatha, Gerald Loogatha and Hazel Roughsey, Wade Loogatha, Mrs Alma Moon (dec.), Mr Teddy Moon and Mrs Bessie Moon, Karla Nathan and Neville Reading (dec.), Shontelle Reid, Lucy Rogers, Cedric Scholes, Ezra Scholes, Jenny Sewter, Roxanne Thomas, Michelle Watt, and Alfred Williams and Margo Dundaman, and all of their children and extended families. I have many fond memories of time on Bentinck Island with Mrs Netta Loogatha, Mrs Dolly Loogatha, Mrs Amy Loogatha, Mrs May Moodoonuthi (dec.), Mrs Ethel Thomas and Mrs Paula Paul. The tenacity of these women in their senior years reminds me of my late maternal grandmother Mrs Mary Dalley (née Leake), and I think of them all often.

In particular I thank Mr Cyril Moon, who taught me first-hand about Aboriginal family by orienting me in the local kinship idiom as his classificatory daughter. Cyril has had an extraordinary life, growing up 'out bush' in the 1940s and then in the mission dormitories, before becoming a father, mission policeman, film star, and later in life a cultural educator. The breadth of Cyril's life experiences and his knowledge of Lardil culture and language has made him an ideal mentor in all manner of contexts. Above all, he has been a reliable fishing companion with a wily sense of humour, with whom I have shared many laughs. I remember our times together with great fondness and appreciation. You be the squid, and I'll be the rat.

Thanks to the *marndagi* (Whitefellas) that I got to know on Mornington Island, especially David Barnes, Dave and Trudy Ives, David Lloyd, Michael and Julie Maat, Jo Manton, and Phil Venables. Outside academia, many friends have nurtured and supported me along the way, though I make special mention here of Kate Adams, Andrew Evans, Adrienne Neilson and Mark Collins, Michael and Louise O'Neill, Sally Potter, and Paul Wood and Mia Garthon.

Thanks to the staff at Berghahn Books, in particular my editor Tom Bonnington and production editor Caroline Kuhtz. I gratefully acknowledge the opportunities afforded by various grants and funding from the University of Queensland. Thanks to Professor Paul Memmott, whose historical knowledge and connections on Mornington Island were invaluable. Time and the intellectual space for writing was provided by the McArthur Postdoctoral Fellowship at the University of Melbourne and the Australian Research Council Discovery Indigenous project IN180100055 'Beyond Recognition: Strengthening Relationality Across Difference in Postcolonial Contexts' at the Alfred Deakin Institute for Citizenship and Globalisation at Deakin University. Thanks to Adrienne Neilson, Daniel Rosendahl, Joel Tarling and Sean Ulm for their assistance with the production of figures.

The realization of this work as a book is attributable in large part to the support and intellectual nurturance that I received over many years from Emeritus Professor David Trigger and Emeritus Professor Nicolas Peterson. Both instilled in me the importance of tackling difficult questions, and in different ways both have encouraged me to see the value of my research and the importance of sharing it with a broader audience.

Over the last fifteen years colleagues at various institutions have become close friends, and their own intellectual accomplishments have been the source of inspiration to me in charting my own trajectory. Thanks to Kalissa Alexeyeff, Ash Barnwell, Rose Butler, John Carty, Brendan Churchill, Simon Correy, Billy Griffiths, Melinda Hinkson, Emma Kowal, Tess Lea, Ian Lilley, David F. Martin, Pam McGrath, Francesca Merlan, Monica Minnegal, John Morton, Sana Nakata, Tim O'Rourke, Yin Paradies, Thao Phan, Diana Romano, Erich Round, Alan

Rumsey, Tori Stead, Sean Ulm, Eve Vincent and Elizabeth Watt. As it relates to this book, particular thanks are owed to Amanda Gilberston, Kelly Greenop, Catie Gressier, Richard Martin, Tim Neale and Daniel Rosendahl, who at different points in time have been unwavering in their encouragement. Jill Lang has been a much-loved part of my family for as long as I can remember. We cherish our memories of Katie 'Boo' Jackson Lang (1981–1997). Finally, thanks to my parents Liz Dalley and Tony Gleeson, and my brother Alex Dalley. Their continuing support and unconditional love have propelled this book forward at every turn.

Notes on Text

Photographs

Aboriginal people are advised that this book contains images of people who are now deceased.

Pseudonyms

In the vast majority of cases, David McKnight, who wrote four books about Mornington Island (1999, 2002, 2004, 2005), opted for the use of real names to identify Aboriginal research participants, including in some of the most sensitive material, such as about sorcery and disputes. It was also the case that the majority of his ethnographic material was published substantially after it was collected, some of it over thirty years later, meaning that many of the people McKnight referred to were deceased at the time of publication.

During my research many Aboriginal people indicated a preference for their real names to be used. However, particularly in examples of large family groups, the use of individuals' names would jeopardize the anonymity of others, especially when such individuals are described in reference to their kinship relationships with one another. In considering the right to privacy for those who requested not to be named, I have opted for the use of pseudonyms in place of people's actual names and have made the use of pseudonyms for specific individuals consistent throughout.

Although attempts have been made to alter the descriptions of specific events to obscure the identities of those concerned, it is unavoidably the case in a small community that some individuals will be identifiable to those who know Mornington Island intimately. It is primarily for this reason that I have chosen (with his permission) to identify my main interlocutor, Mr Cyril Moon, a senior Lardil man. In doing so, I have tried to ensure that his identification did not unduly compromise the anonymity of others, even when they have been referred to using a pseudonym.

Orthography

Where available, the orthography for place names, especially those on Mornington Island, is taken from McKnight (1999), while spelling for other words comes from the Lardil (Ngakulmungan Kangka Leman Language Project Steering Committee 1997) and Kayardild dictionaries (Evans 1992).

Abbreviations

ABS	Australian Bureau of Statistics
ADBT	Aboriginal Development Benefits Trust
AMP	Alcohol Management Plan
CDEP	Community Development Employment Projects (Mornington Island)
CMC	Crime and Misconduct Commission
COAG	Council of Australian Governments
CYWR	Cape York Welfare Reform
GCA	Gulf Communities Agreement
LGRC	Local Government Reform Commission
LIP	Local Implementation Plan
LIPA	Local Indigenous Partnership Agreement
MIRJ	Mornigton Island Restorative Justice
MSC	Mornington Shire Council
NNTT	National Native Title Tribunal
ORIC	Office of the Registrar of Indigenous Corporations
PCYC	Police Citizens' Youth Club (Mornington Island)
PLO	Police Liaison Officer
SEAM	Improving School Enrolment and Attendance through welfare reform Measure
TAFE	Technical and Further Education

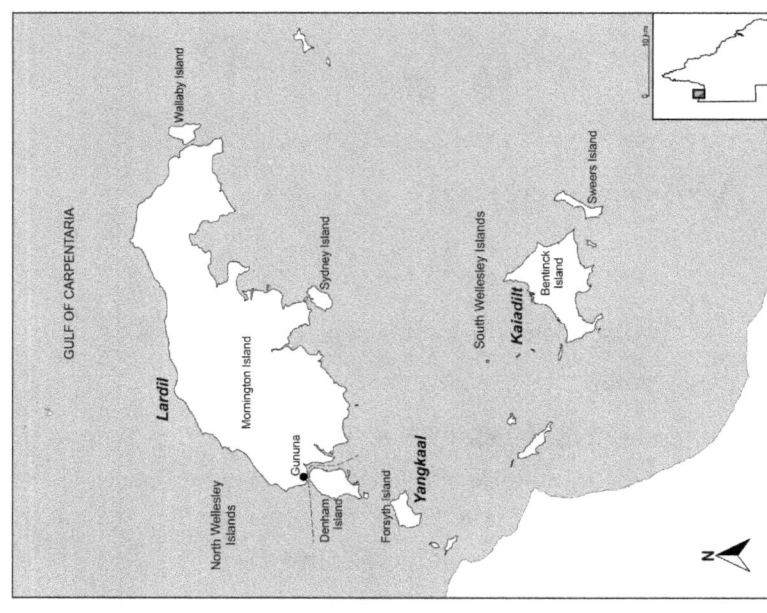

Towns and Aboriginal communities around the southern Gulf of Carpentaria (created by the author).

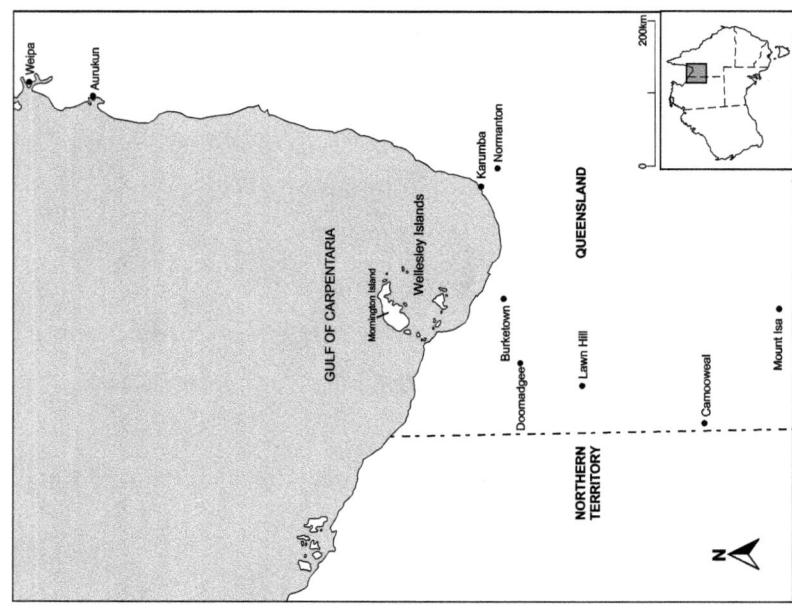

The Wellesley Islands, southern Gulf of Carpentaria showing Aboriginal territorial affiliations by language group in italics (created by the author).

Plan of Gununa, Mornington Island (created by the author).

Introduction

A Return

In Australia's far north, heat greets a visitor like a warm hug, enveloping the body as it exits an air-conditioned aeroplane. It's still some time from what is known as the 'Wet', and residents here will have months of the 'build up' left to contend with before the clouds open and monsoon storms bring sweet relief. For now, I'm covered in sweat, beads springing forth across the bridge of my nose and rivulets forming, running between my shoulder blades, and down the backs of my legs. Waves of heat rise from the tarmac where a small aeroplane waits, baking in the midday sun, and blow towards the small building where a small number of passengers sit on rows of plastic chairs. I'm returning to the small Aboriginal community of Mornington Island in the Gulf of Carpentaria in northern Australia, a very remote island that I have been visiting since 2006 (see first map in the frontmatter). The small commercial plane in which I'm travelling departed from the Australian east-coast city of Cairns, and is now making a brief stop in the small town of Normanton before flying on to the island community. My fellow passengers are the usual mix of Aboriginal people and government workers from the range of service delivery agencies across the region.

The flight attendant calls 'all aboard' and those making the onwards journey from Normanton to Mornington Island trudge across the tarmac and resume their seats for take-off. After crossing the Australian mainland coast, the plane heads out over the ocean, and soon the Wellesley Islands will become visible below. Though located in northern Australia, the Gulf of Carpentaria does not have the crystal-clear turquoise waters of the iconic Great Barrier Reef, known to many from postcards and tourist advertisements. Instead, circulatory tides push and pull sediments, creating pastel-cloudy waters reminiscent of milky tea, but a keen eye can recognize the signs of life that teems in the saltwater below. We cross over the South Wellesley Islands, including the largest Bentinck Island, and then on to the southern end of Mornington Island in the North Wellesley Islands where the community of Gununa is located (see second map in the frontmatter). Gununa is now the only permanently occupied settlement in the Wellesley archipelago; a community of approximately 1,100 people (see third map in the frontmatter), one of many similarly sized remote Aboriginal communities that dot northern and central Australia. Like many of these communities, only a small number of non-Aboriginal people, Whitefellas or *marndagi* as they are referred to locally, live there.

This book is about the everyday lives of Mornington Islanders, both Aboriginal people and Whitefellas. Primarily it is about the lives of Aboriginal Mornington Islanders, as they navigate under conditions that are variously described by others as in 'crisis'. The Australian media is flooded with this crisis narrative, particularly portrayals and images of Aboriginal ill health and violence. The supposed crisis is ongoing and continues to unfold, seeping and leaking out of any contained understanding of the temporal boundedness that might be expected when the term is invoked. What this means is that Aboriginal people continue to find ways to endure and to belong, new ways to create value and meaning and to relate, both in their relationships with one another and to the material world in which they live. It is these modes of enduring and the intensity that these experiences generate that are the core concerns of this book.

In spite of its intellectual and ethical focus on core issues of Aboriginal people's lives, this book is not a manifesto for the necessity of interventions into those lives, nor does it contain suggestions for how to 'fix' the situations that it describes. Rather, it details the range of contexts and conditions under which people already persist, presenting a means of thinking about living in the contemporary in ways which do not foreclose their potential futures. Around the world, studies that focus on endurance are more and more common, a necessary response to the array of social marginalization, economic austerity, militarization and environmental crises which typify late capitalism. Many of these studies draw on the work of anthropologist Elizabeth Povinelli, whose book *Economies of Abandonment: Social Belonging and Endurance in Late Liberalism* (2011) has come to define the field.

Povinelli's particular contribution has been to draw attention to the ubiquitousness with which endurance-related events permeate daily life. These 'quasi-events' are those that do not quite reach the status of an 'aha' moment, Povinelli tells us, and at times slip and slide from view, making them difficult to catch or to hold. It is ethnography's attentiveness to the minutiae of daily life that makes it so well suited to describing the modes of endurance that Povinelli describes, and ethnography forms the methodological basis of this book. Nonetheless, as will be discussed further in this introduction, taking an ethnographic approach to Aboriginal lives is at odds with the opinions of some scholars writing in this space, who argue instead for the taking up of advocacy and political positions which deny anthropology's core practice. As it relates to Mornington Island, what resonates from Povinelli's work is how a committed focus that centres Mornington Islanders does not avoid the difficulties of recognizing the marginal position that they occupy within the contemporary nation state, nor the grittiness of the conditions under which they persist.

By the time that I began visiting there, Mornington Islanders were familiar with anthropologists, having sporadically hosted a number of researchers over the twentieth century. More recently, some Mornington Islanders have been involved with the state-mandated processes of native title, and have become accustomed to articulating their knowledge to researchers for the purposes of having their underlying rights to land and sea recognized by law. Such was the familiarity with the anthropological project that shortly after I had arrived on the Island in 2007, Mr Cyril Moon, a senior Lardil Aboriginal man, knocked on my front door and asked if I was 'the anthropologist'. When I nodded, he responded that I should get my (note) 'book' so that we could 'get goin'. In what would become a pivotal relationship, Cyril began to refer to me as his daughter, thereby incorporating me into the local kinship idiom. The significance of this inculcation was that it provided a shorthand way for others to determine their relationship to me, a means through which Mornington Islanders could make sense of my sociality within their existing schemas. The concentration of my experience was of ten months living on Mornington Island in 2007 and a subsequent six months in 2008, followed by shorter return visits in 2009, 2010, 2012, 2014, 2016 and 2018. For some of this period I was undertaking research towards a PhD in anthropology at the University of Queensland.

In attending to the ideas of endurance and intensity, I speak into the intellectual space created by the ethnographic legacy of a number of researchers who have worked on Mornington Island. In particular, I chart a way of thinking about remote Aboriginal life that does away with tropes that foretell the end of Mornington Island social and cultural identity, something that became the erstwhile task of my anthropological forebear David McKnight (1999, 2002, 2004, 2005). I return to

McKnight's work throughout this book, not only because of his prolific contributions about Mornington Island, but because of the gravity of his pronouncements about those who live there and their future. Though McKnight's ethnographic legacy is voluminous, his analytic is focused almost solely on social and cultural loss, promoting a deficit discourse when it comes to Aboriginal personhood. This perspective has provided little in the way of a foundation on which to build a hopeful future for Mornington Islanders, and it is this absence that provides the rationale for this book.

Mornington Island: A Brief History

Mornington Island is the largest in an archipelago of islands in the southern Gulf of Carpentaria, Queensland, in the northern part of Australia. At the south-west end of Mornington Island is the largest and only permanently occupied settlement in the Wellesley Islands, a community called Gununa. Gununa is what is known in Australia as a 'discrete community', in the sense that the population primarily comprises Aboriginal people and the community exists as a service point for the Aboriginal population that live there, with very little private economic enterprise. Access to the Island is via plane or boat and travel around the Island itself is via a network of unsealed roads, most of which are impassable for several months of each year, including during the annual monsoon from December to February. The Mornington Shire Council is a local government area classed as 'very remote' by the Australian Bureau of Statistics (2010), based on its distance from any major Australian town or city.

During the 2000s Gununa had a fairly stable population of approximately 1,000 Aboriginal people and 100 non-Aboriginal people (ABS 2006: Table B07, 2011: Table B07, 2016: Table G07).[1] The demographic profile of the Aboriginal residents was one of a youthful population, with over 40 per cent under the age of nineteen in 2016 (ABS 2016: Table G07). This mirrors trends Australia-wide, which are of both a youthful and growing Aboriginal population (Langton 2010: 95). Another aspect of growth in the population has been the numbers of non-Aboriginal people living in the community, which has almost doubled from 68 to 130 people in the ten-year period from 2006 to 2016 (ABS 2006: Table B07, 2016: Table G07). Some of this growth reflects large infrastructure-building projects at the local airport and jetty and the expanding population's need for services. It also reflects the glacially slow pace at which Aboriginal people are being supported to develop skills and take up employment in positions to manage and service their own community, making them reliant on skills and expertise from elsewhere.

The non-Aboriginal settlement of the southern Gulf of Carpentaria began during the late 1800s and has had profound and ongoing impacts on Aboriginal residents. Oral history accounts report the brutalization and massacres of Aboriginal people across the islands at this time, including in the South Wellesley Islands. The enslavement of Aboriginal people into *beche-de-mer* and sandalwood industries by non-Aboriginal traders provided the justification for the establishment of a Presbyterian Church mission station at the southern end of Mornington Island in 1914. As has been extensively detailed elsewhere, particularly by McKnight (2002, 2004, 2005) and Memmott (1979), the origins of the contemporary community of Gununa were on the same site as the mission camp. What started as a modest Church mission camp set up by the first mission superintendent Reverend Robert Hall began what would become decades of Church control and the monitoring of Aboriginal people in the region (Wharton 2000: 11). Over subsequent years, Aboriginal people from various parts of the North Wellesley Islands – the Lardil and Yangkaal people – were moved to live within the mission compound and in Aboriginal camps located nearby. The Queensland Government also relocated a number of Aboriginal adults and children from the adjacent Australian mainland, sometimes as punishment for what was described as errant behaviour[2] (Blake 1998: 38; Trigger 1992: 39–40).

Under the guise of 'protection', Aboriginal people became a source of labour exploited by the mission, their intimate knowledge of the local landscape and its resources used to obtain food to fuel mission economies. The murder of Reverend Hall by an Aboriginal man in 1917, and a subsequent siege at the mission house involving mission staff, galvanized the Church and Government's resolve to maintain a permanent presence on the Island. The Aboriginal man responsible for Hall's death, 'Bad Peter', was sent with six other Aboriginal people to the Saint Helena penal colony in Moreton Bay in South East Queensland and was said to have drowned there. Though sometimes framed as a dispute over tobacco, in the historical record this is an extraordinary instance of the rejection of a non-Aboriginal presence in the region and of the occupation of Aboriginal lands.

As relates to Church administration of the Island, a period of relative stability followed from 1918 to 1942 when the Reverend Robert Wilson was mission superintendent. As in many Indigenous communities both in Australia and North America, the Church approach involved removing Aboriginal children from their parents to live in mission dormitories, to work in mission enterprises and to learn English (see Figure 0.1).

This has been exceptionally destructive to Aboriginal social and cultural wellbeing, with enduring and intergenerational effects. Though this period can be characterized as one where Aboriginal culture was increasingly produced in the context of 'intercultural' relationships through interactions with mission staff, there was simultaneous maintenance of a distinct social and spatial Aboriginal domain in which language, local knowledge and kinship relations were paramount (Dalley and Memmott 2010). The maintenance of this domain was integral to the sense of persistence and endurance against non-Aboriginal interference and in the transmission of cultural knowledge.

Over the course of the twentieth century, the Church brought all residents to live in proximity to the mission, and recruited Aboriginal

Figure 0.1. Aboriginal children with school teacher Lucy at the Mornington Island Mission, 1936 (UQFL57, Fryer Library, The University of Queensland Library).

assistants, especially Aboriginal people from the mainland, to convert Aboriginal people to Christianity. In 1947 and 1948, Church authorities moved approximately sixty Kaiadilt Aboriginal people from Sweers and Bentinck Islands in the South Wellesley Islands to the Mornington Island mission[3] (Evans 1998: 47). The trauma associated with this relocation was reflected in Evans' observation that Mornington Island was considered by Kaiadilt people as a place of 'exile' (Evans 1998: 15). In the immediate aftermath of the removal, no babies born to Kaiadilt mothers survived to infancy, a startling reflection on the damage of Church practice and the potency of connection to country. The displacement of Kaiadilt people meant that within forty years the entire Aboriginal population of the Wellesley Islands, who had for millennia lived rich and varied cultural lives across the entire archipelago, were uprooted to live in a single settlement.

From the 1950s, Aboriginal people were sent from Mornington Island to the mainland to work as domestics and station hands on cattle stations, often under horrendous and abusive conditions and for little or no pay. These years, particularly when the Reverend Douglas Belcher was mission superintendent from 1950 to 1969, involved the continued surveillance and control of Aboriginal people. The mission dormitories were permanently closed in 1953 (McKnight 2002: 61). A growing promotion of Aboriginal culture, including its export to the outside world via the selling of handcrafts and performances of a dance group, brought income and travel opportunities for some Mornington Islanders, including the famous Lardil artist Dick Roughsey. Instrumental in the marketing of Roughsey's work was the commercial airline pilot Percy Trezise, in a partnership which began when the men met at a holiday resort in the mainland Gulf town of Karumba (Roughsey 1971: 132). Roughsey's (1971) autobiography and a collection of letters that he wrote to Trezise (held at the Fryer Library at the University of Queensland) detail his experiences during this period. What stands out in Roughsey's letters is the degree to which the daily life of Aboriginal Mornington Islanders was controlled by the mission superintendent, even during the 1970s. In spite of being a highly respected and published author, dancer and senior Aboriginal songman, Roughsey was nonetheless required to seek approval from the mission superintendent (who was referred to by the Lardil kin term *'gu-itha'*, meaning father) in order to travel to the mainland and to spend money that he had earned as part of his artistic endeavours. Roughsey's letters reflect his frustration at the continued infantilization of Aboriginal people by the Church and at his limited access to money and resources that he had earned.

The late 1960s through to the early 1980s were notable for the conducting of anthropologically significant research by David McKnight,[4] Paul Memmott (1979), John Cawte (1972) and Virginia Huffer (1980), and linguistic studies by Ken Hale (which contributed to a Lardil dictionary published in 1997) and Nicholas Evans (1992), who later produced a Kayardild dictionary. Also at this time, Aboriginal people across Australia were agitating to have greater control over the governance of their communities, a position nominally supported by the Presbyterian Church, which was financially unable to provide for the growing population. In somewhat controversial circumstances, the withdrawal of the Church in 1978 (which by then had become the Uniting Church) was followed by Mornington Island being gazetted along with the other Wellesley Islands as a shire under Queensland state legislation, the *Local Government (Aboriginal Lands) Act 1978* (Blake 1998: 42). The special legislation, which also applied to another mission at Aurukun on western Cape York, established a local council responsible for administering the provision of services to residents (Martin 1993: 3). The Mornington Shire Council consisted of a generally elected Mayor and Councillors, usually Aboriginal people, and a non-Aboriginal Shire Clerk. As I discuss in a later chapter, this model of governance, split between an elected Aboriginal board and non-Aboriginal administrators, was also prevalent in Aboriginal corporations being set up on the Island to administer services for Aboriginal residents.

These governance structures became vital to the administration of the Island, particularly as housing was upgraded from basic shacks made out of corrugated iron to permanent housing from the 1960s onwards. Building new accommodation became a priority after 1976, when tropical Cyclone Ted destroyed much of the existing housing on the Island, leaving many Aboriginal people without shelter (Brine 1980). The houses built in the aftermath of Cyclone Ted would form the foundations of what is now the contemporary community of Gununa. In spite of the establishment of permanent housing at Gununa, Aboriginal people continued to advocate for infrastructure to be developed at decentralized locations around the Wellesley Islands, on the country estates to which people maintained spiritual and ancestral connections. During the 1980s and 1990s, injections of funding from the Commonwealth-funded Aboriginal Torres Strait Islander Commission (ATSIC) and the Mornington Shire Council paid for the construction of 'outstations' or 'homelands', as they were also referred to at the time (McKnight 2002: 171). The largest of these was at *Nyinyilki* (also referred to as 'Raft Point' or 'Main Base') on Bentinck Island, which facilitated the return of Kaiadilt people to the South Wellesley Islands for extended periods of time (Evans 1998: 50). An important aspect of the development of outstations was the cutting of roads around the Wellesley Islands and establishment of an airstrip on Bentinck Island, greatly enhancing the access that Aboriginal people had to the more remote parts of their country (McKnight 2002: 172). These endeavours also benefited significantly from the Community Development Employment Projects (CDEP) program that began on Mornington Island in 1980 and provided wages for Aboriginal labour to assist with road and house construction (Memmott and Horsman 1991: 273).

The 'return to country' heralded by the construction of outstations carried over into a more active pursuit of land and sea-based native title rights for Aboriginal people. From the mid-1990s, the Carpentaria Land Council, based in nearby mainland Burketown, managed the administration of a 'Sea Claim' over the waters in the southern Gulf of Carpentaria, which culminated in a legal trial. The determination of the Sea Claim in 2004 found that Aboriginal people had non-exclusive native title rights in waters surrounding the Wellesley Islands, and was a formal recognition of the 'spiritual connection' and ongoing use of marine resources which Aboriginal people had maintained for many generations (National Native Title Tribunal [NNTT] 2004: 23). Four years later, the precedent of the Sea Claim determination provided the basis for a consent (i.e. not litigated) determination that recognized exclusive rights to land over almost all of the twenty-three Wellesley Islands (NNTT 2009). These processes affirmed legally what Aboriginal people had always known; that they were and continue to be the rightful owners of the lands and seas of the Wellesley Islands.

At the same time as these significant developments in access and rights to land were occurring, Aboriginal people were also experiencing the compounding impacts of years of intergenerational trauma and poverty, marked by a proliferation of health and social problems. Alcoholism, self-harm, suicide and inter-personal violence, coupled with high unemployment and poor education outcomes, were becoming increasingly evident (McKnight 2002). A 2009 report found that out of twelve Indigenous communities in Queensland, between 1995 and 2006 Mornington Island had the second-highest prevalence (after the community of Aurukun) of offences against the person, property offences and 'other' offences[5] (CMC 2009: 42). Of particular concern were the rates of reported offences against the person, which were over 18.5 times higher than the Queensland average over the same period (CMC 2009: 42). These social phenomena and their imbrication with alcohol consumption was the focus of McKnight's *From Hunting to Drinking: The Devastating Effects of Alcohol on an Australian Aboriginal Community* (2002), the best-known book about Mornington Island (e.g. Austin-Broos 2011: 134; Langton 2010: 99; Sutton 2009: 40).[6]

The majority of McKnight's (1999, 2004, 2005) research was structural in nature, richly detailing Lardil systems of kinship, animal and plant classification, ritual and sorcery and so on. *From Hunting to Drinking*, though, was a departure in approach and intent, instead taking a highly personalized interpretation of 'the destruction of cultural and social life'. McKnight's most damning assertion was that 'Mornington Island now consists of a community of individuals who are bereft of a social identity except in negative terms; they used to have this or that, they used to be this or the other, but now they have nothing and are no one' (McKnight 2002: 6). In *From Hunting to Drinking*, McKnight yearned for a different time, of Aboriginal people as he had apparently known them to be, socially and culturally intact. He was unable to recognize the endurance of Aboriginal people against the most constrained and trying of conditions. McKnight's book was strongly criticized for its abandonment of critical engagement in lieu of emotional, shattered-Eden 'remarks and opinions' (Sackett 2004: 241; cf. Sutton 2007). Turner (2003: 81) incisively questioned the 'ethics of dwelling on the pathologies of contemporary Aboriginal communities at the expense of people's dignity. What purpose does this serve?'. In attending to this question, the ethnography here is a speaking back to McKnight's narratives about Mornington Islanders.

What Now

The title of this book, 'what now', is a common form of address on Mornington Island, and in some other Aboriginal communities in Australia. Depending on the intonation of the speaker, it can variously mean 'what *now*?' as in, 'given what came before, what do you think will come next?'. It can also mean 'what news do you have of a particular situation or event?'. If said quickly, 'what now!' also acts as a greeting, functioning in the same way as 'hello' or 'hi'. It is the multiplicity of uses and meanings that is instructive. 'What now' elides past and future tense, a way of considering what has been or what has occurred, as well as way of opening a dialogue on what might be to come in the future. It is the concern with both of these aspects of remote Aboriginal life that dominates policymaking in Aboriginal affairs in Australia. What governments are concerned with, and the broader public tasks them with, is how to create or impact change to craft better futures for remote places (Lea 2012).

The time in which I was living on Mornington Island, researching this book and then writing it, was one in which questions about 'Aboriginal issues' were coming to the fore in Australia in unparalleled ways (Dalley and Martin 2015). The constant media attention afforded to such issues was in large part stimulated by the Australian Federal Government's Northern Territory Emergency Intervention (NTER) into Aboriginal communities in the Northern Territory in 2007. The 'Intervention', as it became known, involved the introduction of radical policies guiding the provision of services in remote communities, ostensibly aimed at reducing disadvantage and dysfunction for Aboriginal people (see a range of papers in Altman and Hinkson 2007, 2010). The Intervention was particularly sensational because as part of the implementation of racially particularized policies, the Australian Federal Government suspended anti-discrimination legislation (Sutton 2009: 37). Though not located in the Northern Territory, Mornington Island is one of many communities that has been targeted by particularized policies as part of the 'Closing the Gap' ideology, the Australian Government's attempt to reduce statistical inequality between Aboriginal people and the broader population in areas like health and education (Kowal 2015a; Peterson 2010: 250).

Many viewed the suspension of anti-discrimination legislation in the Northern Territory as extreme and as an affront to the kinds of liberal, multicultural values that drive much of broader Australian society. This effrontery was compounded by the use of uniformed Australian Defence Force personnel to roll out the Government's policies. The imagery of uniformed soldiers moving into Aboriginal communities graced the covers of Australia's national newspapers, crafting an image of order and control to contrast the disordered and dysfunctional people that they had come to assist. In constructing this image of authority, these portrayals sought to reassure a concerned public that something was about to change in remote Aboriginal Australia. But any optimism for positive change was short-lived. In the regularly reported Government statistics on 'Closing the Gap', most indicators point to a widening chasm between Aboriginal and non-Aboriginal statistics of wellbeing, suggesting life for Aboriginal people, particularly in remote Australia, is getting worse rather than better.

As well as in policy, timeliness and temporality are recurrent themes in Aboriginal anthropology. The idea that Aboriginal culture is thousands of years old and on a collision course with modernity is a trope that permeates national media and the broader Australian consciousness (Kowal 2015b). It is also the case that Aboriginal people take great pride in the longevity of their endurance, often describing themselves as the oldest living culture on earth. But to make a rather obvious point, Mornington Islanders are not trapped either in the past or future; they are alive now and deeply embedded in rich social lives. The Mornington Islanders with whom I spent many months over many years did not just have a 'social life' in the way that others might for example, compartmentalize various parts of their lives. Mornington Islanders' sociality permeated every part of their world; it was the centre of their being and the core of the way in which they knew the world. To say that Aboriginal people are social is to understate it; their relationships with others and the desire to continuously reproduce and perform those relationships drives all facets of daily life. So why are Mornington Islanders so committed to the reproduction of these distinct social worlds? To answer this question, it is necessary to understand that the logic of an Aboriginal community begins with the same basic premise of any remote Australian place. That is; with a small population, residents living in close proximity tend to be particularly aware of one another. Compounding this social awareness is the fact that the Mornington Island population is residentially confined to within an extremely small geographic space, half a dozen streets arranged around a main street only 2 km long.

The intensity of social life on Mornington Island was a product of both the isolation and containment of the Island, and particularly in the community of Gununa where the vast majority of residents live. As mentioned previously, by a range of geographic, economic and social measures, the Island is considered 'very remote'. The comings and goings of residents are also influenced by the limited modes of transport on and off the Island: expensive aeroplane travel twice a day and boat travel, generally only undertaken by local Aboriginal people who have intimate knowledge of the tides and seas around the islands. As a destination, Mornington Island seldom draws tourists or visitors, there now being no private tourism businesses active on the Island. In addition, the local Council, composed of Aboriginal representatives elected by permanent residents, has in place a permit system which accounts for the arrivals and departures of non-residents. What this meant is that Aboriginal residents seldom come into contact with those from outside their known social worlds, though this is changing.

The majority of local residents are Aboriginal people whose families have resided on the islands and on the nearby mainland for many hundreds or perhaps thousands of generations. This genealogical intensity has been magnified by high rates of intermarriage among Aboriginal residents, a history that reaches at least as far back as the living memory of the oldest of local residents, and probably stretches back about three thousand years to when the islands were first inhabited (Rosendahl et al. 2014: 258). This means that now virtually all residents consider one another kin or 'family'. David McKnight (2005: 130) referred to this as a form of 'relational density', being the many thousands of kinship relationships between Aboriginal people on the Island. Mornington Islanders' knowledge of one another, of each other's personal histories from conception to the grave, has made them specialists par excellence on the social lives of others, the breadth and depth of which was a constant source of wonder. The orientation towards the social and its proliferation was the guiding force of virtually all being and paramount in all decision-making. Even situations of discord provided opportunities for Aboriginal people to garner support by reorienting the lens of their social world to focus more closely on others.

Mornington Islanders conceive of their own personhood within a richly embedded and illustrated social world, where their kin position and reposition them in an ongoing and dialogic relationship of relatedness. As knowledge of the 'Dreaming', a term used to describe Aboriginal religious and spiritual worlds, begins to lessen, the immediacy of interpersonal relations is affirmed as paramount. This is not to say that particularized knowledge, such as of 'story places', which are physical landscapes inscribed by the activities of ancestor spirits, is unknown to Aboriginal people. Through this book, and particularly in Chapter 5, I will discuss some of the persistent aspects of Mornington Island belief and spirituality which tie particular people to places or animals within their local landscape. It is nonetheless the case that a diminishment in the fully elaborated nature of this knowledge has reduced its potency and hence its transmission to younger generations. The efficacy of transmission has also been tempered by a general reorientation of Aboriginal people away from 'country', and increasingly towards 'town', i.e. community life. In everyday life meeting the growing expectations of government agencies, managing households and money, taking care of children and the demands of kin have come to take precedence. For some, there are also the everyday demands of employment.

Aboriginal people living on Mornington Island have limited integration into the paid workforce, and the meagre value of Australian Government welfare payments results in a particular kind of impoverishment. In 2016, 45 per cent of all Mornington Island residents (Indigenous and non-Indigenous people) aged 15 years and older had a weekly income of less than AUD 399.00. The most common income bracket was those earning AUD 150.00 to AUD 299.00 per week, which is the equivalent of an Australian Government parenting payment or similar (ABS 2016: Table G17b). Though government welfare is not the kind of impoverishment known in many other parts of the world, it creates particular issues in Australia, where the cost of remote living is much higher than in regional and urban centres. Despite offsets and subsidies provided by the government, such as low housing costs and the provision of free health and education services for Aboriginal residents, other basic living costs, especially food, fuel, clothes and household goods, are high on Mornington Island, sometimes astronomically so. Exorbitant prices, which are generally for goods rather than services, reflect both the expense of transporting goods to the Island but also the costs associated with employing staff to sell these goods and the lack of competition in the market where they are sold. Low household incomes combined with the high costs of goods fosters ethics of sharing and borrowing goods and the pooling of resources, practices that are dependent on sustaining relations to the degree that requests to borrow are granted.

Another outcome of low workforce participation is that Mornington Islanders are time-rich. For the most part, the hours of their day can be expended in a manner of their own choosing. It is this excess of available time that generates particular kinds of boredom. Mornington Islanders referred to the quietness that beset the community, or to their own boredom, as being 'slack' or 'too slack', i.e. that there was nothing to do and that there was nothing of interest happening. To occupy time, people played video games and watched TV and DVDs, smoked, washed clothes, cleaned their yards, visited family and sometimes went hunting or fishing. As well as this, open stretches of time gave rise to alcohol consumption and, particularly for younger people, cannabis use, as well as playing cards for money at one of the 'gambling schools' around the community. Though policymakers often discuss how to reduce or ameliorate the nefarious symptoms of boredom, rarely is boredom itself spoken about (Musharbash 2007). The long stretches of time in which no work or formal activities were organized meant that Mornington Islanders were highly dependent on one another for activity and companionship, and it was this reliance that inturn fostered a particular kind of social intensity and belonging to one another and to place.

Writing Ethnography

The research presented here largely reflects a kind of anthropological fieldwork now seldom undertaken in Australia. In bygone eras, anthropologists would head 'out bush' with a swag, a Toyota and a letter of introduction to a missionary or local clerk, and would return twelve or eighteen months later with notebooks filled, and rolls of film waiting to be developed. More often than not the time they had spent in a community was in a kind of total immersion, living with Aboriginal people and gradually coming to understand holistically aspects of the worlds in which they were ensconced. The costs of conducting fieldwork, the time constraints on research and the highly politicized nature of representations of Aboriginal people and places have made this kind of research increasingly uncommon. Aboriginal people have insisted that anthropologists make themselves accountable to the communities that they research, ensuring the continuing transformation of the discipline.

In other parts of the world, Indigenous people are contesting anthropology's project, describing it as one of colonialism, proposing instead a kind of 'ethnographic refusal' (Simpson 2014). As scholar Audra Simpson describes for the Iroquois and Kahnawà:ke of North America, a refusal addresses the 'dissonance between representations that were produced [by anthropologists] and what people say about themselves' (2014: 98). Simpson's work borrows its leading turn of phrase from the anthropologist Sherry Ortner (1995). Ortner's point of view was quite different to that of Simpson, in that while she recognized that ethnographic refusal was a seductive political position, it carried with it the pitfall that a lack of thick description could result in the homogenization of cultures under colonialism. This homogenization stemmed, Ortner argued, from the abandonment of thickness and holism, a kind of 'cultural thinning', without historical depth or the nuances of a culture as an elaborated form, reduced to a reactionary, resistance position.

Of course, who can and should be involved in the writing of these portrayals is a point of contention in the debates as they play out in contemporary Australia. There are many that take the view that assuming an authoritative voice on such matters acts to disempower Aboriginal people, who are after all more than capable of telling their own stories (Wright 2016). Another view, which I share to a degree, is that if we accept that the production of knowledge about others has at times been harmful, we as anthropologists and non-Indigenous scholars must also shoulder some responsibility for righting (or literally re-writing) those discourses. This endeavour, one that I initially undertook with the confidence of naivety, and lately a sense of unease, has nonetheless been underpinned by a sustained commitment to the people and community that I have lived in, visited and been connected to for many years.

My sense of purpose in this undertaking has been heavily influenced by my family's settler-colonial history in Queensland. A key figure in this history is my maternal grandmother's grandfather, Dr Thomas Tate (1842–1934), an Englishman and medically trained naturalist who came to Australia via New Zealand in the 1860s. Part of his story includes being a passenger on the *Maria*, a ship that was infamously wrecked off the Queensland coast in 1872 en route to New Guinea. Some survivors were reported to have been killed by local Aboriginal people. Tate went on to catalogue animals and plants in Cape York as a member of the Hann Northern Exploring Expedition, and was later a school teacher in the Torres Strait. Subsequent generations have inherited Tate's settler-colonial fascinations. During the 1970s, my maternal grandmother collected Aboriginal stone artefacts on the pastoral properties where she lived in Western Queensland and donated them to the Queensland Museum. That my inherited family history centres and speaks of these figures as part of a lauded Australian pioneering spirit sits uneasily with the reality of their involvement in the dispossession of Aboriginal people. Indigenous scholars have highlighted time and again how necessary it is for non-Indigenous scholars, including settler descendants such as myself, to position ourselves within rather than outside narratives about coloniality.

Though these issues are not unique to the discipline, within anthropology there has been what the anthropologist Clifford Geertz (1988) refers to as a 'pervasive nervousness' about representation, particularly in settler contexts. The nervousness that Geertz refers to means that anthropologists are continually asking: 'What should anthropologists be writing about? Are there some issues that anthropologists should not write about?' In Australia, these questions have been debated intensely since 2009, following the release of the anthropologist Peter Sutton's book *The Politics of Suffering*. In his 2009 book and in earlier essays, Sutton's primary contention was that Aboriginal 'culture' could not, and should not, be seen as benign in the formation of dysfunction (Hinkson 2009: 54–55). In making this argument, Sutton largely rejected the notion that historical processes, namely 'colonial conquest', could be considered causal in any singular sense, going so far as to describe such a position 'at best a case of sad ignorance, and at worst an obscene abuse of this appalling disaster for the purpose of scoring cheap political points' (Sutton 2001a: 141). This political point scoring, Sutton argued, was a tactic employed by those of the 'liberal consensus', which included anthropologists and which Sutton defined as having driven Aboriginal policy, particularly during the era of 'self-determination' from the late 1970s onwards (see also Kowal 2008).

Within anthropology, the debate that followed revealed the acrimony between proponents of strongly held political positions, with some welcoming Sutton's exegesis while others were staunchly critical of his ascription of causation. This latter group included Andrew

Lattas, Barry Morris (Lattas and Morris 2010) and Gillian Cowlishaw (2010) with whom Sutton had earlier engaged in debate via a series of journal articles (Cowlishaw 2003; Sutton 2001a, 2005). Cowlishaw had been critical of Sutton for the lack of Aboriginal voices in his discussions of causality, especially given the contention that 'suffering is an experiential rather than objective condition' (2003: 3) and that 'an empirically established, statistically high level of violence and destructive behaviours gives no insight into community relations or the level and meaning of suffering' (2003: 4). Beyond this, Cowlishaw, and those who shared her views, figured a different relationship between history and culture, in which the ongoing failure of government to allow Aboriginal people to determine their own affairs took causal primacy over the influence of culture. Another of Cowlishaw's (2003, 2010) concerns was the view that anthropologists could assist in the meaningful resolution of such complex issues, especially given the highly politicized context and her belief that 'public debate should not be confused with policy formation' (Cowlishaw 2003: 7).

Cutting to the heart of the matter for anthropologists, Aboriginal academic Marcia Langton (2010: 92) noted that 'during this debate, a predictable dilemma has gripped the anthropological imagination in Australia, raising the relevance and efficacy of the discipline in the context of extreme situations in which the state and its subalterns conflict'. Langton's insight is shared by many within and outside the discipline. Unlike the former issue of causality, on this issue Sutton and Cowlishaw seemed to reach some tenuous agreement, albeit for slightly contrasting reasons. For Sutton:

> The in-depth methodology of anthropology and its encompassing theoretical base, not mere assemblages of medical or criminal facts alone, can assist official policies and practices to move beyond their present, tragically ineffectual standing to a point where their communities have a chance of a better life. Yet one should not exaggerate the value of anthropology in this highly politicized context – its role is now always likely to be minor, and indeed we may have seen the end of the era in which it was otherwise. (2001a: 155)

Although not elaborated, Sutton's point is that the role for anthropologists (as distinct from other types of researchers) in interpreting Aboriginal-specific contexts may be diminished. Cowlishaw (2003: 4) similarly asks, 'does Australian anthropology have anything to say about the alleged crisis in Aboriginal society today?' and in the event that it does, 'do scholars such as anthropologists know what to do?'. On both counts, others have proposed some potential answers and solutions. In Central Australia, Ute Eickelkamp (2011: 132), suggests that this question is best understood in the following terms: 'within the limit of the national purview, writing ethnographies of Aboriginal communities (which many no longer be societies) has become a moral issue pivoting on the definition of the real'. Eickelkamp (ibid.) went on to categorize the position of anthropologists on what defined the 'real': 'In the briefest terms: Aboriginalists (Black or White) are divided between those who see the need to address Indigenous suffering and those who see merit in focusing on other issues'. Perhaps a more nuanced approach to undertaking ethnography, however, is not so much about choosing to centre or ignore suffering, but to understand how suffering and endurance exist side by side.

In taking this approach I recall the research of the American anthropologist Lucas Bessire (2014), whose ethnography of Ayoreo people, among the last groups to exit the Amazonian rainforest, addressed many similar issues to those on Mornington Island. Bessire (2014: 7) used the phrase 'a death foretold' to refer to the ways in which his anthropological forebears had conceived of unprecedented upheaval among South American Indians, wherein: 'The supposed death of culture also meant a wider social death' (ibid.). Bessire attempted to redress this conflation by charting a difficult course between recognizing the horrors of the destruction of the rainforest and the apocalyptic changes it wrought on Ayoreo lives, while also not foreclosing what their lives could become.

Endurance and Intensity on Mornington Island

One of the key themes of this book is the endurance of living in a very remote community, contained in space and far from the kinds of life that other Australians might be familiar with. In focusing on daily life and the minutiae that construct and affirm remote distinctiveness and belonging, the emphasis is on the intense nature of relations and the social forms that produce and reproduce particular kinds of personhood. Anthropologists sometimes call this a 'relational ontology', where the primary axis of personal orientation is towards one's own personal kinship network (Poirier 2013). While a focus on relationality is not unique to Aboriginal society, it is the persistent and overriding nature of relations to kin that not only differentiates, but also separates Aboriginal people's lives from those of the broader society. In this sense, this book aims to capture the particular feel of living in a remote Aboriginal community in Australia during the 2000s. It is because of the recursive quality of social processes that the book also explores the dynamically changing nature of Aboriginal people's lives, creating possibilities that are unpredictable, even for those who know the people well.

Mornington Island and the Aboriginal people living there have endured under direct governmental policy since the establishment of the mission in 1914. From that time, Aboriginal people have been influenced by church and government policies which have ultimately transformed the ways in which they live. But to present these forces as external to Aboriginal ways of seeing the world or as the product of governmental policy is only a partial representation; Aboriginal people have also internalized these processes and rendered some of them as their own. To take a relatively benign example, and as will be explored in Chapter 1, in collaboration with Whitefellas, Aboriginal people have established a range of organizations to attract government funding and provide services in their community.

It is true that all Australians undergo change and are influenced by government policies, but the degree of change for Mornington Islanders over a one-hundred-year period has been highly accelerated. It has been the struggle to adapt to rapid change which has led to local conditions that some would describe as a 'crisis'. In particular, Mornington Island has a range of issues associated with low levels of workforce participation, extreme rates of violence and poor health and educational outcomes. Excessive consumption of alcohol and other illicit substances are also part of this milieu. These statistics are not an attempted roll call of dysfunction, but a means of showing that life is not always a kind of remote island utopia for the residents of the Wellesley Islands. It has been the persistent endurance of Mornington Islanders, against such incredibly fraught conditions, which constitutes the most developed sense of optimism for the future.

Chapters 1 and 2 of this book relate Mornington Islanders' experiences with the state and the non-Aboriginal people that come to live in their community. This begins in Chapter 1 with a discussion of the development of Gununa from a Presbyterian mission station to a contemporary Aboriginal community and its governance as a socio-politically defined space within the Australian nation state. Chapter 2 focuses on the experiences of Whitefellas living on Mornington Island, most of whom come to live on the Island to work for government agencies. In spite of the contained and socially intimate nature of the community, these Whitefellas live structurally and spatially separate to Aboriginal people.

Chapter 3 deals more exclusively with contemporary Aboriginal family and households. The chapter begins with an overview of some of the changes to kinship, marriage and the raising of children on Mornington Island and the ways in which these changes have influenced the construction of 'family'. Chapter 4 examines alcohol management and its consumption at the Lelka Murrin Tavern, known locally as the 'Pub'. The permanent closure of the Pub in 2008 and the designation of the Wellesley Islands as an alcohol-free 'dry' zone had particular implications for Aboriginal residents. One of the places that alcohol consumption occurred following the implementation of alcohol restrictions was at outstations located on Mornington Islanders' country across the Wellesley Islands. As is described in Chapter 5, identification with 'country' remains a defining element in the social identities of Mornington Islanders. This salience is derived from extended systems of intergenerational descent which link Mornington Islanders not just to defined areas of land and sea (estates) but also to ancestors who previously lived on country. Changes to systems of descent are discussed in this chapter, as well as how access to country informs the demonstration of connection and the recognition of ownership by others.

The number of books about Mornington Island, notably those by David McKnight, place it among the most-written-about Aboriginal communities in Australia. That such a volume of material exists indicates both the social and cultural complexity and imagination of Mornington Islanders, and broader interest in understanding their lives. Today Mornington Islanders live in perilous conditions, steeped in the cruel practices of settler-colonial and missionary history, made worse by poverty, boredom and excessive alcohol consumption. Such are these circumstances that Mornington Islanders deploy intense sociality to shield themselves from the forces in their lives that they are least able to control. The social intensity that they construct becomes their mode of endurance. The subtlety of these practices, both reflexively produced and otherwise, evades simplistic representation and essentialism, but instead reveals itself most potently in this ethnography of the everyday.

Notes

1. A number of issues have been identified with the ABS enumeration of remote Aboriginal populations in Australia (see Morphy 2006, 2007).
2. Some of these people came from the areas around Turn Off Lagoon, Burketown and Lawn Hill and have thus been thought of as being Waanyi and/or Ganggalida. Based on historical records, Trigger (1992: 39–40) estimated that forty-two adults and children were removed from the mainland to Mornington Island between 1914 and 1942.

3. A number of reasons have been proposed to explain this removal, including the compounding impacts of drought, and a cyclone which spoilt fresh water sources (Evans 1998: 47; Memmott 2008: 19).
4. Most of McKnight's publications, however, came towards the end of his life, with four books published in 1999, 2002, 2004 and 2005. David McKnight died in 2006 (Sutton 2007: 28).
5. 'Offences against the person are homicide (murder), other homicide, assault, sexual offences, robbery, extortion, kidnapping, abduction and deprivation of liberty, and other offences against the person. Offences against property are unlawful entry, arson, other property damage, unlawful use of motor vehicle, other theft, fraud, and handling stolen goods. 'Other' offences are drug offences; prostitution offences; liquor (excluding drunkenness); gaming, racing and betting; breach of domestic violence protection orders; trespassing and vagrancy; *Weapons Act 1990* (Qld) offences; good order offences; stock-related offences; traffic and related offences; and miscellaneous offences' (CMC 2009: 41).
6. It was also the most well-known among Aboriginal Mornington Islanders. On some occasions, I heard Mornington Islanders describe themselves using the analogy in the title of the book, 'from hunting to drinking', to (somewhat flippantly) explain why they had chosen to drink on a particular occasion.

1

LOCATING THE STATE

I sit in a plastic chair in the back row of the cavernous gymnasium on Mornington Island. Children run in and out shrieking at one another, many carrying the vivid plastic flowers that will later be pushed into the sand atop the gravesites in the community's cemetery by the sea. It's 2016, and I'm somewhat unprepared for the funeral of a young Aboriginal woman who has died in tragic circumstances a few weeks before my visit. My cotton trousers, black linen t-shirt and flip-flops are the most appropriate outfit that I can manage from a small bag of clothes that I've brought with me on this visit. My attire is a departure from the more formal and preferred selection of white cotton shirt and black skirt. In this I'm not alone – a sea of ill-fitting clothing abounds; items borrowed or purchased from a limited selection at the local store cover the bodies around me. In front of me, a young Aboriginal woman sits with her long slender legs crossed beneath an off-white chiffon dress. On each of her ankles are stacks of brightly coloured silicon bands, remnant merchandise advertising State and Federal Government programs. On the young woman I count five of these bands on one ankle and eleven on the other. Though these bands are generally worn on the wrist, the fashion among young women at the time is to stretch them up over the foot onto the ankle: no mean feat given their limited manoeuvrability. When programs are brought into remote Aboriginal communities they are promoted with lurid merchandise: t-shirts, caps, lanyards and these silicon bands. Like deflated balloons leftover from children's birthday parties, these bands often outlive the programs that spawned them, hanging around as the debitage of policy and policy failure, of good intentions gone to waste.

A funeral seems an unlikely place to locate the state on Mornington Island, and yet it permeates every corner of Aboriginal people's lives. Over previous decades, anthropologists working in Australia have described relations between Aboriginal people and the 'state' (e.g. Babidge 2010; Kapferer 1995; Morris 1989; B.R. Smith 2005, 2008; von Sturmer 1984). In general terms, the 'state' is used to refer to the norms of administrative representation in any particular place, such as organizations, bureaucracies and institutions, including State and Federal Governments, together with local councils and organizations. This chapter is concerned with the rise and fall of these institutions and organizations that are variously assembled and disassembled to govern Aboriginal people. Like silicon wrist bands, these structures and their effects persist beyond their operation and thus have ongoing impacts on those that they are intended to govern. In particular, this chapter focuses on the ways in which these structures draw in Aboriginal people, often coercively, and variously try to discontinue, mould or mimic aspects of Aboriginal cultural practice. That these various approaches exist side-by-side through time points to the contradictory experiences of the state as locally instantiated.

In Australia, the stage for the discussion of Indigenous issues has primarily been national, extrapolating an enormously complex patchwork of Aboriginal people's lives and circumstances into a broad-scale commentary. It is also at this national level that the signatures of political ideologies that seek to govern Aboriginal people, such as 'self-determination' and 'normalization', are most apparent. These tropes are powerful symbols in the understandings that the broader population have about the management of Indigenous affairs in Australia. Tim Rowse, Australia's best-known historian of Aboriginal policy, has described recent ideology as a shift from 'peoples to populations' (2012), marking the move away from a focus on cultural autonomy towards a statistical accounting of Indigenous people. The most obvious example is the Australian Government's 'Closing the Gap' agenda, which focuses on statistical remediation of Indigenous disadvantage by charting progress across key indicators, relative to the broader population (Kowal 2015a). In public discourse, it has been tropes such as 'Closing the Gap' that are held to account for success and failure to address what the broader population describes in everyday parlance as the 'Aboriginal problem': seemingly intractable differences in Aboriginal standards of living and workforce participation when compared with the rest of Australia. The problematization of Aboriginal people and the forms of governance that dominate within this ameliorative schema have a defining impact on the kinds of places and opportunities that develop.

Sullivan's (2011: 90) 'tools for ethnography of bureaucracy' draw out the broader ideals of a geographically and institutionally amorphous Australian Public Service (APS). The nature of Sullivan's analysis, or rather the presentation of a toolkit for undertaking an analysis, highlights a perennial problem in the interpretation of the state as it relates to the administration of Aboriginal affairs. That is, that few anthropologists have undertaken empirical research to engage the people and places that elaborate this as a social field, though as Sullivan rightly points out, this is changing. For Cowlishaw (2010: 51–52), these investigations need to address questions such as: 'What institutions and individuals do remote Aboriginal people encounter as the state and how is the elaborate and obscure machinery of governance understood there?' This chapter goes to the heart of these questions on Mornington Island. It charts the long-term endurance of these relations over time, and how the rise and fall of bureaucratic entities has become part of Aboriginal people's personhood.

Discussions taking place at a national level do not necessarily reflect people's day-to-day interactions with government, or more specifically, with the individuals, or 'agents', who are employed either directly or indirectly to enact government policy. Both Macdonald's (2013) study of Wiradjuri people of western New South Wales and Purtill's (2017) study of the administration of Ngaanyatjarra Lands in Central Australia highlight a disjuncture between Aboriginal values and norms and those of the state charged with ministering to them. These approaches leave unresolved the question of how to consider those people who occupy what Cowlishaw (1988: 114) describes as 'interstitial', namely Aboriginal people employed by the state in local agencies and administration. Reproducing the categories observed in her fieldwork from the 1980s and 1990s, Cowlishaw (ibid.: 253; 2004: xiv, 116) explains how such people referred to one another and were referred to by others as 'coconuts', i.e. those who were 'black on the outside and white on the inside'. Morton (1998: 360) argues that describing Aboriginal people in such terms creates the potential that 'those who, in one form or another, take up respectable positions or semi-respectable positions in schools, bureaucracies and other institutions' are not considered as 'real' Aboriginal people.

This analysis of Aboriginal people as having worldviews so diametrically opposed to that of the broader society that they are unable to meaningfully understand bureaucratic structures does not resonate with the Mornington Island situation. In fact, many Aboriginal people on Mornington Island interpret bureaucracy and the nuances of bureaucratic culture in order to manipulate its instruments to their own ends. This is not to suggest that Mornington Islanders do not at times encounter administration as antithetical to their own lives and aspirations, but rather that the history of association has been such that they are inseparable from one another. In this analysis I avoid conceptualizing the state as either monolithic or predominately immaterial (Babidge 2010: 12; Lea 2012). Rather, the state is conceived of as instantiated – that is, concretized – through various forms of administration and bureaucracy, as well as being 'peopled' by both Whitefellas and Aboriginal people. Thus, while 'the state' is seen as generative of experience and social relations, the emphasis is on the immediate and local nature of these experiences, rather than those derived from broader Australia. While in this chapter I consider the historical development of particular kinds of bureaucracy on Mornington Island through time, the following Chapter 2 is a contemporary ethnography of the Whitefellas who move to Mornington Island to work in bureaucracies. By exploring these two interconnected elements of the community; types of governance and those who work in it; I contribute to a holistic understanding of the state's presence on Mornington Island, or what Lea (2012: 116) refers to as 'the normative state of *being* the state' [emphasis in original].

Church as State

Aboriginal people all over remote Australia have been impacted by and subject to continual interventions by governments over extended periods of time. Though varying in time and space, a unifying characteristic has been discourses of protection justifying extraordinary actions. The foundational moment of relations between Aboriginal and non-Aboriginal people on Mornington Island was a government-mounted intervention designed to 'protect' Aboriginal people. In 1914 the Northern Protector of Aborigines, Walter E. Roth, acting on behalf of the Queensland Government, approved the establishment of a Presbyterian mission station at the southern end of the Island. This decision was to have profound and enduring impacts across the region.

From its establishment in 1914, the mission superintendent had sustained contact with the Aboriginal residents of Mornington Island, the Lardil Aboriginal people. Over a number of years, the mission increasingly drew in and incorporated Lardil people, and also Yangkaal people who journeyed across from nearby islands (McKnight 2002: 29). This incorporation was achieved in three interconnected ways: through the establishment of a school and dormitories to accommodate Aboriginal children removed from their parents, the establishment of an Aboriginal camp in proximity to the mission, and the use of the camp to source labour for the mission enterprises, such as timber-getting, market gardens, running cattle and the harvest of *beche-de-mer* or sea cucumber (Hall 1986).

As well as Aboriginal people from around the North Wellesley Islands, Aboriginal adults and children from the mainland were also relocated to Mornington Island under the *Aboriginal Protection and Restriction of the Sale of Opium Act 1897* (Blake 1998; see also Trigger 1992: 39–40). The relocation of these people to Mornington Island was a direct result of the processes of 'Wild Time' and its aftermath on the mainland adjacent to Mornington Island (Trigger 1992: 18). As Trigger

Figure 1.1. Aboriginal children and Aboriginal mission staff at the Mornington Island Mission, 1936 (UQFL57, Fryer Library, The University of Queensland Library).

(ibid.) has documented, throughout this period the mainland Gulf of Carpentaria was a frontier where police, pastoralists and Native (Aboriginal) Mounted Police violently dispossessed Aboriginal people, often across large distances. Relationships between people of various ancestries, including Aboriginal, Chinese, Afghan and Whites, resulted in the pejoratively described 'mixed-race' or 'half-caste' children, who were often taken into the state's care (McKnight 2004: 8, 14). This group included mainland Aboriginal people from the Waanyi, Ganggalida, Garawa and Yanyuwa language groups (Trigger 1992; McKnight 2005: 7; Memmott 1979: 343). When on Mornington Island, this group identified collectively as 'Mainland people', a marker reinforced by Lardil and Yangkaal people. Although 'Mainlander' is not a term in regular use today, it is sometimes used to delegitimize the perspectives of those particularly associated (especially through descent) with the mainland southern Gulf country; 'they from Mainland anyway'. Thus, 'Mainlanders' was a term used to enact points of difference and social exclusion, differentiating those who had arrived from elsewhere from

Figure 1.2. Reverend Wilson leads a church service at the Mornington Island Mission, 1936 (UQFL57, Fryer Library, The University of Queensland Library).

the Wellesley Island's original inhabitants: the Lardil, Yangkaal and Kaiadilt people.

Though the total number of 'Mainlanders' removed to Mornington Island was relatively small, less than seventy[1] in total, they nonetheless played an important role in the developing sociocultural relations within the mission (Blake 1998: 38). In 1936, the total population of Mornington Island was recorded as 260–270 Aboriginal people (Nelson 1936: 7), 110–120 of whom were children who had been taken to live in the mission dormitories. The remainder were adults, referred to by the missionaries as 'camp' and 'bush' people, who lived on country, coming in and out of a 'permanent camp just outside the [mission] station compound' (Nelson 1936: 8).

In 1947 and 1948, Kaiadilt Aboriginal people were moved from Sweers and Bentinck Islands to Mornington Island by the mission superintendent Reverend James McCarthy (Evans 1998: 60). The presence of Kaiadilt people altered the social and spatial landscape of the Aboriginal camp, with the most obvious indication of this change being the establishment of a distinct Kaiadilt precinct in the south-eastern part of the settlement (Cawte 1972: 28; McKnight 2005: 10–11; Memmott 1979: 294). Cawte (1972: 27) described this area as an 'enclave' and noted how in the 1960s, after almost twenty years living on Mornington Island, Kaiadilt people continued to be referred to as 'wild Bentincks' (ibid.: 29). Similarly, Nicholas Evans (1998: 34), a linguist who has worked with Kaiadilt people since the 1980s, characterized their history between the 1940s and 1980s as the 'exile years' when almost all Kaiadilt were resident on Mornington Island[2] and were thought of as a 'despised minority' (Evans 1998: 48).

The ongoing maintenance of singular linguistic-group affiliations within the settlement provided challenges to the mission goals of creating a socially harmonious society (McKnight 2004: 14). In order to promote harmony, the missionaries employed strategies to re-order social networks to more fully incorporate 'outsiders'. This included the informal adoption of Mainland and Kaiadilt people by Lardil and Yangkaal families and the arrangement of formal marriages between those of various linguistic affiliations (McKnight 2004: 18). These measures relied on the extension of locally operating Aboriginal kinship relationships and responsibilities to create bonds of social intensity between individuals and family groups.

By the mid-1960s, the Aboriginal population of Mornington Island had grown from the estimated 300 (230 Lardil and 70 Yangkaal) at the time of the first missionary's arrival, to over 600 (McKnight 1999: 120). McKnight (2005: 7) enumerated the distribution of 'Aboriginal Groups' for 1966 as follows: Lardil 253, Yangkaal 70, Kaiadilt 111, Mainland 194 and a total of 628 Aboriginal residents. Fifty years after McKnight's seminal period of fieldwork, the close affiliations between people and their intermarriage has meant that most now identify with more than one sociolinguistic group. In fact, retaining the right to identify with multiple groups (and thus retain a range of interests) through various lines of descent is the norm. As one Aboriginal man aged in his thirties commented, 'we all mix up now'. This 'mixing up' had been occurring for some time, and accelerated as the spatial layout of the settlement changed and the Aboriginal 'camp' transitioned to a 'village' in the 1960s, as McKnight (2005 :8) commented for his first year of fieldwork in 1966:

> The dwellings of the Aborigines were in what I have termed a supercamp but which the missionaries referred to as the village. I could not describe the Mornington Islanders as a tribe for they consist of several tribes. It did not seem accurate to refer to them as a society for they lacked the cohesiveness of a society. It was a community of sorts, an Aboriginal community, and although the term community has been criticized when used for such places as Mornington, mainly because it is favoured by government officials, I think there is some justification for employing this term.

Though it may have 'lacked the cohesiveness of a society', co-residence of various groups became increasingly important from 1970, as permanent housing began to be built on a ridge (and where the community is now based) behind the former mission settlement (Memmott 1979: 319). Being built along a long main street, spatially this layout afforded fewer of the enclaves that had dominated life in the camp (Dalley and Memmott 2010) The need for permanent housing became particularly clear after the devastation caused by a tropical cyclone that made landfall on the Island in 1976. Through the media covering of the event the Queensland State Government was exposed for failing to provide adequate housing for Aboriginal people living in the settlement (Brine 1980: 10).

It was also at this time that political changes across Australia saw the Federal Government become more active in pursuing bureaucratic structures that supported 'self-determination' for Aboriginal people. Within this political climate, the Presbyterian Church promoted what it saw as the need for the Aboriginal people of Mornington Island to take greater responsibility for managing their own affairs. As Memmott (1979: 315) described: 'The church had to re-think its responsibilities and seriously question the past role that its missionaries had played as 'social engineers' changing and maintaining the lifestyle of the Aboriginal people to make "useful and good humanity"'. Having enacted profound and devastating changes to Aboriginal people's lives, the Presbyterian Church supposedly believed that its work on Mornington Island had come to an end, as Aboriginal people were themselves ready to assume key roles in the leadership and administration of the community (Memmott and Horsman 1991: 240). The intended withdrawal of the Presbyterian Church, which had by then become the Uniting Church, was part of a broader sequence of events which led to the formation of the Mornington Shire Council in 1978.

Mornington Shire Council: Democracy and 'Culturally Appropriate' Governance

During the 1970s, a mining company showed interest in extracting bauxite from the Aboriginal reserve around the western Cape York mission community of Aurukun. At that time, Aboriginal reserve land existed outside state and federal control, with independent financial affairs. Realising the potential value of the taxation royalties, both the Queensland Government and the Federal Government were interested in gazetting the area as within their own jurisdictions (Memmott and Horsman 1991: 249). In public and political campaigns, both sides of government debated potential outcomes and in reaching a compromise, it was agreed that the reserve at Aurukun would become its own local authority under legislation specially enacted by the Queensland Government: the *Local Government (Aboriginal Lands) Act 1978* (Martin 1993: 3). In what would become a fortuitous occurrence, Mornington Island and most of the surrounding Wellesley Islands, as the sister mission to Aurukun, were also gazetted, and in 1978 the Mornington Shire Council was formed to manage local affairs (Blake 1998: 42).

When announcing the special legislation, Russell Hinze, the then Queensland Minister for Local Government and Main Roads, noted 'this legislation extends to the Aboriginal people of Aurukun and Mornington Island a degree of self-management and control, through local government, that is not enjoyed by people of Aboriginal extraction anywhere else in Australia' (quoted in Francis 2010). Hinze's use of the term 'self-management' in preference to 'self-determination' reflected the changed political landscape of Australia at the Federal level, which had seen the Whitlam-led liberal (Labor) government replaced by the conservative Fraser-led (Liberal) government in 1975. Will Sanders (2002: 2) described this difference: 'Self-management was a somewhat more conservative and guarded concept than self-determination, with an emphasis on responsibilities as much as, if not more than, on rights'. This emphasis was one which was to gain increasing relevance in Australian Aboriginal affairs over time.

In the case of the Mornington Shire Council, 'self-management' was to be realized through the democratic election of local government officers, a Chairperson (later referred to as the Mayor) and eight Councillors. This locally elected Council for a population of less than 1,000 people differed to the types of governance elsewhere in Australia, where Aboriginal communities were part of much larger local government areas, often including a range of towns and settlements with predominately non-Aboriginal populations (LGRC 2007: 212). Since the first year in which elections were held, all of the elected members have been Aboriginal people.[3] At the same time, the majority of administrative staff responsible for the running and reporting of the Council's affairs, including the Shire Clerk (later the Chief Executive Officer or 'CEO'), have been non-Aboriginal people. Graeme Channells (2000: 404), the first 'Shire Clerk' from 1978 to 1981 and later the Deputy CEO 1993 to 1996, described the Council's operations:

> the elected [Aboriginal] Council relied quite heavily on its [non-Aboriginal] officers for guidance as to the role and powers of a local government council. Councillors were often uncertain about their power to act in a particular situation and would frequently ask for advice about whether they could do a certain thing. As a consequence the Council was frequently advised that it was unable to act in some particular matter. I have advised it that way and many of its other officers would have advised it that way. I do not believe that any Council would have believed it had the power to uphold traditional rights as such. (Channells 2000: 407)

The degree to which Aboriginal 'traditional rights' (referred to by Channells) are integrated in the agenda and outcomes of an organization is sometimes used an indicator of an organization's success. However, David Martin (2005: 195) argued that: 'emphasis should be placed on developing robust relationships between the organization and its clients or constituents, rather than on attempting to mirror customary practice in formal institutional structures and corporate governance mechanisms'. Though the Mornington Shire Council was not empowered to 'uphold traditional rights', Channells' view and that of Robert Carruthers (2000: 412), his successor as Shire Clerk, was that the Council operated within what might be described as a:

> culturally appropriate' paradigm, albeit within the boundaries of its capacity: the Council, in carrying out its own activities did so in a manner which respected the traditional owners. If Council's activities would affect a partic-

ular area then it would ask the people from that area. The Council was comprised of people from the Island so there was no difficulty in determining who should be asked. (Channells 2000: 407)

This concept of 'who should be asked' related to the notion of 'asking permission' from Aboriginal people to access country to which they were traditionally affiliated (a point further elaborated in Chapter 5). This example is suggestive of discussions about the ability of administrative organizations, especially Aboriginal corporations, to incorporate (or indeed become) Aboriginal models of governance, particularly in remote areas where Aboriginal people are seen to have maintained distinct structures of authority (Martin 2005; Martin and Finlayson 1996; Townley 2001). These studies highlighted that 'such organisations, of course, while they "incorporate" Indigenous practices and values, by their very nature frame and constrain them, and are thus sites of their transformation' (Martin 2005: 189).

However, that the Mornington Shire Council was not empowered to specifically 'uphold traditional rights' was part of a critique of the structure and imposition of the Council by Channells, and also by McKnight (2002: 3), who described it as a form of 'colonialism' and an 'anathema for Aboriginal people'. McKnight's critique was that the Council was not a 'democratic body'.

> The councillors claim that they are a democratically elected body. But it is not a true democratic body. True democracy existed when the Mornington Islanders held meetings and everybody had a right to a say. During the initial years of my fieldwork there was a bell in the middle of the village which was rung when somebody wanted to make an announcement or to hold a public meeting. (McKnight 2002: 112)

It is difficult to interpret McKnight's contention that community meetings were a 'true democracy', if democracy involves the election of representatives to act on behalf of a particular group of people. Meetings are in fact far from democratic, as they privilege and recreate existing structures of patrimony, which are underscored by gender and age inequities. As Trigger (1992: 166), for example, noted of 'public' meetings in the nearby Aboriginal community of Doomadgee, 'most [attendees] were disinclined to speak' and 'the small number of people who did speak were usually councillors, police, church elders, or people who had once occupied one of these offices'.

Creating the time and space for people to contribute meaningfully was also limited by the impossibility that all those attending a meeting could have such an opportunity, especially given the size of the local population. Further, Mornington Islanders have embraced their role in the election of local representatives (Councillors and the Mayor) to the Mornington Shire Council. In all three recent local government election cycles – 2008, 2012 and 2016 – over 400 Mornington Islanders cast a ballot to elect a Mayor (Electoral Commission Queensland 2010, 2012, 2016).[4] In each of the three elections, the voter participation represented over two thirds of the total number of registered voters, a significant turnout.

The role and structure of the Council on Mornington Island has undergone continual change, including in recent times. Since 2005, successive reviews and the establishment of new legislation have significantly altered systems of local government across Queensland, including in Indigenous communities. The most significant of these reviews was undertaken by the Local Government Reform Commission (LGRC) in 2007 and resulted in large-scale amalgamations of councils, reducing the total number from 157 to 73 (LGRC 2007: 13). Primarily because of their 'different land tenure arrangements' which created 'impediments to amalgamation', the Mornington Shire Council and Aurukun Shire Council were able to remain as distinct entities (ibid.: 213). However, following the 2007 review, the number of elected Councillors was reduced from eight to four (plus a Mayor). Even under the new arrangements, Mornington Island has the highest ratio in Queensland of elected representatives to electors (ibid.: 212). The LGRC (ibid.: 59) noted of Indigenous councils across Queensland that they:

> have a small population, are remote, and rely heavily on grant funding for the delivery of council services. They also face key capacity difficulties in attracting appropriate staff to manage the services required to build the sustainability of these communities … are relied upon by their communities to provide a range of day-to-day services over and above the municipal services provided by other local governments throughout Queensland.

Part of the reason that the Mornington Shire Council assumed such a key role in service provision to residents was because it had a local presence (in the form of offices and staff), and also because there was often an absence of other agencies willing and able to do so. In 2010, the then Mornington Shire Council CEO Chris Francis discussed the central role of the Council in service delivery, using the example of banking facilities. As he put it, the Council: 'is the bank and we operate this service on the basis of being a community service obligation. We cash cheques, we do third party transfers, we bank cash for local businesses. This is not our core business, but it is essential' (Francis 2010: 9). Between 2006 and 2010, the Council also managed other essential services such as housing and housing maintenance and the upkeep of the airport runway and all roads, and had the contract for the local Community Development Employment Projects (CDEP) program (Maat 2007). As well as this, it operated smaller but socially important services, such as an aged persons' facility which allowed older persons to remain living on the Island, and the financial administration of pay deductions for funeral arrangements which helped families to afford the cost of burying their loved ones in the local cemetery. The role of the Council in financial matters on the Island was such that, as the CEO described it in 2010, the 'Council sits at the heart of the local economy' (Francis 2010: 5).

The extensive involvement of the Council in service delivery and the social and economic dependence of its constituents created a kind of 'localism' (Martin and Finlayson 1996: 5). Although Martin and Finlayson (ibid.) used the term as a way of referring to the Aboriginal domain, the central role of the Council in administering such a wide variety of services was similar to their description in which the 'priority' of functions was: 'accorded to the values and issues which are grounded in the particular and local, rather than in the general and regional or national'. This localism was also seen in the forms of Aboriginal corporations which operated on Mornington Island.

Aboriginal Corporations: Accountability and Capacity

At a similar time to the establishment of the Mornington Shire Council, a growing 'Indigenous sector' was being created across Australia to administer State and Federal Government funding (Hunt 2008: 28; Rowse 2005; Sanders 2002: 3). A prolific example of the 'Indigenous sector' has been Aboriginal corporations and organizations, created in the thousands from the mid-1970s under various legislative acts including the *Aboriginal Councils and Associations Act 1976 (Cwth)* (Martin 2003: 1; Rowse 2000: 1516). The operations and outcomes of such corporations have been widely reviewed, especially as relating to the notions of Aboriginal 'self-determination' or 'self-management' (Martin and Finlayson 1996; Sanders 2002). As Morgan (2006: 22) pointed out though, such organizations: 'have an ambiguous status. On the one hand they are symbolic spaces in which something called self-determination can be practiced and community cultivated – ideologically a milieu separate, and apparently protected, from the everyday regulation of the state. On the other they have a formal legal relationship to the state'. This 'formal legal relationship' became the undoing of many such organizations as they struggled to meet the expectations of accountability placed on them by funding bodies.

As has been the case across Australia, many of the organizations established on Mornington Island operate for a limited period of time, often to access a particular grant funding opportunity or while there is a local administrator to maintain the functions of the organization. What this means is that locally constituted organizations are constantly being established and dissolved (McKnight 2002: 132). Since 2009, twelve organizations were registered with the Office of the Registrar of Indigenous Corporations (ORIC) under the *Corporations (Aboriginal and Torres Strait Islander) Act 2006 (Cwth)* (CATSI Act) to administer funding for Mornington Island. Two of the corporations were also Prescribed Body Corporates (PBCs), dually incorporated under the CATSI Act and set up to administer the provisions of the *Native Title Act 1993 (Cwth)*. There was also an incorporated company, Gununamanda Limited, which was started in 1974 and had a governance structure very similar to the Aboriginal corporations (McKnight 2002: 82).

The activities undertaken by these organizations ranged from administering the local art centre (Mirndiyan Gununa Aboriginal Corporation) to operating a safe haven (shelter) for women and children (Yuenmanda Aboriginal Corporation). Based on information available online from the Office of the Registrar of Indigenous Corporations, in the 2009/2010 financial year the nine corporations ranged in membership size from nine (Werne Ngal Karan Aboriginal Corporation) to almost 500 members (Mirndiyan Gununa Aboriginal Corporation). The high degree of Aboriginal involvement, as directors and members, led McKnight (2002: 133) to facetiously comment that 'one might be forgiven for concluding that the main activity on Mornington is getting elected to committees'. Being a member or director, however, did not necessarily equate to taking an active role in the day-to-day affairs and running of such organizations. Rather, these tasks tended to fall to the Aboriginal and non-Aboriginal personnel who had the capacity to manage the affairs of the organization.

The interrelated nature of accountability, capacity and personnel was demonstrated in an example provided by the Federal Government Coordinator on Mornington Island in 2007. The example was of what was referred to locally as the 'Men's Group', which was running on the Island during the mid-2000s:

> One of the previous drivers of the Men's Group was [an Aboriginal man from Cape York]. He has since moved on, however he was one of the members with a vision towards the future for the group. He was able to galvanize the men into a workable body. During his leadership, the men met regularly and discussed their role in the community and devised plans for how they would find their place in the community. During that time the men began to

link their future to economic independence with visions of enterprise development on a grand scale, all of which was to be funded by government and other providers. At this time the Men's Group was given suggestions about how to develop their corporate and administrative skills, however this was not progressed. As a consequence, some of the men's group blame the government for not providing them with the capital they needed to begin business ventures, which they say then led to the demise of the Men's Group. (Maat 2007: 40)

That the Men's Group had operated during the 1990s in another guise, the Guba Dangka (meaning 'Good People') Aboriginal Corporation (Memmott et al. 2001: 66, 109), is further evidence of the cyclical histories of local corporations. The establishment of a new organization in 2013, the Thuwathu Wellesley Islands Sport & Recreation Aboriginal Corporation, whose members are all Mornington Island men, suggests a renewed attempt to reinvigorate male-specific services. The Men's Group is just one example of the ebbs and flows of such organizations on Mornington Island over time.

Financially, there was also considerable variation in the annual turnover of the organizations registered on Mornington Island, from several million dollars annually in the case of the Mirndiyan Gununa Aboriginal Corporation, which ran the local art centre and an Aboriginal dance group, to those that had no current financial dealings. Importantly, in meeting their responsibilities of accountability, the employment of an administrator, usually a non-Aboriginal person or an Aboriginal person from elsewhere, ensured that an organization had a degree of accounting and reporting capability when most Aboriginal Mornington Islanders had very few skills in this area (McKnight 2002: 83). Local Aboriginal people were often employed in a casual capacity, and moved through organizations in a similar way to that described by Christen (2009: 87) in the town of Tennant Creek: 'rather than following a "career path" in the vernacular of training institutions, many people move from job to job within and between organizations, with little worry about definitive "skill sets"'.

The high mobility of staff between organizations created a lack of accountability in their management of particular affairs, especially those relating to finances. Gaps in accounting or failure to deliver on stated outcomes thus had the potential to be considered an inherited problem from the previous management, creating systemic and cyclical processes of emergence and decay. In a review of a major agreement between Aboriginal groups and a mining company in the Gulf region including Mornington Island, Martin (2003: 7) commented on 'the almost total absence of competent and broadly supported Aboriginal organizations in the region'. This lack of 'competence' and 'support' was exemplified by my own experiences on Mornington Island in 2007. An elderly Aboriginal woman, a director of a local corporation, had received an overdue notice from a telecommunications company demanding payment for the corporation's telephone bill. The woman was uncertain as to how to respond to the notice, and asked me to place a telephone call to the organization's accountant in Townsville on her behalf. After five minutes on the phone resolving the issue, the accountant asked if I would consider being employed by the organization in an administrative capacity. The request identified the difficulties that some organizations faced in recruiting and maintaining staff to administer their most basic functions and their reliance on those who had few skills in the area.

One notable exception over the last ten years has been Mirndiyan Gununa Aboriginal Corporation, which employed non-Aboriginal men in the roles of General Manager and Manager of the art centre. The income stream created via successfully obtaining government grants (approximately AUD 800,000 in 2009 and AUD 1.4 million in 2010) and the sale of art (approximately AUD 900,000 in 2009 and AUD 1 million in 2010) through the art centre that the Corporation managed was instrumental in its ability to recruit and retain staff, including creating ten new positions in 2009 (Mirndiyan Gununa Aboriginal Corporation 2009: 6). The outlay is reflected in the 2009/2010 financial year, when the Corporation spent over AUD 700,000 on employee benefit expenses (Mirndiyan Gununa Aboriginal Corporation 2010). Also working in the Corporation's favour was that one of the non-Aboriginal men was a long-time resident of Mornington Island, married to a local Aboriginal woman who was also an artist represented by the art centre that he managed. The achievements of the Corporation were particularly impressive given that in 2008 it had been issued with a 'compliance order' relating to bookkeeping and accounts by the Office of the Registrar of Indigenous Corporations (ORIC), the body overseeing the CATSI Act (Mirndiyan Gununa Aboriginal Corporation 2009: 5).

Nevertheless, the impressive rise of the Corporation was relatively short-lived, and in 2017 it was placed into voluntary administration following concerns raised by the board of directors relating to the financial position of the organization. In documents arising from this administration, the Special Administrator asserted that the organization was in 'financial crisis' and that: 'Mirndiyan's money problems have been serious for some time. The Corporation had become accustomed to receiving significant revenue from the sale of paintings from the famous and well-respected late Mrs Sally Gabori. That's one reason it was spending more money than it was earning'. While Mrs Gabori's works adorn countless private and publicly owned buildings across Australia, and her work has been celebrated in a number of books and major exhibition retrospectives, the art centre that nurtured and supported her talent during her life now struggles to stay financially viable.

In the case of Aboriginal organizations, ORIC rarely intervenes unless to contain misappropriation after the fact, often when hundreds of thousands or millions of dollars have gone missing or been inappropriately spent. As Morgan (2006: 23) described it: 'The state has been reluctant to intervene in the affairs of self-determining organizations where things go awry, whether as a result of political cowardice or a misplaced cultural relativism. Both black and white Australia have been guilty of papering over the cracks, covering up the significant cleavages'. The continuous rolling nature of corporations makes it likely that the ebb and flow will continue and that most organizations which are established will sparkle and fade into the bureaucratic history of the Island. The state's supposed desire to remain, wherever possible, external to such organizations unless their intervention was called for contrasted to the types of service delivery for which they were more directly connected.

State and Federal Government: Responsibility and Enforcement

Over the last decade governmental approaches to the administration of Aboriginal people on Mornington Island have been geared towards engendering a greater sense of 'responsibility' or 'obligation', partially through various kinds of 'enforcement'. This ethos mirrors changes in the administration of Aboriginal communities Australia-wide, following in the wake of the Northern Territory Emergency Response (also known as 'the Intervention') into Aboriginal communities (Peterson 2010). Rather than facilitating 'self-determination' or 'self-management', 'responsibility' and 'obligation' have become foils for the enactment of punitive policies against Aboriginal people. Though situated in Queensland and not under the policy regime of the Northern Territory Intervention, on Mornington Island these approaches were most observable in areas where government service delivery was direct, as distinct from those where funding was provided via an interlocutory organization, such as the Council or an Aboriginal corporation.

As in most remote communities in Australia, on Mornington Island the State and Federal Government's key realms of service delivery were health, education, law enforcement and social security, also known as 'welfare'. The mantra of 'responsibility' in the Aboriginal sector can largely be attributed to the Aboriginal lawyer and political figure Noel Pearson, whose 2000 position paper, *Our Right to Take Responsibility*, marked the beginning of a decade of influential commentary in Aboriginal affairs (Langton 2010: 94). Pearson's (2000) paper contrasted the governmental ethos of previous decades, based on rights (particularly land rights), with the concept of responsibilities, attempting to address growing concerns about the symptoms of social dysfunction in Aboriginal communities. As I explained in the Introduction, these issues were particularly relevant on Mornington Island which, for example, had one of the highest rates (per capita) of reported violence in Queensland from the mid-1990s to 2006 (CMC 2009: 42; Memmott et al. 2001: 14).

Closely associated with this violence was the excessive consumption of alcohol. An early example of the intervention of government in this sector was the Queensland State Government's introduction of a range of restrictions on the sale and consumption of alcohol within the Mornington Shire Council jurisdiction. The changes were implemented via an Alcohol Management Plan (AMP), variations of which were introduced locally in seventeen Queensland Aboriginal communities (Queensland Government 2003). From its inception in 2003, the Mornington Shire AMP was modified by the State Government with increasingly prohibitive functions. I discuss the Pub and the consumption of alcohol and Aboriginal people's specific responses to the restrictions in detail in Chapter 4, though here I note that the initial introduction of the AMP was presented as a measure to 'reduce harm' by creating a more responsible drinking culture. However, in the end, the failure of the AMP to sufficiently impact drinking behaviour resulted in total prohibition, including the closure of the local Pub in 2008 (Queensland Government 2008a). This was indicative of the more stringent enforcement by government of its policy responses to Mornington Islanders.

In an attempt to broaden the introduction of 'responsibilities' to other areas, in 2007 the Federal Government signed a 'Local Indigenous Partnership Agreement' (LIPA) with the Mornington Island community following discussions at a 'negotiation table'. The LIPA set out five target areas; education, health, housing, family lands and leadership In 2009 Mornington Island became a community of interest for the Council of Australian Governments (COAG) 'Closing the Gap' program, and subsequently a Local Implementation Plan 2010–2014 was formatted. The LIP had seven priority themes similar to the existing LIPA, while including additional elements such as early childhood education and economic development. Each element was assigned a 'symbol' to give the priority themes 'local resonance' in 'traditional culture' through a system of marketing identification developed by the Mirndiyan Gununa Aboriginal Corporation (COAG 2010: 1). The marketing also included the translation of the theme titles into Lardil and Kayardild Aboriginal language, together with an accompanying 'cultural story' (ibid.).

At a similar time to these changes, a number of projects being run elsewhere in Queensland under the collective banner of the Cape York Welfare Reform (CYWR) trial were beginning to report positive outcomes. The CYWR was based on the more policy-defined visions of Noel Pearson (2009) who had been lobbying governments to 'recognize the failures of the previous policy paradigm' (ibid.: 274). In doing so, Pearson argued, government and Aboriginal people needed to 'attack passive welfare and tackle substance abuse' and 'focus on health, education and community life and on supporting people's efforts to build their lives' (ibid.: 275). One of the trial projects implemented in the communities of Aurukun, Coen, Hope Vale and Mossman Gorge was the tying of welfare payments for parents to their children's school attendance, or what was known as 'welfare quarantining', as overseen by a Family Responsibilities Commission (FRC). Reported anecdotal success of the trial in the Cape communities resulted in the development of a similar project by the Federal Government and Queensland State Government on Mornington Island, as well as at the nearby Aboriginal community of Doomadgee and the suburb of Logan to the south of Brisbane (Department of Education, Employment and Workplace Relations [DEEWR] 2011).[5]

The Improving School Enrolment and Attendance through welfare reform Measure (SEAM) trial, under which Aboriginal parents receiving Federal Government social security payments[6] via Centrelink could have their payments suspended or revoked if their child had repeated and unexplained absences from school or was not enrolled, commenced in Term 4 2009 (DEEWR 2014). At the discretion of teachers and the school principal, when a 'breach' was believed to have occurred, parents could be sent a letter and asked to provide details of their child's enrolment and an explanation for any absences. In 2011, it was reported that overall school attendance on Mornington Island showed moderate statistical increases, which the then Federal Minister Jenny Macklin interpreted to mean that the measure was 'having an impact on behaviour' (Karvelas 2011: 9).[7] However, after the trial ended in 2012 an evaluation report found that the increases in attendance were largely attributable to the 'threat effect' associated with the trial announcement and instances where breach letters were issued (but suspension of payments did not necessarily occur) (DEEWR 2014: 76–78).

The threat effect was also said to have lessened over time, eventually having no statistically observable impact on attendance. In comparison with the more urbanized trial locations, the evaluation report also noted the concern of teachers at Doomadgee and Mornington Island about the potential for 'consequences of their referrals', including personal safety, suggesting a reluctance for reporting to take place. The expectation that teachers would implement punitive measures against fellow residents in small-community settings is indicative of the burdensome nature of the policy on education providers. In 2012, the Queensland Government Minister announced the discontinuation of the trial, noting that the Federal Government's own data showed that the suspension of payments had 'no impact on improving school attendance'.

Another example of governmental approaches to problematic social issues was the Mornington Island Restorative Justice (MIRJ) Project, which commenced on Mornington Island in 2009. The MIRJ Project was funded by the Australian Attorney-General's Department in partnership with the Dispute Resolution Branch of the Queensland Department of Justice and Attorney-General (CMC 2009: 291). Although operating within the existing justice framework, the MIRJ Project set out to 'enhance the capacity of the community to deal with and manage its own disputes without violence, by providing ongoing training, support, supervision and remuneration for local mediators' (ibid.). Though many of the disputes were between younger persons, including children, local mediators were often older men, referred to as 'Elders', and selected for their authority in the community. A key part of the Project was enabling Mornington Islanders to resolve disputes so as to avoid the need for (further) police or judicial intervention. In 2017, the Project was reported as undertaking 160 mediations each year, and a recent review touted it as 'a spontaneous appropriation of mediation as a customary initiative' (Brigg et al. 2018: 347).

Aboriginal Mediators and White Administrators

Common to all of the bureaucratic structures operating on Mornington Island was the cultivation of professional relationships between 'White administrators' and 'Aboriginal mediators'. In some cases, Aboriginal people were formally employed by agencies as, for example, Community Liaison Officers with the local CDEP or Indigenous Engagement

Officers under the LIP (COAG 2010: 11). The impact of these kinds of relationships has been noted in other remote settings by those who recognized the complex interrelationships formed between those purportedly representing the state at the local level and those who they were governing (e.g. Batty 2005; Gerritsen 1982; Smith 2008). Such relationships often involved tensions and ambiguities for both Whitefellas and Aboriginal people, where each sacrificed or 'leased' their ideals and aspects of their identity in the formation of relationships. Through engagement, such partnerships became 'significant sites of administrative and cultural mediation, both delineating and channelling the aspirations of Aboriginal people and government' (Batty 2005: 216). Their partnerships were similar to those described by Kimberly Christen (2009: viii) in the Northern-Territory town of Tennant Creek where: 'Alliance-making as an analytical category opens up the possibility of seeing the intricacies of these relations, the rerouting of power, and the agency culled by those who may seem to be firmly in the grip of hegemonic power'. On Mornington Island, relationships between Aboriginal mediators and Whitefella administrators dissolved any nexus between the conceivably autonomous 'administrative agency' and 'the community'. The Coordinator of Federal Government services on Mornington Island in 2007, for example, referred to an Aboriginal colleague as being instrumental in his understandings of community politics and in identifying avenues for policy development. As he described, 'I guess you do latch onto people or get to know people that you get used to, more than anybody else. You just find someone that you have an affinity with and get used to'.

Another example was of two local Aboriginal Police Liaison Officers (PLOs) employed by the local Police Citizens Youth Club (PCYC). In an interview in 2009, the Whitefella Manager of the PCYC reflected on the close working relationship that he had with the PLOs, describing their involvement in PCYC projects as 'not important, it's just vital':

> right from the word go they gave me the orientation around the community, especially to people ... letting me know about different relationships ... proper terms and proper titles for people from *thabu* [Lardil kin term meaning older brother] to uncle and to whatever, and why they're called that and how they appear in the community, which is really important for me because if I have any kind of issue on the community, especially the youth, I know the most appropriate person I should be contacting.

The Manager also believed that this relationship enabled a degree of operational transparency and advocacy within the community:

first of all those guys [the PLOs] feel part of the management and second of all they have this ongoing ability for me to communicate with the community ... I'm not here to be popular and there are sometimes, there are decisions that I have to make which don't make me popular ... But the decision is made in all fairness and with a degree of justice and transparency and this is where the Police Liaison Officers ... are able to really lay it down to the community and explain things when questions are asked.

The way in which relationships or alliances between individuals extrapolated to a broader relationship with the 'community' formed the cornerstone of a model of 'community engagement' as described by the Federal Government Coordinator (Maat 2008: 2). The Coordinator, though, cast some doubt over the ability to achieve 'community engagement' based on such a model. As he pointed out: 'The government attempts to engage the 'community'. What it tends to do is engage the community leaders and elders of the community. The community leaders and elders talk to government, expressing what it [sic] perceives to be the concerns from the broader community' (ibid.).

The Coordinator's comments emphasised that the most intensive engagement occurred between the 'government and agencies' and the 'community leaders and Elders', while the degree to which 'community leaders and Elders' related to the broader 'Mornington Island community' was unclear. On Mornington Island 'community leaders' were largely men and women aged between their early thirties and late forties, who had particular skills in interpreting and negotiating bureaucracy. Some of these people were identified in a Mornington Island Leadership program in 2007, which singled out 'drivers' associated with particular priority themes such as education, health and employment (Hearn 2007). Examples of these individuals included local government Councillors, staff at the CDEP and Council office, supervisors in the CDEP work groups, and Aboriginal people employed by the local Council and State Government. Often, they were also members of local Aboriginal organizations, some involved as directors across a number of organizations.

The second group, who the Federal Government Coordinator and other Whitefellas called 'Elders', referred to Aboriginal people of varying ages but especially those aged in their sixties and seventies. As Peters-Little (2000) found of the term in south-eastern Australia, on Mornington Island 'their identities were rooted in their ability to survive mission and station life, as opposed to identifying with a traditional life'. It was notable that in my experience the term 'Elders' was not in any regular use among Aboriginal Mornington Islanders other than in the presence of Whitefellas. Thus, it appeared to demarcate a particular governmental discourse in the same way as the honorific terms 'Uncle' and 'Aunty', as I discuss further in Chapter 2 (see also Babidge 2010: Chapter 7). In the 'Closing the Gap' Local Implementation Plan (LIP), an Elder is defined as a 'widely respected man of authority who has gone through many rituals and ceremonies and has a deep knowledge of traditional lore' (COAG 2010: 26). Examples of 'Elders' included those associated with the Justice Group and Granny Group, and those who were employed as 'songmen' and 'culture teachers' with the Mirndiyan Gununa Aboriginal Corporation.

Day-to-day, 'Elders' and especially 'community leaders' were sought out by both Whitefellas and Aboriginal people, the latter often for basic assistance, such as with the interpretation of a letter received from a government agency such as Centrelink. Despite the importance of these individuals in communication between bureaucracy and Aboriginal people, the Federal Government Coordinator was not naïve about the degree to which they modelled the kinds of behaviour that bureaucracy advocated, as he described: 'leaders of the community are not immune from issues such as adherence to law and order, domestic and family violence, lack of a work ethic, personal responsibility and true leadership. This can create a "credibility gap" between what the community leaders say and what they are seen to do' (Maat 2008: 2). One example of this 'credibility gap' was that in 2010, the then Mayor of Mornington Island was charged with obtaining financial advantage through social security fraud for offences relating to the period prior to him becoming Mayor in 2008 (Tapim 2010; Electoral Commission Queensland 2010).

The Rise of the NGO Sector

The bust and boom cycle of Aboriginal corporations created an opportunity for other organizations to take on service delivery roles through funding made available through the Federal and State Governments. Over the last twenty years, non-government organizations (NGOs), also known as not-for-profits and better known for their work in parts of Africa and Asia, have increasingly expanded their operations into Aboriginal communities. Examples include Oxfam, Save the Children, Mission Australia and World Vision. Setting them apart from other providers, these organizations are heavily reliant on a workforce drawn from the local Aboriginal population. This is likewise the case on Mornington Island, where they send in non-Indigenous trainers and managers on an as-needs basis for short periods rather than being permanently located on the Island. The first of these organizations to have a local presence on Mornington Island was Oxfam, who from 2007 to 2011 employed two local Aboriginal people. In 2014, Mission Australia and Save the Children each constructed purpose-built state-of-the-art facilities. These organizations had also managed to recruit a local Aboriginal workforce, the vast majority of whom were women who had previously worked in a range of other organizations on the Island. As part of their employment, staff at these organizations often underwent training towards qualifications, sometimes involving trainers sent to the Island to deliver components of TAFE (Technical and Further Education) courses.

A key to their success appears to have been gradual development from small-scale operations. Save the Children, for example, began their operations on Mornington Island with Luuli, a small mobile playgroup for children aged up to four years of age. By 2014, these modest beginnings had been up scaled to a variety of programs, also including an after-school homework program for primary school-aged children and a thirty-nine-place childcare centre. In the context of the burgeoning local Aboriginal workforce, the day-care centre offered women wanting to enter the workforce the opportunity for their children to be cared for. Mission Australia operates three services at Mornington Island: a safe haven, safe house and women's shelter, services previously operated by local Aboriginal corporations. The focus in these areas, on increasing access to structured learning opportunities for preschool-aged children and facilitating access between children taken into care and their parents, reflects much of the increasing attentiveness to early interventions in child development and the importance of early childhood socialization. The position of these organizations, and their relationship with the Federal and State Governments, gives insight into the direction of service delivery for remote-living Aboriginal people, that is, the shift from direct service delivery by Federal and State employees to NGOs acting as intermediaries providing such services.

Private Enterprise: A New Form of Autonomy?

Another notable change occurring on Mornington Island has been the development of small Aboriginal-run businesses. Some businesses were assisted by start-up funding provided by the Aboriginal Development Benefits Trust (ADBT) as part of the Gulf Communities Agreement established in 1997 (Grant 2011; Martin 1998: 4). The GCA set out the obligations of companies (sequentially Pasminco, Zinifex and Oz

Minerals) who owned and operated a large zinc mine at Lawn Hill on the mainland to three Aboriginal groups, registered native title claimants in the areas which were to be particularly impacted by the mine (Grant 2011; Martin 1998: 4; Trigger 1998: 157). Many of the people that identified as part of these three groups were resident in the Gulf communities of Burketown, Doomadgee, Mornington Island and Normanton (Martin 1998: 4; Trigger 1998: 157).

David Martin (1998), who was particularly involved in negotiating the GCA, noted that it established a number of programs and initiatives in areas such as training, employment and education, and had economic goals including: 'the movement away from welfare dependency, the promotion of economic self-sufficiency to the greatest extent possible, and the enablement of local Aboriginal people to participate as fully as possible in the project' (ibid.: 4). Within the Agreement, the purpose of the ADBT was to 'provide loans or grants for small business skills training, start-up finance for small businesses and finance for equity in joint ventures and land purchases' (ibid.: 5). Some of the projects that the ADBT helped to set up on Mornington Island between 2008 and 2010 included a local bus service that operated as a taxi, a hire-car company, a convenience store and a shop that sold camping and fishing equipment (Francis 2010: 7; Grant 2011; Rowling 2010).

One of the first of the small businesses to be assisted by the ADBT was KJ's & Co., a home wares and bric-a-brac store established by a local Aboriginal woman aged in her thirties at the home that she shared with her Aboriginal husband and their young children in 2008. The woman started the business after holding a garage sale of her sons' baby clothes where she made AUD 500.00. Integral to the woman's business was her knowledge of the local community: 'Even though it's not the first business on Mornington, it is a pretty big thing, I am local, we are local. Like they'll come and ask for certain things, but we been here for that long, but we pretty much know what they're after, especially with the young mothers an' that. Things that I like, they tend to like as well'. This knowledge, she argued, gave her business a point of difference from the main local store, where 'you stand up half the day to get served'. In contrast, she told me, KJ's & Co. was 'more personal' and a 'gathering place' where women in particular came for a cup of tea and a 'yarn' as well as to purchase goods.

While 'local' knowledge was sometimes useful in selecting stock, and identifying a price point that was acceptable to the consumers, it also provided challenges. As the owner of the camping and fishing business reflected on his experience of balancing these two factors: 'been a bit of a journey so far, a challenge I suppose, meeting the needs of what the people want and good price for what they want' (Bradley Wilson speaking in Grant 2011). Being a local Aboriginal person and business owner also created quandaries when kin who were customers asked to lay by (purchase by small payments spread over time) or 'book up' (in this instance, to purchase something entirely on credit), thus delaying payment until a later date.

For the woman operating KJ's & Co., there were times when customers failed to pay off the balance owing on a lay by item, or continually asked to put off payment on an item of high monetary value (on a no-deposit basis); she reminded the customer that their failure to pay meant that she was in effect 'paying for this'. Another tactic that the woman used to avoid this problem was to only stock items that were 'inexpensive, affordable'. This reduced her own outlay in purchasing stock, made items cheaper to buy (and thus, more economically affordable) and reduced the potential loss if a customer 'booked up' and failed to pay. In spite of this, she noted that 'most people do come back and pick up their stuff' and that her general strategy was to only let people 'book up' when the item was 'really important, a funeral or something like that'.

The imposition on the business owner, however, did not always relate to finances. One of the main drawcards of the convenience store was that it was open on weekdays from 4 to 7pm as well as weekends, all times when the local store (supermarket) was closed. In spite of this, the Aboriginal woman who operated the convenience store noted: 'I don't think a lot of people on the Island can tell the time. We close at 7pm but we still have people walking up our steps and knocking on our door at midnight wanting to buy a can of drink. Hopefully we'll be able to put a stop to that soon' (Helen Reid quoted in Rowling 2010). Thus, both the home wares and convenience store business owners had developed strategies for balancing the needs of the market, as the example of 'laying by' suggests, but also ones that were 'personalized' and responsive to the local context.

These examples are suggestive of the model of economic engagement termed the 'frontier economy', as developed by McDonnell and Martin (2002) to describe Aboriginal community stores. These stores were developed under particular government legislation aimed to ensure the availability of food to Aboriginal people in remote locations. It was because of their position between the 'competitive' market-driven non-Aboriginal domain and the Aboriginal domain 'informed by the cultural context of business' that McDonnell and Martin (2002: 4) described them as occupying conceptually an 'interstitial space'. This in-between position was likewise the case for the Mornington Island store

Gununamanda, which was operated by a board of Aboriginal people but run within a 'market economy' (the buying and selling of goods using cash).

In remote locations, the ability of businesses to remain viable in the long term was dependent on their ability to remain either in the 'non-Aboriginal domain' and hence be guided overwhelmingly by market forces, or to operate in the interstitial space of the 'frontier economy'. Those which operated solely or at least predominately within the Aboriginal domain appeared more likely to fail (McDonnell and Martin 2002: 7). A comment by the (Whitefella) Chief Executive Officer of the local Mornington Shire Council illustrates this point using examples of three businesses, which might be conceptualized as belonging to each of the three spheres:

> We have seen two local indigenous businesses thrive but on very different terms. Whereas the hire car business is doing very well because it is used almost exclusively by visiting Government and business people, the corner [convenience] store is doing well because its customers are local people willing to buy items when the community store is not open. However, the local bus service has not thrived – the feedback was that local people were resistant to paying for travel. (Francis 2010: 7)

One explanation for this might be that residents were unaccustomed to paying for travel when they were able to demand a similar (or more preferable) service from kin who owned a car. It also reflected a point made by Francis (ibid.: 6) that 'indigenous people tend to purchase products and not services', especially when they were able to procure the latter through their networks of kin and for free or a cost far less than the market would demand.

In spite of the issues associated with balancing market-based and Aboriginal economic values, the owners of small businesses were enthusiastic when discussing their enterprises, some even suggesting that their success had broader implications for local Aboriginal people. In May 2011, an episode of the Australian television program *Living Black* (on the Special Broadcasting Service, or SBS, channel) focused on these businesses; the presenter Larteasha Smith (speaking in Grant 2011) noted how 'many residents here [on Mornington Island] are dependent on some form of welfare'. Within this context, the owners of the hire car company suggested that small businesses broke this 'dependency': 'Doing this sort of stuff makes us self-sufficient and gives us a sense of pride what we can achieve in this community and that's something that they can't take away from us' (Richard Sewter speaking in Grant 2011). Though it is somewhat unclear in this quote who was being referred to by 'us' and 'they', one interpretation might be that the reference is to the Aboriginal residents of Mornington Island (us) and government (they), given that welfare, the predominating form of income, was provided and structured by government (Francis 2010: 5).

Figured out of the assessment of these private businesses as a form of 'self-sufficiency' were the particular roles played by two major sectors which were both conceivably set outside the Aboriginal domain. The first of these was the assistance provided by the ADBT, which was funded by the profits of a privately listed company, at that time Oz Minerals. As has already been mentioned, the ADBT provided funding as part of their agreement with Aboriginal people in the Gulf region, where they own and operate what was once said to be the 'biggest zinc mine in the world' (Trigger 1998: 157). The second sector was government, specifically the Mornington Shire Council and the Queensland State Government, who were implicated in the success or otherwise of the businesses in a variety of ways, depending on the type of service being operated.

In some instances, they provided premises for the businesses to operate out of, either as an extension to an existing residential house (the infrastructure for which was provided by the Queensland State Government[8]), or in the case of one business, in a refurbished part of the Council chambers themselves (Francis 2010: 9; Rowling 2010). For one of the businesses, the hire car company, government employees visiting from the mainland were 'almost exclusively' responsible for rental demand (Francis 2010: 7). The Mornington Shire Council also assisted in other less visible ways by handling financial transactions and cash, given that there was no bank or credit union present on the Island to provide such services (Francis 2010: 9). Though no figures are available, it would also seem that most of the money which came through the community was derived from welfare payments and CDEP participation (ibid.: 5). In spite of these entanglements, the business owners on Mornington Island were overwhelmingly positive of their experiences, in two instances encouraging others to contemplate running a business (Helen Reid speaking in Grant 2011).

Enduring and Becoming the State

In this chapter I have described the ways in which Aboriginal people on Mornington Island are neither fully incorporated into, nor remain wholly outside, the state. In interpreting the rise, fall and decay of various government agencies and other administrative bodies, I have charted the means by which Aboriginal people have at various times been impacted by these processes. This has included forms of colonial violence, the most impactful being the containment of Aboriginal children in mission dormitories during the twentieth century. Perversely, the dispossession of people and their relocation into a single settlement, and the reordering of kin relations that occurred during this time, were justified by a paternalistic logic of protection. More recent experiments in policymaking have been geared towards recrafting Aboriginal people into the kinds of citizens that the state desires, often with limited effects. This is consistent with related policy manoeuvrings in the nearby Northern Territory, where the Intervention became a means for government to trial punitive policy approaches. Nevertheless, what appear first to be incisive changes often unravel over time, as the example of the School Enrolment Attendance Measure demonstrated.

In parallel, Aboriginal people have punctuated the inhale and exhale of these changes with their own explorations into state structures, as employees of organizations or in establishing their own private companies. One aspect of this experience has been to mimic and adapt the state's functions to suit their own ends. The example of the Mornington Shire Council and of Aboriginal people's enthusiastic participation in the electoral system both as candidates and as voters illustrates this point. What is elsewhere in Australia a non-Aboriginal domain has on Mornington Island been embraced locally as a form of Aboriginal representation. Charting the administrative apparatus of a remote community and its continual ebb and flow gives some sense of the constant management that Aboriginal people must undertake in their dealings with the state. The fatigue that Aboriginal people experience is largely a product of the state's continual reinvention of itself and of ways to govern Aboriginal people. Some of these experiments are deemed successful and become permanent fixtures in the policy landscape, while others are temporarily abandoned, to be later resurrected under the guise of a 'new' approach. All impact on Aboriginal people's lives in ongoing ways.

Notes

1. Blake (1998: 38) estimates sixty Aboriginal people as removed from the mainland between 1919 and 1936. However, there is some evidence, including from the missionary Hall's photograph captions, that children and adults from the mainland were being sent to Mornington Island as early as 1916.
2. As a form of punishment, missionaries periodically sent Aboriginal people to live in missions elsewhere (Memmott 1979: 273). For example, in 1941 thirteen Kaiadilt peo-

ple were sent to live in Aurukun, following their involvement in an attack and killing of a Mornington Island man on a mission boat (McKnight 2002: 39). Evans (1998: 62) reports that most relocated back to Mornington Island in 1953, though some settled permanently in Aurukun
3. The first non-Aboriginal councillor was elected in March 2020.
4. Numbers of ballots cast were 420 in 2008, 408 in 2012 and 441 in 2016. Figures include informal votes.
5. The trial was also adopted in the Northern Territory in the communities of Katherine, Katherine Town Camps, Hermannsburg, Wallace Rockhole, Tiwi Islands and Wadeye (DEEWR 2014: 2–3).
6. Including Youth Allowance, Newstart Allowance, Parenting Allowance, Parenting Payment Partnered, Parenting Payment Single, Age Pension and Carer Payment (DEEWR 2014: 8).
7. One of the issues with available data is that it is counted as the total number of potential attendance days for the entire population of registered children, rather than, for example, as an average attendance per child. It may be the case that a range of other factors also contributed to this moderate increase.
8. Residential housing on Mornington Island was managed under the 'One Social Housing System' (Queensland Government Department of Housing 2008: 3). The system meant that housing infrastructure was provided by the Queensland State Government and managed by the Mornington Shire Council through tenancy agreements with Aboriginal residents (ibid.). Further discussion of this system is provided in Chapters 2 and 3.

2

WHITEFELLAS AND BLACKFELLAS

It's 2007, and I walk from the supermarket down the main street towards the house where I'm staying. The ground is uneven, strewn with rubbish, and I'm keeping an eye out for Snowy, the large white dog that lives around here and has taken a particular dislike to me. It's unbelievably hot, and I can feel sweat run down the inside of my legs. The weight of a plastic bag full of overpriced groceries cuts into my hand, making my fingertips swell and tingle. I pass a 'high-house' where a group of Mornington Islanders are playing cards in the shade of a bauhinia tree. A middle-aged Aboriginal woman looks up and sings out, 'Cammy! Cammy!', gesturing for me to walk over to her. It's the first time in weeks that anyone has sought me out, and I feel a brief jolt of recognition, a moment of excitement just to hear my name called. I cross the road to the gateway. A man at the card game looks up and growls, 'Don't come in here! Don't you fucking come in here. Got a lot of cheeky dogs here.' The woman that called to me now laughs and looks away. 'Never mind!' she yells. 'Catch you after!' I don't understand what just happened but it is clear that I am not welcome. I keep walking.

In this chapter I address the experiences of the non-Aboriginal population, or those called 'Whitefellas' or *marndagi* in the local vernacular, who for the most part come to Mornington Island to deliver services to the Aboriginal community. For many Whitefellas, leaving their homes in metropolitan centres to take up residence on the Island is a confronting experience which is unparalleled in their professional or social lives, having transformative impacts on their short and long-term careers. The isolation of the community, the small population and limited access to the services and entertainment of more urbanized settings prove challenging, particularly for younger people. It is also in remote communities that workers, who are sometimes straight out of completing their professional degrees, are presented with challenges quite different to those in the towns and cities where they may have gained their majority of experiences and expectations of the workplace. Without the support of more senior colleagues with a greater depth of experience and skill, workers often find themselves managing complex and unfamiliar situations, leaving them feeling as though they are lurching from one catastrophe to another.

The immediacy of the geographic and professional isolation that such workers face is stark and relatively unyielding, yet these workers are the 'front-line', charged with being the physical presence to execute the policy mandates set out by State and Federal Governments (Purtill 2017). The vagaries of policy mandates make the targets almost impossible to achieve and eventually most Whitefellas move on, feeling burnt out and without having achieved any of the idealistic expectations for positive change that they arrived with. For some, the contractual nature of much of this work, and the cyclical funding regimes that support it, prevent greater professional investment. At the same time, not all Whitefellas go to Aboriginal places to 'help', and some of them are not committed to 'making a difference' at all. Many, especially teachers and police, take up positions in remote locations because of the entitlements and forms of career progression that it facilitates when they return to more urbanized locations.

The relentless turnover of non-Aboriginal people also has profound impacts on Aboriginal people's experiences and expectations of the state and of interactions with Whitefellas more generally. On Mornington Island, these impacts are pronounced, in that virtually all of the non-Aboriginal population of the Island, which over the last ten years has been approximately 10 per cent of the population at any time (or 100–160 people), move to the Island in order to take up jobs there, and move on a few years later. There are very few Whitefellas who have lived in the community for longer than five years. For the most part, Whitefellas and Aboriginal people lived parallel but distinct lives, socially and spatially separate from one another. As I argue in this chapter, my own experiences as a Whitefella on Mornington Island, and those of other Whitefellas, suggested that a range of interrelated factors contributed to this mutually enacted separation. This experience reflects Rowse's (2007: 90) conclusion for Australia more generally that 'social distance and cultural difference continue to be valued by both Indigenous and non-Indigenous Australians'.

In a journal at the start of my first stay on Mornington Island in 2007, I wrote that non-Aboriginal people occupied the 'bottom rung in the social ladder' and that as a woman, and as the most recently arrived Whitefella, I was 'invisible'. As I would come to understand, my feelings of 'invisibility' were not an accurate accounting, and certainly did not reflect the failure of Aboriginal people to see me. Rather they reflected my inability, at least at the outset, to read the dense and intricately crafted Aboriginal social world and to reconcile this with the confronting nature of my own isolation, exclusion and uncertainty. My experiences, together with those of other Whitefellas, demonstrate the importance of such perspectives in gaining a holistic understanding of the varying social lives of Mornington Islanders, both Whitefellas and Aboriginal people. To provide ethnography which elucidates Whitefella experiences recognizes the centrality of these people in attempting to operationalize broader policy agendas.

Writing about Whitefellas in Aboriginal Places

Despite the importance of non-Aboriginal people in the delivery of services in remote Aboriginal places, anthropologists have tended to pay only cursory attention to their day-to-day experiences and practices (Cowlishaw 2003: 11, 2010: 51). Instead, ethnographers have predominately focused on interpreting Aboriginal subjectivities in these locales, some commenting on the moral ambiguity of studying Whites, arguing the primacy of generating knowledge about disadvantaged people in the hope of improving their situations (Kowal 2015a: 25). This lack of critical engagement has had a twofold effect. The first of these is that the lack of ethnographic accounts about Whitefellas has rendered them out of the social landscape, without sufficient attention having been paid to the ways in which they inform Aboriginal people's perceptions of non-Aboriginal people more generally. These social dynamics are arguably a vital part of the expectations that Aboriginal people have of the outside world. Second, and as Cowlishaw argued, the lack of attentiveness created the potential for Whitefellas in such locales to be 'viewed as homogenous in thought and practice, when the reality is more complex' (2003: 11). In a homogenous rendering, Whitefellas simply blend into a broader monolithic state. With this 'displacement' comes 'a falsifying sense of a disembodied state operating as a coherent and even rational ordering device' (Lea 2012: 117).

One differentiation that has been lost under these conditions is as between what Lea calls a 'bureau-professional' (ibid.) and what I refer to as a 'worker'. One effect of the collapsing of these categories has been to misunderstand the roles that the various cohorts have, or see themselves as having, in addressing the symptoms or structures of inequities. While in locations such as Darwin and Brisbane, there may be considerable overlap in the roles performed by bureaucrats and workers, in more remote settings the task of formulating policy is at a level of abstraction beyond the daily workings of communities. On Mornington Island and in other remote communities, this boundary is particularly stark because of the distance to the regional centres where policy decision-making takes place. Policymakers are confined to 'elbow-tipping' visits, so called as they look worryingly at their watches to ensure that they do not miss their flight home. Their experiences are of brief and voyeuristic exoticism, the novelty of remote travel and the chance to be 'out of the office'. For these reasons, Purtill argues 'there is an enormous gap – an experiential and informational gap – between the level of policymaker and bureaucrat and that of the remote community staff member' (2017: 11).

Though there is undoubtedly interdependency between the components of the state apparatus that manage Aboriginal communities, one important distinction remains. While Lea (2012) has argued that bureaucrats desire intervention, by first 'projecting' a kind of anarchy onto Aboriginal subjects, I would argue that this can only occur when there is a degree of physical abstraction between the bureaucrats and the realities of everyday life. For those living and working in communities, there is no need to develop visions of this anarchy; their inability to read the social field means that anarchy appears to them in their everyday interactions with Aboriginal people. As my own experience at the vignette at the start of this chapter indicates, the hope for a kind of social inclusion was replaced by confusion, resulting in the more permanent closing off of social worlds.

Gillian Cowlishaw has been a staunch advocate for writing about Whitefellas. Since the 1980s, she has studied cross-cultural relations in the western New South Wales town of Bourke, and more recently in urban Sydney. Two of Cowlishaw's acolytes, Tess Lea (2008) and Emma Kowal (2015a) took up this challenge in their studies of bureaucrats working in Aboriginal health in the Northern Territory. Lea and Kowal considered a particular kind of Whitefella, generally bureaucrats or what Lea (2008: 3) described as the 'helping Whites' or 'bleeding hearts', people who had chosen to work with Aboriginal people in an effort to 'do good'. As previously mentioned for Mornington Island, however, not all Whitefellas working in service delivery for Aboriginal people might be defined or define themselves in similar terms. Elsewhere, for example, the demographer Will Sanders (2007: 65) has contrasted those wanting to 'do good' with those who want to 'make good', the latter more interested in the financial or professional incentives attached to working in remote communities than in securing positive outcomes for Aboriginal people. From time to time the worst of the 'make good' Whitefellas are splashed across the pages of Australia's daily newspapers, described as 'carpetbaggers' or 'shysters', accused of ripping off unknowing and vulnerable Aboriginal people for their own financial gain.

Sanders' analogy is reminiscent of the first two parts of the 'mercenaries, missionaries and misfits' metaphor, three categories often used to characterize Whitefellas working in remote Aboriginal communities. Like Sanders' 'make good', 'mercenaries' were those who worked in Aboriginal communities for financial or material benefit, while missionaries were motivated by their belief in the transformative potential of Christianity. Kowal (2011: 323) has described how the 'missionaries' moniker was the most 'serious' to level at the group she calls 'White anti-racists', on account of its association with colonial history. For White anti-racists, missionizing also cut across a dedication to both preserving Aboriginal people's social and cultural difference and improving their statistical outcomes against the broader population. The final category, that of the 'misfit', similarly suggests a kind of fetishization of the difference of Aboriginal people, largely by Whitefellas who were estranged from their own society. David McKnight described these Whitefellas on Mornington Island as those who find it 'irksome or dull' (2002: 221) to live with non-Aboriginal people. It was not uncommon during my time on Mornington Island for other Whitefellas to pose the question: 'which is it: mercenary, missionary or misfit?'

Though anthropologists are only now beginning to take seriously the experiences of Whitefellas in these settings, a number of published memoirs have provided accounts of their experiences (e.g. Brown 2005; Jordan 2005; Moss 2010; Shaw 2009). In a variety of ways, each of these accounts, which sit between memoir and non-fiction, chart the good intentions of these workers, their frustrations and gradual disillusionment with both Indigenous and non-Indigenous community management. In doing so, they also point to the marked social divides between Aboriginal and non-Aboriginal residents. Jordan (2005: 8), for example, explained: 'I vaguely expected it to be a mishmash of black and white – but in fact there is a sharp social divide. I had thought that the white people, a tenth or less of the community, would have both black and white friends, but we socialize amongst ourselves, while the Aboriginal communities keep to themselves'. Such accounts provide ready fodder for academics keen to point out the paternalism and naivety of Whitefellas intent on changing Aboriginal people (Probyn-Rapsey 2007; Reed 2005; cf. Trigger 2009). Discussing those involved in the Northern Territory Emergency Intervention, Cowlishaw (2010: 52) says they 'are vigorously attempting to change the everyday practices, internal social organization and structural position of a whole people. Obviously they cannot know what they do'. Whether or not they 'know what they do' is a difficult question to answer, as what 'they do' is as much a question of what the broader society expects them to do. The weight of this expectation, Tess Lea (2012: 111) argued, contributed to a kind of 'addictive … headiness' among bureaucrats working in the Northern Territory Intervention. Lea's point about the state being 'peopled' is a useful one, as it highlights the 'anarchic' ways in which policy is developed and implemented. As to whether or not this peopling means, as Lea seems to suggest, that the power of these feelings is such that they would encourage the overstating or embellishment of problems in remote communities so as to justify an ongoing need for the state to intervene in the lives of Aboriginal people, is a riskier proposition to contemplate. The risk is to understate problems so as to encourage a kind of apathy or ignorant acceptance for the disadvantage that Aboriginal people are forced to live with.

It is perhaps also the intensity of such experience and the frustrations it entails which often lead to disillusionment and withdrawal among bureaucrats and those working at the coalface in remote communities. On this burnout, Kim Mahood (2012) reports an Aboriginal person on the edge of the Western Desert commenting that 'Kartiya [Whitefellas] are like Toyotas', the punchline being that when they are broken down they can be replaced with another. While some may take this as a humorous anecdote of Aboriginal people's expectations of non-Aboriginal workers in remote Australia, it also highlights the callous disregard that some Aboriginal people and Whitefellas have for the lives and well-being of these people, while ignoring their pivotal role in the service-delivery needs of such communities. To imagine that Aboriginal places, particularly those in remote settings, might survive without the involvement of non-Aboriginal people in service delivery perpetuates a structural fantasy for a particular kind of self-determination which continues to show no signs of being realized in the short or long-term. It remains the case that now and into the foreseeable future, Aboriginal people will be dependent on the skills and expertise of non-Aboriginal people to successfully maintain and manage their communities. The challenge is to imagine ways in which these relationships can be mutually enacted from positions of strength, which enable sustainable investment in such partnerships.

White as a Category

Across Australia, a variety of terms are used to refer to those designated as 'non-Indigenous'. This includes words derived from Aboriginal languages, such as *kardiya*, used in the Kimberley and parts of the Western Desert, *balanda* in Arnhem Land and *marndagi* in the Gulf of Carpentaria. While the specific uses and meanings of these terms vary both geographically and contextually, they all act to reproduce a foundational dichotomy between the identities of Aboriginal and non-Aboriginal people. On Mornington Island, despite the ubiquitous local use of the term, the 'Whitefella' portion of the community is ethnically diverse and has lately included people with a range of ancestral backgrounds including Filipino, German, Indian (including Sri Lankan), Maori and South African (ABS 2006: Table B08, 2011: Table B08; 2016: Table G08). Given this heterogeneity, 'Whitefella' is a signifier used to designate more than skin colour or ancestry, but rather to enact a particular social category.

Most of the Whitefellas living on Mornington Island over the last fifteen years have worked in one of the service delivery agencies operating on the Island. According to the Australian Census, the non-Indigenous population of the Island has been steadily increasing over the same time period, almost doubling between 2006 and 2016 (ABS 2006: Table I01a, 2011: Table I01a, 2016: Table I01a).[1] Some of the more recent growth is attributable to large-scale infrastructure projects, namely the building of a new barge facility and the upgrading of the local airstrip. In her study of 'White anti-racists' working in the health system in the Northern Territory, Emma Kowal (2015a) discussed the contexts in which Whites performed aspects of their Whiteness in both public and private spaces. In this way, Kowal's use of the term 'White' in her research stemmed from a desire to categorize those who enacted particular kinds of 'Whiteness' in everyday life, built on a foundation of 'Western education, income, class privilege'. Kowal's account was particular in the sense that most of her research subjects identified as 'anti-racist', a political positioning that Kowal saw as emerging from their status as 'non-Indigenous, left-wing, middle-class professionals' (2015a: 33).

The collapsing of racial identities in the accounting of non-Aboriginal people has been reported elsewhere in Australia. Myrna Tonkinson (1994), for example, a Jamaican woman with black skin, wrote of being regarded as a Whitefella when she accompanied her White husband (the anthropologist Robert Tonkinson) to his field research site in Central Australia. She described how she had anticipated that her shared skin colour would craft a kind of affinity with Mardu Aboriginal people, but that 'in the few discussions I had with people about this I was never able to persuade them that my skin colour signified any special link with them' (ibid.: 166). Being called a 'Whitefella' by Mardu people, Tonkinson (ibid.: 167) argued, 'was consistent with their giving salience to culture' above skin colour in the interpretation of identity.

On Mornington Island, skin colour was just one of the markers at play in determining whether a particular person was thought of by Aboriginal people as 'White' or a 'Whitefella'. Other factors included having material items like cars and boats, having a full-time job and whether they interacted socially with other Whitefellas. Another marker was what an elderly Aboriginal woman once described to me as talking 'real proper', using plain English rather than Aboriginal English when engaging with Aboriginal people. What most defined Whitefellas as other, however, was their lack of shared historical experience with local Aboriginal people. To highlight a particular point: for a number of reasons, including the designation of the Wellesley Islands as an Aboriginal reserve, the overwhelming majority of Whitefellas living there have moved to the Island as adults to work for the Queensland State Government or the local Mornington Shire Council.

In other parts of Australia and other post-settler countries, non-Indigenous people's assertions of autochthonous identities have been derived from successive generations remaining in the one locale, where the development of relationships with land and the generative nature of ancestry and memory propelled the development of connection (e.g. Dominy 2001; Martin 2015; Redmond 2005; Trigger and Martin 2016). In contrast, the high turnover of Whitefellas on Mornington Island, and the short amount of time that they spent there, resulted in diminished forms of connection. This was exemplified by the fact that Whitefellas referred to Aboriginal people as 'locals' or 'local people'. Conversely, Aboriginal people referred to non-Aboriginal people as 'outsiders', a term used intermittently with 'Whitefella'. These mutually enacted expressions of those who belonged, 'locals', with those who did not, 'outsiders', illustrate how categories of identities were used to enact forms of social categorization.

At times Aboriginal people used acts of consubstantiation to blur the boundaries of categories in order to demonstrate their fondness or affinity for particular individuals. For example, in 2009 an Aboriginal woman in her thirties, with whom I had developed a particularly close friendship, asked me, 'But you not really White aye [are you]? You're like black, but on the inside'. Consubstantiation, or the sharing of substances like skin colour and blood, materializes relationality by acting as a generative bridge between what might otherwise be unrelated bodies (Carsten 2011). Whether I was actually 'black on the inside' was immaterial; the performative nature of the woman's expression made clear her intent for me to feel and consider myself socially incorporated in a particular way. In another instance, the woman's husband made a similar comment to another Aboriginal man who had questioned my knowledge of a remote outstation on the northeast end of Mornington Island. After I outlined the Aboriginal place name and described the location of the outstation and the curves of the access track, the man laughed, telling those present, 'yeah, she a proper Lardil woman her'. These examples, suggestive perhaps of playful social incorporation rather than of serious intent, are indicative of gestures by Aboriginal people to expand categories of identity to include others.

As part of my research, I interviewed Whitefellas employed in a range of roles on the Island, including a school teacher, hospital staff, Aboriginal corporation employees, the Manager of the local Police Citizens Youth Club, the Federal Government Coordinator and employees of the local Council. At the time that I interviewed them, the participants ranged in age from their late twenties to their mid-fifties, and each had spent varying amounts of time living on Mornington Island, from several months to several years. For many of these Whitefellas, Mornington Island was their first experience of working in a remote Aboriginal community, and some spoke of their arrival as associated with a sense of uncertainty or fear. A doctor aged in his thirties, who was on a short-term placement at the local health service, described his arrival on the Island in 2007 as akin to travelling to Indonesia. This description related to the unfamiliarity of negotiating the intricacies of travelling on a small aircraft and the searching of passengers' luggage by the police on arrival (as part of the Alcohol Management Plan), compounded by the sensory overload when stepping off the plane for the first time: smells of burning rubbish from the nearby rubbish dump and the 'dilapidated' appearance of the community.

Another observation made by the doctor was how many 'unfamiliar faces' he encountered upon his arrival. In interpreting that these faces were 'unfamiliar', the doctor was not just recognizing that most residents were unknown to him, but also that they were Aboriginal faces. In broader Australia, Indigenous people comprise less than 5 per cent of the Australian population and few Australians report encountering Indigenous people on a regular basis. As Indigenous scholar Yin Paradies (2006: 359) has pointed out, 'it is clear that skin colour and physicality are exceptionally important in the recognition and validation of Aboriginal identity'. It is generally the case that Aboriginal people on Mornington Island conform to a particular stereotype that allows them to be easily recognized as Aboriginal, notably that they have dark skin. When arriving on Mornington Island, the doctor experienced an immersion with people that he visually coded as Aboriginal. This inversion, where Whitefellas find themselves in a minority, destabilizes their expectations of being a racial majority, an experience which undermines the primacy of their belonging, taking them into 'unfamiliar' territory.

For some Whitefellas arriving on the Island for the first time, the sensory overload was paired with unease about safety. A single school teacher in her forties recalled: 'I arrived here [Mornington Island] on a Sunday evening about 5.30[pm] and it was very hot and I was really quite frightened'. For some this fear had been built up before even arriving on the Island itself. A middle-aged couple who travelled to the mainland town of Mount Isa to receive induction training before moving to the Island, were confronted with others' stories about the place: 'We were told some horrendous stories and about living and working there … I think people relate the most shocking ones [stories] because they think they're the best ones to tell'. Another middle-aged couple that had worked in other remote settings previously had familiarized themselves with what the community looked like before their arrival using the Internet video site YouTube and other online media. As they drove through the community for the first time, some Whitefellas reported being shocked by its appearance, describing it as 'desolate'. Feelings of uncertainty, fear and the appearance of the community made some Whitefellas desirous of an instant separation between themselves and Aboriginal people. A woman in her forties who worked for a local Aboriginal organization reflected on her early days on the Island: 'I needed to be physically separate from them [Aboriginal people], as I got more used to them yes, but in the beginning I wanted to go into a cave and just say "I'm not sure about this"'. For most Whitefellas the desire for 'physical separation' was realized through the layout of the community, with some areas predominately occupied by Whitefellas and others by Aboriginal people.

Space and the Production of Race

In Australia, the spatial demarcation of settlements has been a major feature of studies of race relations. In many towns and cities, Aboriginal people and those of other ethnic minorities were historically prevented from entering particular locales. Contemporary street names, such as

'Boundary' streets in Brisbane and 'Separation' streets in Melbourne, continue to bear this legacy. Though not always constituted by named streets, in country towns and Aboriginal communities these divisions were similarly stark. In Oenpelli, a settlement in West Arnhem Land, for example, von Sturmer (1984: 222) discussed how in the 1980s, a 'causeway marked the boundary' between the area used by Whitefella tourists and where Aboriginal people lived. Divisions between areas used by Whitefellas and Aboriginal people in the Aboriginal community of Doomadgee were mapped by David Trigger (1992: 80) during the 1980s. In his description of the boundary between the two spheres, Trigger (ibid.: 79) explained how 'an open strip of bare ground, 100–200 metres wide separated the two areas'. While both areas included residential housing, it was only in the Whitefella domain that Aboriginal people could access services such as schools and the local hospital (ibid.: 81). Similar divisions were discussed by McKnight (2002: 7) and Memmott (1979: 479) for Mornington Island, at least until the 1980s when the church withdrew administration and new housing was built on the ridge behind the mission.

For the 1970s, Memmott (1979: 392–93) described how the Aboriginal domain was a place of residence and also included particular kinds of 'social behaviour', which he described as 'traditionally Aboriginal':

> gossiping, gambling, fighting, square-up, traditional dancing, outdoor church services, children's play, drawing water from communal taps, and occasional sports such as boxing and football. The origin of many of these activities is traditionally Aboriginal, and all except church service are controlled and directed by Aboriginal people. Most of these activities thus share a sense of Aboriginality.

Though it is unclear the basis on which such activities were deemed to be 'traditionally Aboriginal', Memmott (ibid.: 393) made it clear that this area was 'a most Aboriginal place', clearly defined against the 'mission precinct' where 'mission imposed rules' dictated the behaviour of Aboriginal people.

Though not as clearly demarcated as they were reported for the 1970s, similar spatial and behavioural divisions were evident in Gununa during the 2000s. In 2008, there were 178 dwellings[2] on Mornington Island, managed by the local Council through tenancy agreements with Aboriginal residents (Queensland Government Department of Housing 2008: 13). Part of this 'One Social Housing' stock was also dwellings used to accommodate (mostly) Whitefella staff of external service delivery agencies, such as Education Queensland, the Queensland Police Service and Queensland Health (ibid.: 22). Whitefella residences, in-

Figure 2.1. Gate and fencing on the northern side of the hospital compound (photograph by the author).

cluding housing for teachers, police, medical staff, tradesmen, employees of the local Shire Council and Aboriginal corporations, comprised fifty-four,[3] or approximately 30 per cent, of the total number of dwellings. Given that Whitefellas comprised less than 10 per cent of the total population, the small number of occupants that each of these houses accommodated is indicative of the privileged position that Whitefellas had in the social demarcation of space. These houses were clustered in particular parts of the community, often surrounding or in proximity to the place of employment. For example, the hospital 'compound', as it was referred to by both Aboriginal and Whitefella residents, encompassed the hospital itself together with accommodation for hospital and paramedic staff.

Taking up almost an entire block, the 'compound' was surrounded by a seven-foot mesh fence topped with barbed wire (see Figure 2.1). When viewed from surrounding roads, it was rare to see people in the compound, as I observed in my fieldnotes in 2007: 'I wanted to see whether there were many White people out and about in the compound. Although I could hear some voices I couldn't see anyone'. The main gates to the residential side of the hospital compound were held together with a heavy chain and lock, though as one of the health workers, a young man aged in his thirties, observed, 'it was never actually locked'. Rather, the fence and lock acted as:

> a visual deterrent, something that creates a distinction between us [Whitefellas] and them [Aboriginal people] and implies ... that separateness. They don't come into our space, our area. Somewhere separate. I think that they [Aboriginal people] understand that different sanctions apply if they stepped into that area and they expect to be treated differently than if they stepped into someone else's place in the community.

Another resident, a middle-aged woman who had lived in the hospital compound for over three years with her husband who was a health worker, perceived the fence differently. She explained that she could 'visually see it' but that to her it did not 'mean anything'. The woman worked for the local Council and spent much of her time outside the compound confines. She also gave an account of how an Aboriginal co-worker at the local Council described the hospital compound as 'Guantanamo Bay'. In the context of race relations, the Guantanamo Bay analogy has relevance as a reversal of roles, re-crafting the non-Aboriginal inhabitants of the compound as somehow deviant to the societal norms of the predominately Aboriginal population who lived outside the compound. In considering the analogy, the woman explained that her Aboriginal co-worker 'believes that the Health Department don't want their employees to associate with local [Aboriginal] people. I don't see it as that at all but maybe locals [Aboriginal people] do, they might see it that way'. Although the woman was not prepared to recognize the racialized implications of living within the compound, she did acknowledge that some Aboriginal people had a different view.

In the case of hospital workers, cloistering was facilitated by arrangements made by Queensland Health, meaning that it was possible for hospital staff to live and work entirely within the compound confines, without having to visit other parts of the community. Food, including meat, vegetables, fruit and dry goods were brought off the weekly barge and placed in a storeroom within the compound and made available to Queensland Health employees. This meant that health workers could bypass visits to the local store, a vibrant and pivotal meeting place for Aboriginal people. Those living in some other State Government accommodation, staff of the Queensland Police Service and Education Queensland in particular, also had perimeter fences surrounding their individual residential houses, as shown in Figure 2.2.

Though not all the fences were as substantial as those at the hospital compound, a Whitefella resident living in the Queensland Police

Figure 2.2. Example of Queensland Police Service House (photograph by the author).

Service house shown at the left in Figure 2.2 explained that the fence around the these houses contributed to a 'compound mentality':

> the mentality when they were built twenty years ago was to build a big high fence that locals [Aboriginal people] couldn't get into.[4] So we lived in a house that was adjacent to the police station, and there were seven houses there. It's less of a compound than a precinct, but it does in fact have a high fence but the gates were never locked but ... there was that compound mentality.

Not all Whitefellas, though, lived in compounds or houses surrounded by imposing fences. Some Whitefellas who were employed by the State Government or the local Mornington Shire Council, such as contract tradesmen (simply referred to as 'contractors'), lived in the area known as the 'caravan park' or 'contractors' camp' on the north-eastern side of the community. Although not physically far from nearby Aboriginal housing, the contractors' camp was set apart by having a singular access road that lead only to the camp itself. Thus, any car or person driving or walking up the access road could only be going to visit one of the Whitefellas living there. Musharbash (2010) undertook a related study of Whitefellas' use of particular roads in and out of the Aboriginal communities of Yuendumu and Wari Wari in the Northern Territory. She noted how Whitefellas – teachers, policemen and contractors and employees of the Australian Federal Government as part of the Northern Territory Emergency Response (also known as 'the Intervention') – only used the 'long road' into Yuendumu. In contrast, Blackfellas (Aboriginal people) used the 'back roads', an unsigned network of unsealed roads around the towns (ibid.: 214, 216).

The differential frequenting of different roads was used as a metaphor for the distinctive ways in which Whitefellas and Aboriginal people lived 'parallel lives, simply avoiding each other' (ibid.: 223). Musharbash (ibid.: 224) suggests that these types of social relations were somewhat 'dormant' in the community before the Intervention, after which there was a dramatic increase in the number of Whitefellas working in particular Aboriginal settlements. The increase, she suggested, 'detrimentally intensified' relations of separation between Aboriginal people and Whitefellas in the Yuendumu region (ibid.: 223).

In Gununa, Whitefella Council employees other than contract tradesmen lived clustered together at the top (western) end of Lardil Street and down along the Appel Channel in proximity to the Council offices. These residential areas were not as clearly demarcated as the hospital compound and police precinct, and from time to time Aboriginal people took up co-residence in these domains, for temporary emergency housing or as a de facto partner to a Whitefella. Such cohabitation made these domains immediately more accessible to other Aboriginal people, and sometimes family members of the Aboriginal partner could be seen sitting outside the house 'yarning' with their relative. During some of my visits to the Island between 2008 and 2012, I was likewise accommodated in Council-managed properties, either in the contractors' camp or in these areas. My frustration at being spatially and therefore socially distant from Aboriginal people led me to ponder the rationale for this positioning: 'maybe it's because they [the Council] want to segregate us Whities [sic] together'. In reality, there was a 'critical shortage' of housing for staff, visitors and 'workers from outside the community' (Queensland Government Department of Housing 2008: 21) and for most of the Whitefellas living on Mornington Island, their place of residence was determined solely by arrangements made by their employer, involving very little 'choice' on their part.

The security measures and fencing around houses were also predetermined by the Queensland Government, which at that time was particularly aware of the security concerns of employees in remote communities, especially health workers. This concern was heightened by tragic events in 2008, which involved a 27-year-old nurse being raped in her sleeping quarters on a remote island in Torres Strait, prompting a public outcry about safety and accommodation (Koch 2003). A subsequent audit of 1,200 such residences concluded that security for health workers in remote communities was mostly sufficient and that the rape was an 'isolated incident' (Wenham 2008: 8). Nevertheless, media around the incident considerably damaged the reputation of the then Queensland Health Minister Stephen Robertson and the then State Government (Wray 2005). In 2016, the brutal rape and murder of Gayle Woodford, a paramedic nurse on a solo callout in the remote Anangu Pitjatjantjara Yunkunatjara community of Fregon in South Australia, prompted renewed calls for enhanced safety measures for remote health workers. The Aboriginal man convicted of Woodford's murder was sentenced to the longest non-parole custodial period in South Australia's history (thirty-two years), and the South Australia Government subsequently introduced legislation ('Gayle's Law') preventing health workers from attending solo callouts. An alleged historical assault of a nurse by an Aboriginal man on Mornington Island was attributed by at least one health worker as the reason for the security fence around hospital accommodation, which was reportedly designed to 'make the nurses feel safer'.

More than just a question of safety, the provision of spatially separate housing was endorsed by some as an important element in attracting and retaining competent Whitefellas to work on the Island. The Federal Government Coordinator in 2007, for example, suggested that:

> If you expect quality people to work in these places you need to give them their own space. It's almost counterintuitive because … the best way [to deliver services] is to know the community well. But when you have down time, you need your own space … that allows you to choose to visit people or walk through town. If you live in the centre of the community, that's not a choice.

This 'choice' related to the idea that segregated housing gave greater choice to Whitefellas to control incidental encounters with Aboriginal people. In an experience in 2008 where short-term housing in Whitefella domains was extensively booked, I was accommodated in a house in the middle part of the community, surrounded by Aboriginal housing. My time staying at that particular house was characterized by much more frequent incidental interactions with Aboriginal people. Taking out the rubbish, watering the garden and other simple household tasks held the potential to encounter Aboriginal neighbours or passers-by. Segregated housing, however, also had the opposite effect, giving Aboriginal people the chance to eschew social interactions with Whitefellas.

The Appearance of Autonomy and Homogeneity

The physical appearance of Whitefella spatial domains, particularly the hospital compound and police precinct, contributed to other Whitefellas' perceptions of them as socially contained and harmonious social entities. As a school teacher explained, 'from the time I've been here, the hospital staff all have one section and more of a community sort of style and it appears to me that the police also have that little community, because they're all grouped'. Although a police officer himself, the Police Citizens Youth Club (PCYC) Manager also described this 'little community': 'There are any number of cliques on the Island but unfortunately they're of different departments' making and the police … the police socialize with themselves. They get behind the barbed wire fence, have BBQs by themselves, go to Birri [Lodge] by themselves. They become very dependent on one another and live in each other's pockets'.

Birri Lodge was a fishing venture with a liquor licence and restaurant on the northern coast of Mornington Island, approximately forty minutes' drive from the main settlement of Gununa, where patrons could 'book in' for an evening meal and (alcoholic) drinks. Though 'Birri', as it was referred to locally, was closed in 2015, for many years it served as a retreat for local Whitefellas, and to a lesser extent Aboriginal people, wanting to escape the intensity of community life for a 'night out'. Groups of Whitefellas such as the police, teachers and health workers living in Gununa often went out to Birri. Nevertheless, these interactions were not opportunities available to all. For example, although employed by the Queensland Police Service, the Police Citizens Youth Club Manager and his wife, both Whitefellas, described how they were socially excluded when general-duties police made trips to Birri.

It appeared that some of the younger teachers (aged in their twenties) also had similar kinds of close social relationships as those described for general-duties police, interacting regularly with one another after hours and on the weekends. In 2009, for example, it was not uncommon to see a group of young teachers sitting out the front of one of the Education Queensland houses on the main street of Gununa in the late afternoon. A teacher in her forties noted that while she did not experience this propinquity, 'a lot of the teachers are younger than I am, so perhaps between themselves they have a lot more social interaction than what I do'. At the same time, there was recognition that just being a Whitefella did not constitute enough grounds of similarity for enjoyable interaction with other Whitefellas. As a young Queensland Health worker asked rhetorically, 'How do you socialize with people that you have very little in common with?'

It did appear that age was a factor in the degree to which individuals were socially active, and older Whitefellas, particularly couples, spent much of their out-of-work time at home. Two middle-aged couples who worked in different types of service delivery, for example, described how they spent most of their time at home reading or watching television, as they were often exhausted from long days at work. These couples commented that they did not particularly crave or miss social interaction with others, but that they did periodically feel 'isolated'. One of the women that I interviewed became quite emotional when she contrasted these experiences with those in a similar-sized town where she and her husband had lived on Queensland's Sunshine Coast. In that situation, she noted how she and her husband had never felt like 'outsiders'. In 2009, the couple, who had then lived on the Island for three years, was offered accommodation outside the hospital compound. The house being offered was much larger than the duplex where they had been living, and was situated in one of the more scenic parts of the community, overlooking the channel between Mornington and Denham Islands. In spite of this, the couple turned down the offer to move, as the woman explained:

> One of the reasons was because of my husband's job [as a health worker], we felt that if we were out in the community, then [Aboriginal] people would come over and want to talk or want things. I know one of the ladies that was working here and she had a government position, and she found that [Aboriginal] people were knocking on her door at 11pm at night and wanting a lift from the pub, money for a Powercard[6] at 1am, kinds of really unreasonable requests. That's why we wanted to stay in the compound, then you didn't have to deal with those issues.

In this case the couple did not seek out interactions with Aboriginal people, and used their housing arrangements as a means of countering and denying any potential requests for assistance from Aboriginal people. As was the case here and more generally, stories of negative encounters between Aboriginal people and Whitefellas elsewhere in the community informed the decisions that Whitefellas made about their place of residence.

One of the better-known examples often discussed in the 2000s involved a local Aboriginal man and his Whitefella supervisor. Both men were employed by the local Council, and according to the Aboriginal man involved, a dispute had arisen out of disagreements in the men's workplace. When the Whitefella and his wife moved out of the contractors' camp and into a house next door to the Aboriginal man, the dispute then spilled over. As the local Council was responsible for the allocation of housing and was already aware that the two men did not get along, the Aboriginal man interpreted the Whitefella's relocation as a deliberate act on the part of the local Council to get him to resign from his job:

> Like they trying to find a hole, to get in there and tear you apart. That was just their ploy I reckon putting him [the Whitefella] there. They knew that we weren't going to get on. It never worked at work, when he was in the [contractors'] camp there. I told all the people I worked with, I tried and tried but there's only so far I'll try. After all he is in my hometown, my home community so I wasn't going to try anymore. But they put 'im next door, which was a real bad move.

Over the following months, tensions escalated when the Whitefella began feeding the Aboriginal man's guard dog. As the Aboriginal man explained, police were called to an incident between the men, and the Aboriginal man was taken into custody after spitting on an attending police officer. While being placed in a cell to 'sober up', the Aboriginal man's hand was injured and he subsequently wrote 'KKK'[7] in his own blood on the watch house walls. Later, the Aboriginal man began a petition to be signed by Aboriginal residents, demanding that the local Council eject the Whitefella from the community, something that they were empowered to do under provisions of the *Local Government Act 1993 (Qld)*. Sometime later, the Whitefella and his wife left the Island, after apparently being offered employment elsewhere. When questioned how the incident made the Aboriginal man feel about having Whitefellas living and working in the community he replied:

> It's not so much colour, it's your attitude. If you come into the community and willing to share your knowledge, share what you know an' that, empower people, people'll embrace you. But most times when people come in here they see an opportunity to make a lot of money and they don't really want us to be self-reliant or self-sufficient or whatever fancy term, you know.

This observation, that it was 'attitude' and not 'colour', was replete in accounts by Aboriginal people. A middle-aged Aboriginal woman reflected on her experiences of Whitefellas: 'Some good ones ... But you can always pick the no-good ones, pick them straight out. You look them in the eye and say "no good" and you can tell'. Another Aboriginal woman, aged in her fifties, described this situation for Whitefellas, and noted that when compared to the 'mission times': 'It is a lot better now, white people and black people talk. Some here, some are just what they are I suppose. They're just people brought up the way they're brought up. You won't change them. On the whole I don't care, I don't mind'. Though perhaps an obvious point, recognitions of heterogeneity, that there were 'some good, some bad', is indicative of the varied experiences that both Aboriginal people and Whitefellas had in their encounters with one another (see also Tonkinson 1994).

Racial Encounters

In her 2004 book, *Blackfellas, Whitefellas and the Hidden Injuries of Race*, Gillian Cowlishaw described race relations in the western-New South Wales town of Bourke. Cowlishaw detailed the multiple ways in which Aboriginal people and Whites 'performed boundaries', providing examples of encounters including those marked by 'an overwhelming moralistic flavour, and occasional chilling nastiness' (2004: 113). Many of the encounters described by Cowlishaw were overtly racialized, including the use of racist terms as a means to 'shore up the racial boundary' (ibid.). On Mornington Island, encounters between Aboriginal people and Whitefellas were mostly defined by the necessity of interaction. This interaction was coded with the structure of racialized categories, or as one health worker described it, as a 'privileged interaction', where 'you're there providing the service, they're the person relying on that service'. Beyond that, there was a subtle but generalized disinterest in cultivating relationships beyond those defined by the service delivery framework.

This disinterest was exemplified by the fact that during the 2000s, there were few instances where Aboriginal people visited Whitefellas for predominately social purposes or vice versa. Even some of the Whitefellas that I interviewed who prided themselves on the extent of their interaction with the community as part of their professional role rarely invited Aboriginal people along to social events or into their residential areas, and vice versa. In contextualizing this situation, some Whitefellas cited the awkwardness of the interactions, where expectations and social mores were disproportionate, resulting in mutually disappointing experiences. Thus, the majority of forays made by Whitefellas into the Aboriginal domain (and vice versa) were made within the context of service delivery and related activities. Examples of these interactions included nurses reminding patients to attend the hospital for follow-up treatments or school teachers visiting the parents of a truant child.

These incursions were often noted with irritation by Aboriginal people, who resented the paternalistic intent and embarrassment at being ministered to in what was their own spatial domain. Some Aboriginal people had such an aversion to these kinds of interactions that on at least two occasions, Aboriginal people that I was attempting to visit at their homes initially hid from me, later humorously suggesting that they thought I was either a policewoman or someone from the local hospital. That these justifications were offered as reasonable explanations for Aboriginal people's avoidance of me (as a Whitefella) demonstrates the normalization of such behaviours in everyday life. In one of the two instances, when I entered a yard (without invitation) and knocked on the front door, two elderly Aboriginal women that I wanted to see peeked out from behind a curtain in a nearby window. Having been 'spotted', they opened the front door and exclaimed: 'Oh it's *you*! We thought you was one lady from the hospital!'

At other times, and as the vignette at the start of this chapter indicates, Aboriginal people would warn that they had a 'cheeky' (i.e. aggressive) dog as a way of ensuring that Whitefellas remained outside a house's perimeter fence, at least until the person they were looking for emerged (Corbert 2010). Whitefellas' behaviour in these encounters only strengthened the sometimes-held view that they had no understanding of Aboriginal social norms. Some of these social norms were structural, such as understanding the local kinship relationships between Aboriginal persons, while others were subtler, relating to locally defined conventions often associated with an awareness of spatiality, such as the physical orientation of the body in relation to others. Other examples included Whitefellas parking their car on the road, rather than pulling up onto the curb as Aboriginal people did, and standing to face an Aboriginal person directly, rather than standing alongside them. Similar observations were made by Trigger (1992: 96) of Whitefellas living in Doomadgee in the 1980s: 'Whites would walk or pass things across the direction of someone's path of movement, vision or personal orientation, rather than proceeding behind such lines of personal social presentation; they would hardly ever sit on the ground, and would abruptly arrive at and leave social interaction rather than more slowly announcing arrivals and departures'.

Such behaviour sometimes contributed to the sense in which the subsequent encounters were awkward or jarred with the flow of social life. Compounding the irritation was that Whitefellas were often in the Aboriginal domain to follow-up on an unsatisfactory situation, such as a police matter or a child who had been badly behaved at school. When a Whitefella departed after such a visit, Aboriginal people present would sometimes make derogatory comments, for example, that they were a (proverbial) 'White cunt', and that the way that they had behaved (or the organization that they were working for more generally) was incongruous with local styles of behaviour, ideals or aspirations. This was exemplified by the oft-heard phrase among Aboriginal people when referring to Whitefellas on Mornington Island: 'I don't see why they gotta…'.

Whitefellas' failure to adopt Aboriginal etiquette stemmed largely from their lack of regular exposure to normalized behaviours therein. This applied even to the places that could be considered relevant destinations for both Aboriginal people and Whitefellas, such as the local store. Though the practice diminished following a change to the barge services in 2009, in earlier years, Whitefellas often ordered food on the Internet from the supermarket Coles in Cairns, and collected it off the barge each week. Thus, in 2007 and 2008 they were rarely seen at the local store, a major meeting point for Aboriginal people, and where (at least in the mid-2000s) it was not unusual to queue for over half an hour to buy even a single item (Francis 2010).[8] Another way in which some Whitefellas were able to eschew interaction with Aboriginal people was to drive rather than walk through the community. Walking was the only means of transport for many Aboriginal people, and a way that mundane tasks, such as a visit to the post office, became opportunities to see and interact with Aboriginal people who lived in other parts of the community.

For the first six months of my time on Mornington Island I only had intermittent access to a vehicle, meaning I spent much of my time walking around the community. During a visit to the hospital, a young nurse told me that other Whitefellas living in the community thought of me as 'really mad [stupid] for walking round'. This view reflected various considerations: a number of aggressive dogs, perceived threats to personal safety and the oppressive heat, but also because it was not the 'done thing' for Whitefellas. Almost the only time that Whitefellas were seen walking was in the late afternoon or early morning, when they exercised on the road leading out of the community towards the dam, or the roads around the Council offices, routes which were mostly away from Aboriginal residential areas.

The corollary to these situations was when Aboriginal people sought out Whitefellas or entered Whitefella domains to access services. These work domains included the hospital, the school, the shop and the range of organization offices including the Mornington Shire Council, CDEP and Justice Group. For the most part, these locations were considered part of the Whitefella domain, and Aboriginal people adopted particular types of behaviour when visiting or moving through these areas. When Aboriginal people, particularly older people, entered these domains they did so with a degree of reverence, casting their eyes downward and speaking in hushed tones among one another. Men sometimes removed their hats, especially Akubras (colloquially known as 'cowboy hats'), and Aboriginal children who played boisterously were scolded for being noisy. Aboriginal people also abstained from swearing and chastised one another for doing so – 'Aye! Don' swear!' – while at the same time gesturing (often with a nod of the head) at any Whitefellas present. As Sansom (1980: 30–31) observed of the Aboriginal campers around the fringe of Darwin: 'the rate of production of swears is thus responsive to the presence of high-talking white outsiders in English-speaking Aboriginal society'. Though often used in the everyday vernacular of the Aboriginal domain on Mornington Island, words like 'fuck' and 'cunt' were almost entirely absent in the Whitefella domain other than to denote extreme anger or frustration. However, once Aboriginal people moved out of these areas, they reverted to their usual demeanour, uninhibited by the presence of Whitefellas. Despite this general formality, some Aboriginal people did work in these domains, making them less intimidating to Aboriginal 'clients'. Examples of Aboriginal workers included the cashier at the Council office, checkout assistants at the local store and health workers at the local hospital.

One example that I observed of the transition that Aboriginal people underwent when moving from the Aboriginal domain to the Whitefella domain took place when I accompanied an Aboriginal man aged in his seventies to the hospital for an eye examination by a visiting ophthalmologist. On the morning of the ophthalmologist's visit, I found the man making his way along the main street, having already been to a few houses around the community, visiting Aboriginal kin for cups of tea and an early morning yarn. When I reminded him about his upcoming eye examination, he protested, saying, 'but I never even have bogey [bath/shower] yet girl!' (see similar discussion in Trigger 1992: 89). We went back to the house where he was staying and he changed into a clean shirt. As we walked up towards the hospital, he tucked his shirt in and asked me, 'what I look like girl, alright?' Thus, while having already spent a number of hours interacting with Aboriginal people around the community, a visit to the ostensibly Whitefella domain of the hospital made the man conscious of his appearance.

It would be incorrect, however, to define all interactions between Whitefellas and Aboriginal people as rigidly bound by concerns about etiquette and dress, and there were a number of examples where friendships had been cultivated. One Whitefella couple, for example, provided a space for a young Aboriginal artist to work on her canvases under their house on weekends. In another example, a school teacher went out fishing on weekends with an elderly Aboriginal woman. As the school teacher explained it: 'So she [the Aboriginal woman] used to take me out to different places and go fishing and make damper in the sand and cook fish on the beach and get crabs. Because she didn't have any transport she was very happy for someone to pick her up and take her places.' In both instances, though, the Whitefellas involved also observed the social discontinuities that prevented the friendships from progressing as they may have expected. In the first example, the Whitefella couple felt that the painter did not especially welcome the potential social interaction that the situation created: 'I'd go down and I'd talk to her [the painter] but she almost didn't want me to intrude. And you'd say "how are you going, want a cup of tea?" and she sorta say "piss off". You'd think that she would want company, but she didn't'. In fact, it appeared that the painter was using the house as an opportunity to eschew the distractions and social demands of both Aboriginal and non-Aboriginal people.

In the case of the school teacher, sometime after the elderly Aboriginal woman began to periodically stay overnight at the teacher's house, the local school principal contacted the teacher to inform her that she would need to obtain written permission from the school if she was to have visitors. The rationale for this was that Education Queensland leased the house, and that it was in their interests to control who was able to come and go. However, the teacher explained that: 'I know [that] if I said that it was local [Aboriginal] people or probably someone with colour, then it would be stopped'. There were those, Whitefellas and Aboriginal people, who perceived these kinds of rules or locally constituted understandings of the maintenance of barriers between workers and Aboriginal people, particularly for those employed by the Queensland State Government, as oppressive. It was often related that nurses, police and teachers were 'not allowed' to 'mix'[9] with Aboriginal people. Despite the discontinuities, cross-cultural relationships were identified by Whitefellas living in the community as defining features of their stay and the source of some of their most cherished experiences of living in a remote location.

Personal Names and Kin Relationships

Both in the previous chapter and here, I discuss the professional alliances sometimes developed between Aboriginal people and Whitefellas. I noted that while these partnerships were exceptional, they had the potential to substantially impact on the experiences of both parties, especially in the operation of particular agencies. In spite of this, Aboriginal people only sometimes learned the personal names of Whitefellas living on the Island, even those who had lived there for a number of years. This was indicated when Aboriginal people often asked me the names of Whitefellas – 'what-her-name?' or 'what-'is-name?' – assuming that all White people knew each other's names. In the 1980s, McKnight (2002: 94) noted how such was the rapidly expanding number of Whitefellas on the Island at that time, that: 'Sometimes when I ask [Aboriginal] people who someone [Whitefella] is I am told that they do not know, but "He must be somebody"'.

For those whose names were learned, particularly teachers and doctors, mention of their first name (almost never the surname) was accompanied by a prefix such as 'Teacher Sandra' or 'Doctor Albert', clearly indicating the service that they were responsible for providing. In other cases, the name was mispronounced, particularly if it was unusual. That Aboriginal people did not know precisely or correctly the full names of Whitefellas was noteworthy because it contrasted so starkly to the remarkable recall that Aboriginal people had for long and complex Aboriginal people's names, particularly those of young children. Often with more than two 'middle names', some of the more elaborate included newly composed names, created by the splicing of one or two African-American names (McKnight 1999: 69; see also Sutton quoted in Toohey 2009: 3).

Aboriginal people also usually knew the names of any 'new' Aboriginal people visiting the Island from another community, to attend a funeral, visit family or for school holidays, for example. When questioned, Aboriginal Mornington Islanders could often immediately name the individual, their family and the reason for their visit. Partly, this was because visiting Aboriginal people fitted into the pre-existing Aboriginal system of kinship. Thus while 'new' in one sense, any family connection to Mornington Island, however tenuous, meant that they were immediately related and a known part of the Aboriginal social world. The extrapolation of the kinship system to include Aboriginal people visiting from elsewhere also acted as a guideline for the kinds of behaviour that would inform their interaction.

In contrast, few Whitefellas were adopted into the local Aboriginal kinship system. This is unlike Redmond's (2005: 234) example from the northern Kimberley, where Ngarinyin Aboriginal people extended their kinship systems to incorporate some non-Aboriginal pastoralists. As Redmond (ibid.: 237) pointed out, this incorporation occurred as a result of subsequent generations of the same Aboriginal and Whitefella families remaining in the same area and intermarrying. In that case, rendering one another as kin was beneficial for both parties as it affirmed intergenerational relationships, or 'mutualities and dependencies', which extended beyond the usual employer/employee dynamic. Similar observations have been made by the anthropologist Richard Martin (2015), in reference to Aboriginal and non-Aboriginal people resident on pastoral properties around the Queensland/Northern Territory border. These relationships were driven in large part by the pastoralists' need for local Aboriginal labour and knowledge of the local landscape, and conversely Aboriginal people's desire to access and live on their country. In the case of Mornington Island, the majority of Whitefellas living on the Island at any one time were there for a relatively short period (years, not generations) and had no tenured entitlement to the lands and waters on which they resided. Hence, very few Whitefellas had been integrated into the local Aboriginal kinship system in the ways described by Redmond (2005) and Martin (2015).

Instead, many Whitefellas working in service delivery used the 'culturally aware' honorific terms of 'Aunty' and 'Uncle', commonly used to refer to older Aboriginal people in urban contexts (Sutton 1998: 71). As Sutton (ibid.) explained the use of the terms in broader contexts, though such terms evoked the kinship idiom, they were in fact 'more like titles than actual kin terms'. On Mornington Island, two particular examples of this involved the Federal Government Coordinator and the PCYC Manager. Both men used the terms to refer to Aboriginal men and women with whom they worked. Local Aboriginal people, however, almost exclusively used the terms when a person was their aunt (father's sister) or uncle (mother's brother), i.e. for a limited number of people, as traced through kinship relations. Thus, in the case of Mornington Island, the improvised use of 'Aunty' and 'Uncle' somewhat ironically highlighted Whitefellas' externality to the kinship system, rather than their integration. As I mentioned in Chapter 1 regarding the term 'Elders', use of 'Aunty' and 'Uncle' also reflected the lack of intricate knowledge that Whitefellas had of local Aboriginal kinship. One hospital employee, discussing events following a motor vehicle accident in 2007 in which a man aged in his twenties died, commented: 'Because that community is so interwoven, the number of people that would attend [the hospital] and say "I'm the grandmother, the aunty" and *everyone* would be the grandmother and they feel like they have a right to be at the bedside. And you'd have to say "no" to everyone. And you have to ask who the *real* parents were'.

In this instance, the hospital employee recognized that the community was 'interwoven', yet still sought clarification of who the 'real' parents were, when in fact the patient's 'family' and those identifying themselves as close kin were a broader group of people. Those few

Whitefellas who were taught local kinship terms and systems, generally through adoption by a particular Aboriginal individual, were expected to both know and demonstrate their knowledge. For example, I asked a man what our appropriate kinship relationship was, to which he responded (with irritation) '*thabu* [older brother]. I told you that last time!'

Similarly, Aboriginal people were sometimes ill informed about Whitefellas' relationships. A middle-aged woman who moved to the Island in 2006 with her husband relayed one of the more extreme examples of this. The woman worked for the local Council, while her husband was a health worker at the local hospital. In 2009, the couple attended a school fete, a rare community event, and walked hand-in-hand around the small number of stalls. Despite having already lived in the community for three years, the woman noted how a small number of local Aboriginal people at the fete had commented that they were unaware that they were a couple. The couple were somewhat unusual as, unlike many of the Whitefella couples on the Island who were employed by the same agencies and seen together at work, this couple worked in different places in the community. The couple also lived in the hospital compound and thus were rarely seen together in public places around the community.

One of the obvious explanations for these gaps in knowledge was the high turnover of Whitefellas living in the community. This 'anonymity', as McKnight (2002: 94) interpreted it, had arisen because of the increasing size of the bureaucracy tasked with managing Aboriginal affairs and services, and also because of the relatively short time frames that Whitefellas spent in the community. The size of the bureaucracy, though, was arguably proportionate to the growing population of Aboriginal Mornington Islanders and the State and Federal Governments' commitments to reduce disadvantage by 'Closing the Gap' (COAG 2010). To take a specific example, the number of police on the Island rose from six in 2007 to ten in 2011 (CMC 2009: 374). As in most remote parts of Australia, in order to fill vacancies and attract staff, the State Government generally set tenure for positions at two years and attached significant financial rewards and professional benefits, via 'points' and permanency systems linked to career progression (e.g. for police see ibid.: 174).

As a number of Whitefellas noted, it was only 'over time' that they felt they had become 'known' in the community, and that the most obvious changes in their experience began to occur after their first two years and then again after four years (two consecutive contracts each of two years). As one woman recalled, 'It just seemed to us to take two years to get accepted and two years to get momentum. I don't know whether it was that idea that I had in mind, but I did feel that after those two years there was a shift'. This turnover made it difficult for some Whitefellas, especially those who would have preferred to be living elsewhere, to invest emotionally or professionally. As one teacher aged in her forties explained of some of the teachers who came to the Island straight out of university, 'they're here to get permanency [with Education Queensland], and do their two years and go back home again'. Cutting across those Whitefellas working in service delivery was a smaller group of men who intermarried with Aboriginal women and remained on the Island in the longer term.

A Different Kind of Whitefella

In contrast to the Whitefellas that had moved to Mornington Island to work in service delivery and stayed only a short period of time were those who had stayed over much longer periods of time and partnered with local Aboriginal women. In recent times, there have been between fifteen and twenty such men living on Mornington Island, as the married or de facto partner of an Aboriginal woman.[10] Most of the men had moved to the Island between the 1970s and mid-2000s, some as fishermen and others as tradesmen, and had remained there since that time.

During the 2000s, most of these Whitefellas lived in the Aboriginal domain, usually with their Aboriginal partners and children, in housing which was administered by the Mornington Shire Council, and they tended to be employed by the local Council or a local Aboriginal corporation, undertaking specific tasks. As Gerritsen (1982: 29) observed for a similar group of men in the Northern Territory, on Mornington Island they were mechanics or tradesmen, or ran the post office, radio station, power station, airstrip or art centre. Though vital in the upkeep of basic services, such tasks were relatively free from the politics of positions relating to the management of the community, such as the Council CEO, Deputy CEO and State Government employees. The choice to work in these roles may have reflected their desires to be more autonomous from bureaucracy, or to conceive of themselves in similar terms as Kapferer (1995: 72) described Mossman in north Queensland, 'as a place at the edge of the state, at the extremity of its controlling tendrils'. Beyond the work domains and for a variety of reasons, these men might be thought of as existing in an interstitial space, neither wholly incorporated into the Whitefella or Aboriginal domains.

Despite intermarriage with Aboriginal women and often long associations with the community, these men occupied a peripheral social position, being partially marginalized within the locally operating societies by both other Whitefellas and Aboriginal people. Some other Whitefellas thought of them as 'crazy', analogous to the 'misfits' component of the 'mercenaries, missionaries and misfits' stereotype. One middle-aged White woman living on Mornington Island described her experiences with these men as the 'biggest eye-opener – more so than the locals [Aboriginal people]', adding, 'you just go "holy smokes" ... and you know they can't fit in mainstream society, and then they come here and you just go "oh my goodness"'. This perspective was evidently shared by McKnight (2002: 221), who commented that they 'find it irksome and dull living with White Australians' and 'are no longer able to cope with the outside world'. McKnight (ibid.: 93) was generally scathing in describing such men, characterizing them as having 'drifted into the community ... linked up with local girls' (ibid.) while showing 'little concern for the future' and being 'heavy drinkers, congenial and well-liked by Aborigines' (ibid.: 221).

While it was generally the case that the men were indeed 'well-liked', particularly by family members, Aboriginal people too sometimes found the behaviour of such Whitefellas inexplicable and demonstrative of their lack of understanding of Aboriginal social norms. On one such occasion in 2007, during a smoking ceremony[11] held to release the spirit of a deceased Aboriginal man at the workplace where he died, a number of vehicles were parked across an adjacent road to block traffic as a mark of respect. A Whitefella who had lived on the Island for more than twenty years, with an Aboriginal partner for much of this time, drove in between the parked cars and through the middle of the ceremony. Standing behind me, the Whitefella's Aboriginal brother-in-law commented 'you think 'e'd know, 'e live on this Island long enough'.

It was with a mixed sense of guilt and glee that Aboriginal people sometimes related the unfortunate stories of some of these men, such as how their house had been burgled or their car had broken down. This exclusion was felt by at least one of the Whitefellas, as I wrote at the time: 'He was talking today about how you're always a stranger here. Even him with a little baby to a local woman says that he still feels like an outsider. Being white and not having been brought up here seems to mean that you never really fit in'. This predicament was similarly discussed by Gerritsen (1982) of the 'wayfarers' in the Katherine region of the Northern Territory. In his terms, wayfarers were 'in the community but can never be of it' and their actions 'stem from their reactions to their situation and the imperatives of their survival' (ibid.: 29).

On Mornington Island, one hypothesis for this was explained to me in an interview with a Whitefella who had young children with a local Aboriginal woman and had lived on the Island since 2003. He recalled an experience where another Whitefella living on the Island had approached him and reportedly said: 'What a situation you're in, the locals [Aboriginal people] hate you for being a Whiteman living with a black woman and other White people hate you for living off the system'. In reflecting on these comments, the man noted that, 'I wouldn't say that people hate me just because I'm a Whiteman. I think some people hate me because I'm with an Aboriginal woman, some older men maybe think that I shouldn't be'. During the 2000s, there were instances where Aboriginal people expressed disappointment and sometimes anger at Whitefellas, particularly short-term contractors who were reported to be 'going with'[12] local Aboriginal girls or women. In one instance in 2007, an Aboriginal woman's grandsons reportedly assaulted a Whitefella on the basis that he had walked the woman home late one night after a drinking session at the local Pub. Incidences in which the innuendo was that sexual encounters had occurred were different to those where a mixed-race couple showed genuine commitment to one another by living together in a de facto or married relationship.

As one young Aboriginal woman whose partner was a Whitefella explained, there were incentives to such couplings. By her own account, the woman had purposefully chosen to live with a Whitefella because 'all MI [Aboriginal Mornington Islanders] men are dogs, it's better to get a Whiteman that will look after you' (see similar comments in Huffer 1980: 109–10). The reference to 'dogs' related to the view that White men were more likely to be faithful than Aboriginal men, who were (supposedly) more sexually indiscreet (i.e. like 'dogs'). Being 'looked after' correlated with the view that having a Whitefella partner offered Aboriginal women a better quality of life than with an Aboriginal partner. Elsewhere, Peterson and Taylor's (2002, 2003) research on the 'domestic moral economy' in western New South Wales considered socioeconomic outcomes for mixed-race couples, based on data collected during the 1996 Australian Bureau of Statistics Census. Peterson and Taylor (2003: 112) found that mixed-couple households, comprising an Aboriginal and other-than-Aboriginal partner, were more likely than Aboriginal couples to own their own home and have higher median annual household income, and were less likely to live in community housing or have more than fifteen children. These factors were identified as being more consistent with contemporary mainstream Australia (Peterson and Taylor ibid.: 106).

Though racially identified data of this nature was not available for Mornington Islanders, one related indicator of the difference between mixed-race couples and Aboriginal couples was the degree to which houses (as distinct from 'households' as discussed in Chapter 3) accommodated extended family. In a survey of houses that I conducted in 2009 (see Appendix 1), more than 80 per cent of the houses where mixed-race couples lived accommodated only the Whitefella, their female partner and children. In the same survey, however, among houses with solely Aboriginal residents, less than 25 per cent were comprised solely of a couple and their children (see Appendix 1). Thus, unlike most Aboriginal houses, mixed-race couples tended not to accommodate extended Aboriginal family.

There is one particular factor, however, which differentiated the Mornington Island situation from that described by Peterson and Taylor for western New South Wales. While in western New South Wales, mixed couples were able to purchase or rent private housing, however uncommon it may have been (Peterson and Taylor 2002: 15), on Mornington Island all housing was administered through an agreement between the Aboriginal and Torres Strait Islander Housing section of the Queensland Department of Housing and the Mornington Shire Council (Queensland Government Department of Housing 2008: 3). As it was intended for Aboriginal people, Whitefellas were only able to occupy housing as the partner of an Aboriginal person or with their part-Aboriginal children. Even in those cases, the men or their partners had to 'make a case' to the housing committee as to why there were special circumstances that should allow a Whitefella to become a registered tenant. This system meant that Whitefellas were in a far more tenuous position than Aboriginal people to remain living in the community long-term. This uncertainty about place of residence contributed to feelings of wider uncertainty, as one Whitefella described: 'I always have this feeling in the back of my mind that I can't stay here forever'. At the same time, though, the man was committed to the place, saying: 'I want to know what goes on here, not that I have any right to or even any real reason I guess. I don't leave too because I think my sons deserve the opportunity to grow up here and be part of the community ... And my families stick up for me cause they care about me. But it's a very uncertain life with a very uncertain future'.

These sentiments suggest an alternative to McKnight's (2002: 221) assessment that such men showed 'little concern about the future' or that 'they evidently find it irksome and dull living with White Australians'. Nor does it accord with Gerritsen's (1982: 29) proposition for such men in the Northern Territory, that they 'can come and go from a community without too much trouble'. Further, the exclusion felt by some Whitefellas on Mornington Island did not negate the connections that some made with Aboriginal people, especially those who had become family. For example, two Whitefellas who died from cancer in 2007 and 2011 were buried in the Mornington Island cemetery. At least one of the men had his Aboriginal language (Lardil) name, *Banbadji*, the Torres Strait pigeon, engraved on his tombstone alongside his first name and surname. The burial of Whitefellas in the local cemetery was an almost-unknown occurrence prior to this[13] and could be seen as an indicator of their integration into the Aboriginal polity. It would seem that many of the Whitefellas on Mornington Island – who had ended up staying in the community for a variety of reasons, including the love of their partner – were committed to the community, and in particular to the opportunity for their children to be brought up amongst their Aboriginal relatives. Their feelings of uncertainty for the future were justified by the tenuous nature of their housing arrangements.

This uncertainty was brought to a head if they separated from their Aboriginal partner, became a widower or retired from work. When this happened, the Whitefella was likely to be at the mercy of the Council to secure ongoing residency in housing otherwise intended for Aboriginal people. In one instance, when one of these Whitefellas departed the Island, Aboriginal people spoke with great fondness about him, saying that he was being 'chased off the Island' when he had become part of the community, and had 'lived amongst Aboriginal people all his life'. In spite of their difficulties in accessing housing, this different kind of Whitefella was in some ways similar to the pastoralists that Redmond studied in the Kimberley (2005). In the Kimberley, Whitefellas' incorporation into Aboriginal kinship was the result of sustained and intimate contact that they had with Aboriginal people, which sometimes included fathering children (ibid.: 235). In the Kimberley as on Mornington Island, these children became part of the Aboriginal kinship polity at birth and thus, their Whitefella father's social position could be traced or 'reckoned' through their children (ibid.).

Over the last fifteen years, I have observed increases in the prevalence of relationships between young local Aboriginal people and Whitefellas, including young White women, and with Aboriginal people from more distant parts of Queensland. These developments replicated the Queensland-wide pattern noted by Birrell and Hirst (2002: 25–26), where marriage or de facto partnerships between Aboriginal people and others had become an increasingly large proportion of couplings for Aboriginal people from 1996 to 2001. In the 'rest of Queensland' category (i.e. other than Brisbane), mixed-race partnerships made up 63 per cent of all couplings for Aboriginal people in 2001 (ibid.: 26). Though not a new occurrence for Mornington Islanders, attending boarding schools on the mainland and returning with a partner appeared to be part of the explanation for this increase (Dalley 2018). Often on Mornington Island, though, especially in the case of young White women, such relationships did not persist and usually the women left the community, taking their mixed-descent children with them (see also McKnight 2002: 225). Obviously, such developments are likely to relate to the dynamics within the relationships, but potentially also to some of the issues of isolation and exclusion discussed here.

Conclusion: Service Delivery and Race Relations

A Whitefella who had lived on Mornington Island for an extended period with his Aboriginal wife and mixed-descent children noted: 'Race relations are a big problem here and there's good reasons. But that stuff is used as smoke-screen for some … Sometimes I feel that I'm just a simple individual who ends up being indicative of a race of an entire people. And I don't want to be indicative of a race of people'. The issues identified in this quote represent some of the complexities of relationships between Aboriginal people and Whitefellas on Mornington Island. On the one hand are the underlying tensions and discontinuities evident when people from very different historical and cultural backgrounds are brought together in an extremely remote and isolated community. In one sense, this conclusion might appear to support the idea that the discontinuities were solely the product of interracial difference; as Cowlishaw (2004: 111) put it, 'Aboriginal communities remain as coherent groups, and continue to be self-defined as against another category – whitefellas'. However, on the other hand, a number of factors indicated (at least in the Mornington Island example) that the realities of social relations and identity created complexities that impacted on the coherence and autonomy of each group. For example, there was little to suggest that Whitefellas conceived of themselves in socially or ideologically unified terms, and they were often highly critical or at least uninterested in one another.

That separate Aboriginal and Whitefella domains did exist, both spatially and socially, and were mutually constituted, has the potential to be interpreted in different ways, as described by Rowse (2007: 92):

> Voluntary separatism, as I understand it, rests on the assumption that Indigenous Australians possess their own codes of respectability that are distinguishable from what they perceive to be the non-Indigenous system of

values. Describing and understanding these alternative codes is the most challenging task in the contemporary analysis of Indigenous affairs, for voluntary separatism is open to contradictory readings: social pathology or cultural autonomy?

A 'social pathology' reading might include those where relations are interpreted as an enacted power hierarchy. In a study of race relations in the town of Mossman in north Queensland, for example, Kapferer (1995: 74) describes 'multi-layered separations' but 'above all, the racial hierarchy of the town, the domination of whites over black'. While in the 1970s Memmott (1979: 297) concluded that 'many Aborigines in the village regard the spatially-separated staff housing as an inequality which they resent', my interpretation of similar (though less encompassing) spatial segregation in the recent period is somewhat different. That is to say that while there were undoubtedly those people, Aboriginal and otherwise, who held the view that such segregation was undesirable or indicative of unequal power relations, there were also those who viewed the situation with disinterest or ambivalence. Thus, to conceive of Mornington Island social relations in a similar way to Kapferer, as the domination of one racial group over another, would be to fail to capture the nuanced ways in which power was locally created and expressed.

Some of the local conditions which contributed to this separation included that the majority of Whitefellas living on the Island relocated there for a limited period of time and had little intention of remaining. As a result, they were often socially disconnected from Aboriginal people and instead became ensconced in their own spatial and social domains, with their interactions with Aboriginal people confined to work contexts. Kapferer (1995: 73) points to 'a prejudice or a prejudice created in a white fear, a fear or terror generated in a non-Aboriginal discourse in which individuality and personal integrity are perceived to be under threat from the control and institutions of the state'. Yet in the Mornington Island example, fear and apprehension was perhaps derived not so much from the state but from the potential for Aboriginal people to infringe on Whitefella autonomy and their notions of personal security. Justification for this threat was framed as the level of intrusion that it was 'reasonable' to ask Whitefellas to accept in their day-to-day lives.

While it may be partially true that, as Cowlishaw (2010: 52) argued, 'the sharp racial division and the harsh barriers that often exist between the government officials and other residents in remote communities are characteristic elements of a particular way of governing a particular kind of people', Aboriginal people sometimes had little to say about Whitefellas living on Mornington Island. For some, there was a begrudging acceptance that Whitefellas were in the community providing necessary services, and how they interacted socially was their own business. As an example of this view and as previously noted, an Aboriginal woman aged in her late fifties noted: 'they're brought up the way they're brought up. You won't change them. On the whole I don't care, I don't mind'. Other Aboriginal people recognized a degree of diversity among the Whitefellas they interacted with, making comments like 'some good, some bad', and noting that the tenor of relations came down to the individuals concerned.

As a result of these views, Whitefellas and Aboriginal people had little social knowledge of one another, as evidenced by the lack of knowledge of personal names. This suggests a slightly different set of social relations than those investigated by Redmond (2005: 236) in the Kimberley and Martin (2015) in the mainland Gulf country. As I have shown, on Mornington, Aboriginal people and Whitefellas acted deliberately, both socially and spatially, to reduce their interaction. Thus, according to Redmond's (2005: 236) categories, most Whitefellas remained as 'relative strangers' (rather than 'strange relatives') whose relationships were defined by the boundaries of their roles in the community. This production of social domains is highly suggestive of the relations characterized by Trigger et al. during the 1980s and 1990s (Rowse 1992; Trigger 1986; von Sturmer 1984) and is illustrative of Rowse's (2007: 90) point that: 'People who want to coexist within the one nation need not be attracted to the idea of sharing domestic space … A tough-minded approach to social cohesion between Indigenous and non-Indigenous Australians must consider the possibility that social distance and cultural difference continue to be valued by both Indigenous and non-Indigenous Australians'. The counterpoint to this was the smaller group of Whitefellas who did share 'domestic space' with their Aboriginal partners, occupying an interstitial space both physically and socially, neither wholly embedded in either domain. When referring to issues of identity, such men posed challenging questions about the meaning and experiences of categories of race, not dissimilar to those of Paradies (2006: 361), a man of mixed descent who finds himself in a 'strange in between space'.

In keeping their social worlds separate, Aboriginal people are able to preserve a sense of autonomy, or at least independence, from Whitefellas in their personal lives. This sense of autonomy was contrasted with the reality that Aboriginal people were reliant on Whitefellas to ensure the running of the Island's most basic of services. The hospital, school, store and even maintenance of basic services such as running water and sanitation relied on the skills of Whitefellas. Despite this, on Mornington Island as in Doomadgee during the 1980s (Trigger 1986), the Aboriginal domain, and the social interactions which occurred within it, formed the key setting in which Mornington Islanders constructed their identity. Aboriginal domains, though, were not predicated on a form of 'traditional life' in which Whitefella culture did not intrude, as has been suggested in critiques of the domains approach (e.g. Holcombe 2005: 224). Rather, Aboriginal people lived socially and spatially separate from Whitefellas, while at the same time, both purposefully and less deliberately via processes of exposure, accommodated and embraced intercultural subjectivities. It is these Aboriginal domains which I explore more fully in subsequent chapters of this book, beginning with an analysis of the notions of family and household in the next chapter.

Notes

1. This ranged from 91 in 2006 and 131 in 2011 to 160 in 2016. This accounted for 8 per cent to 14 per cent of the total Mornington Island population at any one time.
2. Dwelling types were predominately standard houses, but also included 'dongas' (a one- or two-bedroom fibro, demountable house often found in mining camps) and flats.
3. 11 Education Queensland, 7 Queensland Police Service, 8 Queensland Health, 10 Mornington Shire Council, 2 Aboriginal corporations, 6 short-term visitors, 10 for contractors (mostly tradesmen).
4. Though such fences were high, it seems implausible that they would be sufficient to prevent access to any committed and able-bodied person.
5. I have used the masculine term here and elsewhere to emphasise the point that to my knowledge, all of the Whitefellas employed in this capacity were men.
6. Electricity on Mornington Island is paid for through a 'Powercard' credit system. Residents purchase powercards of AUD 20.00 or AUD 50.00 value, which are then swiped at the power box mounted on individual houses. Power to the house is metered and the credit diminishes until it expires and power is cut off to the house.
7. A reference to the North American organization the Klu Klux Klan, infamous for their White supremacist activities.
8. Previously, a larger barge travelled from Cairns each week, but the company operating the service changed to a smaller barge operating out of Normanton, which did not have a Coles supermarket.
9. 'Mix' in this sense refers to the development of ongoing or sustained social relationships, rather than simply knowing or meeting Aboriginal people.
10. During my research, two young White women moved (temporarily) to the Island to live with their Aboriginal partners. Neither remained on the Island long-term. It is significant to note that in the past, there have been a number of examples of Aboriginal men from Mornington Island forming relationships with White women and having children, including one instance in the 1980s where a local Aboriginal man married a White school teacher.

11. See Memmott and Horsman (1991: 316–17) for an explanation of the development of this practice on Mornington Island.
12. This term was used in a variety of ways, but generally to describe those in a sexual relationship with varying degrees of socially demonstrated commitment to one another.
13. The first mission superintendent, Robert Hall, was murdered on Mornington Island in 1917 and buried in a shallow grave. His body was later exhumed and re-buried near the mission house. The Reverend Douglas Belcher's ashes were interred at the Mornington Island cemetery in the late 1990s.

 3

Contemporary Aboriginal Family

> Everyone down this street, they all relations.
>
> —Aboriginal man aged in his late twenties

> We're not living here for family, we like our space. We like it. It's quite good this little area because you don't see much people, don't hear much, right out of the way and it's always been.
>
> —Aboriginal man aged in his mid-thirties

These two quotes, from Aboriginal men living in Gununa, introduce two experiences of family on Mornington Island, where connections to kin and the ongoing constitution of such relationships were defining aspects of social life. That is to say that Aboriginal people spent the bulk of their daily lives interacting with people to whom they could 'trace' a kinship relationship. As has been detailed extensively by David McKnight (2004, 2005), kinship relations, as sets of defined systems of relationships between people, have undergone considerable change on Mornington Island over time. These changes included the influence of Presbyterian missionaries, the coming together of previously disparate groups in a single settlement, resulting in population growth and increasing intermarriage with Whitefellas and Aboriginal people from places other than Mornington Island. In view of such changes, of particular importance was the constitution of relationships based on 'performative kinship' (Sansom 1988: 170), or what Peterson and Taylor (2003: 108) described as 'the extent to which social relations have to be produced and reproduced by social action'. In this sense, 'social action' included a range of interactions, from intimate interpersonal encounters, such as the care of children, to economic transactions, including 'demand sharing' among kin (Peterson 1993). The significance of resource sharing relates to the widespread impoverishment experienced by Mornington Islanders, a product of dependence on various forms of government welfare, limiting access to cash and facilitating extensive periods of time available to spend with family.

On Mornington Island, as in studies of Aboriginal sociality in other parts of Australia, 'family' is a 'key unit, at both an actual and conceptual level, in Indigenous social and economic life' (Smith 2000: 176; see also Finlayson 1991). Studies elsewhere have identified variations in the ways in which 'family' is enacted locally through processes of social action and in response to a range of contextual factors, such as native title (Babidge 2010: 112; Sutton 1998; Vincent 2017). A term related to 'family' is 'household', used to denote variously a place of shared residence or those who make 'common provision for food or other essentials for living' (Morphy 2006: 28). In this chapter, I discuss the contemporary situation on Mornington Island with reference some of the important developments in kinship and the constitution of family over time. I place particular emphasis on transformations in the knowledge and observance of kinship systems, subsections, marriage and the care of children. I analyse two case studies of family on Mornington Island, avoiding Diane Smith's (2005: 175) concern that 'researchers today are less willing to spend the longer, intimate time on the ground with families that is needed to convey the dynamic environment of their daily life'.

The first case study is of the 'Middle families', as I refer to them: an interconnected set of kin, spread amongst proximate residences in a particular part of Gununa, who were reliant on one another in daily life. It was these types of networks that were pervasive in Gununa sociality during the 2000s, and are a common model of contemporary Aboriginal family found in a range of geographic contexts (e.g. Finlayson 1991). The second case study is of a much smaller family, 'Neil and Clare', who lived in a single dwelling with their children and asserted a relatively autonomous social and economic identity. This other kind of family is proposed as an example of Peterson and Taylor's (2003: 107) 'inwardly focused household', and what seems likely to be an example of a 'significant yet under-analysed economic change that is currently taking place in the lives of Indigenous Australians' (ibid.: 109). In some ways, these case studies encapsulate two exemplars of the tension that Myers (1986: 160) defined as an emphasis either on 'relatedness' or 'differentiation'. Relatedness, in the sense that Myers used the term (and others adapted it), refers to the bonds between individuals, partially the product of complex a priori Aboriginal kin relations, but also instantiated, that is, rendered particularly meaningful, through extensive networks of sharing. Alternately, differentiation means the incremental changes being made by Aboriginal people towards more independent forms of social life.

Family, Household and Sharing in Aboriginal Australia

Studies of Aboriginal sociality in Australia over previous decades have emphasized the concept of 'family' as the defining feature of social life (Babidge 2010; Birdsall 1988; Finlayson 1991; Rowse 2007; Yanagisako 1979). Despite its commonality in anthropological research, Sutton (1998: 57) noted how understandings of Aboriginal family vary across Australia, partly because of the tendency for anthropologists to conduct research in single case studies or regions, rather than comparatively across a number of settings. In an early paper which foreshadowed many of the key issues in the differentiation between the concepts of 'family' and 'household', Yanagisako (1979) synthesized literature from a range of contexts including Australia. A major conclusion of Yanagisako's (ibid.: 174) was that:

> The evidence that societies contain different frequencies of a range of household types surely challenges the classification of whole societies into two categories of those with "extended family households" versus those with "independent family households." Our goal of understanding and explaining domestic organization maybe better achieved by investigations of the diversity of domestic units in societies and the articulation of these domestic units with one another, rather than by comparisons that reduce whole societies to a single household type, family structure, or marriage transaction.

The task of explaining the diversity of family and household types within particular societies has been taken up by a number of anthropologists conducting research in Australia. One of the most detailed of these ethnographies undertaken in a single location was by Julie Finlayson (1991) in Kuranda, north Queensland. Finlayson investigated changes to Aboriginal family that occurred between 1913, when an Anglican mission was opened at Mona Mona, through to the early 1990s. Part of the missionaries' success in the conversion of Aboriginal people to Christianity was the imposition of the European nuclear family in place of the previously more extensive patterns of Aboriginal kin relations (ibid.: 124). Similar observations have been made in other parts of Australia, including Mornington Island, where the degradation of Aboriginal kinship by missionaries via the segregation of children from their parents and the orchestration of marriages between non-appropriate kin had both transformative and ongoing impacts (Martin 1993: 54; Memmott 1979: 288).

Finlayson also examined the relationship between the notions of 'family' and 'household' in 1990s Kuranda, particularly as they related to the sharing of resources. A 'household' was defined as a single physical dwelling (house) within which a number of 'economic units' resided (Finlayson 1991: 192). Each of the economic units shared amongst themselves money and food, and each unit was also expected to contribute to the overall upkeep of the house (ibid.: 193). As economic units tended to include kin, some households were composed entirely of kin (ibid.: 195). Mobility, particularly of children and young adults, and the continual dissolution and reconstitution of households, including as a result of economic instability, were important features of household cycles (ibid.: 200–1). Finlayson modelled these cycles in diagrams, which showed the arrival and departure of household residents through time (ibid.: 206–7). Central to Finlayson's research was the finding that, despite the economic importance of resource cycles to their long-term viability, 'households are not organized according to any determining principle such as the communal sharing of resources' (ibid.: 190; see also 192–93).

The distinctions between family, household and dwelling have also been central themes in the research of Yasmine Musharbash (2000, 2001, 2008) at Yuendumu in Central Australia. Musharbash (2008: 7) has focused on the three themes of intimacy, immediacy and mobility as defining features of the patterns of co-residence among Warlpiri people. She showed how ongoing changes in the sleeping arrangements of Warlpiri in camps, particularly women's camps or *jilimi*, demonstrated how individuals sleeping side-by-side evidenced and created intimacy and reflected the desires of people to express their relationships as such. The ongoing movements of women and children between *jilimi* challenged any notion of household in which the composition of residents was static or unchanging (Musharbash 2008: 60). High rates of mobility between locally proximate Aboriginal dwellings have also been demonstrated over greater distances between communities and regions (Memmott et al. 2006).

Definitional issues raised by the diversity of interpretations of family have posed particular questions for the numeration of Aboriginal people in the Australian Bureau of Statistics' (ABS) Census of Australian households. In various critiques of the Census collection methods, anthropologists have pointed out that the key terms of 'family' and 'household' might be interpreted differently by Aboriginal people in their completion of the survey, as against the broader understandings (Martin et al. 2002; Morphy 2006, 2007). One potential result of this differentiation was that the data collected could be 'misleading' or provide only 'misrepresentations' by recruiting Aboriginal 'members according to the same nuclear family principles that most Australians find "normal"' (Rowse 2011: 41).

This propensity was noted by Frances Morphy (2006, 2007), based on her research with Yolngu Aboriginal people in the Northern Territory and other case studies from around Australia. Morphy (2007) argued instead for a 'nodal network' model of interaction as a more accurate representation of the extensive bonds of interrelatedness between people in different dwellings. As others had previously (e.g. Musharbash 2001: 4), Morphy (ibid.: 165) noted that: 'the container metaphor is an inadequate basis for modelling the characteristics of the Aboriginal populations of remote Australia. Instead these are characterized by nodal points in space, connected by extensive, overlapping kinship networks, within which individuals are highly – but not randomly – mobile'. Attentiveness to the use of space and of dwellings has particular policy implications for the allocation of housing resources and architectural design. Others, though, such as Babidge (2010), Sutton (1998) and Peterson and Taylor (2002, 2003) have been more focused on changes occurring in Aboriginal kinship across a range of contexts, urban, rural and remote.

In a major review of existing ethnographic literature on Aboriginal family, Sutton (1998: 56) identified forms of 'post-classical' sociality, which he termed 'families of polity'. One particular 'family of polity' was the 'surnamed family group', a collation of cognates; the descendants of a single apical ancestor, who predominantly 'carried'[1] the same surname (ibid.: 57). Despite having emerged over an earlier period, surnamed family groups became particularly evident in the native title era, during which social allegiance to a collective identity was associated with the potential benefits of formal recognition of rights to land and seas under Australian law. The politics around the composition of Sutton's 'surnamed family groups' were at the centre of research undertaken by Sally Babidge (2010) in the north Queensland town of Charters Towers.

Babidge focused on the ways in which notions of Aboriginal family, including examples of surnamed family groups, were mobilized through processes of native title, which were active in the region where she was undertaking fieldwork in the early 2000s. More broadly, in the case study region, Babidge (ibid.: 101) noted that: 'when people spoke of "family", the term referred to their residential unit, bilateral kin, an ancestor focused construct such as cognatic descent group, inclusive combination of all 'close' kin including affines, and "one big family", being all those related in some way'. Babidge's analysis was similar to that of Chris Birdsall (1988) in Perth with Nyungars (Aboriginal people of the south-west region of Western Australia) during the 1980s. Birdsall (ibid.: 140) concluded that the term 'all one family' was used to gloss over smaller group identities, which might be termed 'lots', 'mob' or a particular 'part' of a bigger family (ibid.: 141).

As well as these connotations, when it came to native title, the concept of 'family group' was used in meetings and other bureaucratic situations to denote politically utilitarian relationships with others (Babidge 2010: 114). Another aspect of Aboriginal families investigated by Babidge was the distribution of resource sharing between individuals and the ways in which such relationships instanced bonds of relatedness. Individuals sharing resources in this way were not always co-resident, and as a result, there could be a number of residences of resource significance for a particular individual (ibid.: 106).

The place of economic factors, primarily the sharing of resources, and the degree to which such behaviours were integral to the definition of relationships with others was at the heart of Peterson's influential notion of 'demand sharing' (1993). Peterson used the term to explain a particular kind of sharing practice among Aboriginal people, based on the largely unrefusable claims for cash and resources made by Aboriginal people against their kin. Peterson's concept (ibid.: 862) built on his own field research and the ethnographic accounts of others, including that of Basil Sansom (1988), who, like Peterson, undertook research in the Northern Territory. Although in the early 1990s Peterson (1991: 68) described in his research findings that 'cash and commoditization have led to only limited transformations', changes in the previously sheltered economic and social lives of Aboriginal people, particularly in remote settings, were gathering pace. A decade later Peterson and Taylor (2003) began discussing the 'modernizing of the domestic moral economy', whereby the practices associated with demand sharing were undergoing modernization as they became increasingly exposed to capitalist mores. One example of this modernization was 'the emergence of the inwardly focused household' (2003: 107).

Taking a similar conceptual approach and at the same time, Austin-Broos (2003) charted the distributions of cash and commodities among Arrernte in Central Australia. In this seminal 2003 paper, Austin-Broos considered the transformation of Arrernte kinship relations to articulate with the major drivers of the capitalist state: cash and commodities. Austin-Broos (ibid.: 119) argued that this had enacted fundamental change, away from 'place-based' economies towards the more 'mobile' currencies (cash and commodities). As Austin-Broos (ibid.) described, 'the circulation of cars, nondurables, and cash, as well as the access to entertainments brought by mobility, all act to prise kinship away from country and redefine its significance'. Two decades after first discussing the role of demand-sharing practices, Peterson (2010: 251; 2013) reflected on the inevitability of processes of modernization as a kind of 'secular assimilation', where material (economic) changes necessarily have ramifications for culture and social identity, while nonetheless noting the 'persistence' of sharing practices. Such conclusions were suggestive of the redefinitions of kinship and family occurring in Aboriginal Australia over a relatively short period of time.

The Transformation of Kinship

As has been discussed at length elsewhere by David McKnight (2004, 2005), since the arrival of missionaries on Mornington Island in 1914 there have been dramatic changes to local systems of kinship and marriage among Aboriginal residents. The shift towards greater fluidity in the adherence to kinship structures, McKnight (2004: 226) argued, was not solely the result of interference by or engagement with Whitefellas or other Aboriginal people, but rather had been an inherent part of social interaction, and hence 'part and parcel of the "system" of kinship and marriage'. While in the past, geographic and social distance had ensured a degree of autonomy in the social life of each of the traditional owner groups of the Wellesley Islands, as detailed in McKnight (1999: Chapter 3, 2004: Chapters 2–4), Memmott (1979: Chapter 4), and Evans (1998: 17–24), the coming together of the groups in a single settlement on Mornington Island resulted in the redefinition of relationships toward a common shared identity.

A common feature of kin relations across the Wellesley Islands in pre-contact and early contact, and a particular aspect which persisted in some forms during the 2000s, as in many parts of Australia (Sutton 1998: 19), was the system of 'classificatory' kinship. As is usual for Aboriginal kinship, classificatory kin were regarded as of the same order as immediate or actual kin. For example, mother's sisters (MZs[2]) were classed in the same way as the mother, and father's brothers (FBs) were classed in the same way as the father. By extension, the children of a 'classificatory' mother or father also became one's brothers (Bs) and sisters (Zs). To indicate such a relationship, it was not uncommon for a person to refer to their 'cousin-sister' or 'cousin-brother', as a way of distinguishing between their actual or 'full' siblings. The children of a person's aunt (FZ) and uncle (MB) were referred to as 'cousins'.

The significance of classificatory relatives was that they formed part of large suites of relationships extending outwards from any particular person to include paternal, maternal and affinal related others (McKnight 1999: 34). Traditionally, Lardil kin terms existed for twenty-two different categories of relative, and each kin term was associated with particular types of behaviour and the performance of designated roles within those relationships. During the 2000s, some of the eldest living generation of Mornington Islanders, born approximately between 1925 and 1945, had extensive knowledge of Lardil or Kaiadilt kin terms and understood the associated behaviour and relationships.[3] The linguist Erich Round, who between 2006 and 2009 studied the language spoken by Kaiadilt people (spelled as 'Kayardild') resident on Mornington Island, noted that the eldest generation of living Kaiadilt used 'close to the full range of Kayardild kinship terms' (based on lists recorded by another linguist, Nicholas Evans, in 1992) while subsequent generations, who speak Aboriginal English, 'usually use Lardil terms' (Erich Round, The University of Queensland, pers. comm. 2011).

With some exceptions, younger people, especially those born in post-mission times (1978) were aware of a significantly reduced number of kin terms, and a much smaller set were in regular use. The most commonly used Lardil kin terms were those for 'close' kin: *thabu* (older brother), *kungku* (brother), *yaku* (sister), *jembe* (mothers' father), *karda* (mother's brother) and *babe* (fathers' mother). It appeared that many of the kin terms for affines (relatives via marriage) and more genealogically distant relationships, especially terms for those more than one generation level removed (i.e. great-grandparents), were generally unknown during the 2000s. Indicative of this was that Mornington Islanders used the term *banji* to refer to brother/sister in-law, this being a term used throughout Aboriginal Australia rather than being derived from local languages.

The consolidation of known kin terms can be understood partly as a product of the reduction in the number of fluent language speakers, across Lardil, Kaiadilt and Yangkaal, and the transition to Aboriginal English as the dominant language (McKnight 2004: 18). Currently there are between five and ten fluent Lardil and Kaiadilt speakers, with a much larger number of people able to understand some basic terms, especially nouns and verbs. By the time McKnight visited Mornington in 1966, there were only 'one or two fluent Yangkaal speakers' (ibid.), and during the 2000s I was unaware of anyone (other than linguists) who was able to speak Yangkaal or distinguish it from Lardil. Despite the loss of the specific kin terms for those in a person's extended network of family, Mornington Islanders instead used English words to refer to relations and observe the types of relationships recorded by McKnight.

Another aspect of the incorporation of kin was that at least until recent times, Aboriginal groups in the Gulf of Carpentaria (with the exception of Kaiadilt) were organized around an eight-subsection system, also known as 'skins' for social and ritual purposes (McKnight 2004: 3; Memmott 1979: 69). The eight subsections were known in Lardil as *Burrarangi, Kangal, Yakimarr, Kamarrangi, Bangarinyi, Balyarrinyi, Ngarrijbalangi* and *Burany* (McKnight 1999: 44). Subsections were a cornerstone of sociality as they constituted a way of understanding correct marriage partners for individuals, or what are referred to as 'straight-head' marriages (or de facto relationships): that is, individuals from appropriate subsections marrying one another (ibid.: 45). The subsection system was one of the social categories that worked in concert with the kinship system. For Lardil, the ideal marriage was between (distant) second cross-cousins, i.e. 'between the children of female cross-cousins or male cross-cousins' (ibid.).[4] In the case of 'irregular marriages', i.e. when a person had a child with someone of an inappropriate subsection, a choice would have to be made as to who the child would 'follow' to obtain their subsection /skin, this either being via their mother or father. A number of examples of 'irregular' subsection derivations are provided and discussed in McKnight (2004: 114–24). Though there has been some debate about the inheritance of subsections for Lardil people, particularly following Sharp's (1935: 162) assertion that even in straight marriages, children took their subsection 'through the mother', the more recent interpretation has been that in the case of straight skin individuals marrying, the resulting children derived their subsection 'through the father' (McKnight 2004: 113; Paul Memmott, The University of Queensland, pers. comm. 2011). Rapid changes, however, including the number of children fathered by non-Aboriginal men and Aboriginal men from parts of Australia where the subsection system was not used, were likely to have dramatically increased the number of children determining their skin through their mother, particularly from the 1940s onwards.

An important event in the transmission of information relating to subsections was the practice of male initiation. As part of this process, older men, who had themselves undergone initiation into law, took young men away from their family to prepare them in the lead up to their circumcision, an integral aspect of the initiation process. Part of the preparation included the transmission of various types of knowledge, including a form of sign language (known as *demiin*) and appropriate types of behaviour for men and women as designated by their relationships in terms of skins (McKnight 1999: 24–25, 27). From the arrival of missionaries in 1914, initiation ceremonies were discouraged and thus only held periodically and for small numbers of young men, in 1932, 1958, 1972, 1974 and 1979 and subsequently through the 1990s and early 2000s (McKnight 1999: 32; Memmott and Horsmann 1991: 311).

In some years, young men were taken to regional ceremonies on the mainland, particularly at Borroloola in the Northern Territory (or people from Borroloola were brought to Mornington Island), where knowledge of initiation rituals had persisted among Garawa and Yanyuwa people (McKnight 1999: 249; Memmott and Horsmann 1991: 312; Trigger 1992: 75). One man aged in his late thirties explained that he:

> went through the law on Mornington. Camped out bush for one whole month. Got taught our ways through them. Long time ago they used to have them nearly every year. You're growing up with it and it's there you know. Them say come for dance and you know what to do. You go straight out bush and dance and that ... Someone probably start it back up. Got families in Borroloola they come back here. Hmm they help, oh they run the whole show. Everyone here on Mornington, they go along with it sort of thing. Everybody helps out. They go do hunting and all that stuff. The young boys, when they go through law, they go bush and do all that work.

The infrequency of these ceremonies[5] had resulted in the lack of maintenance of a coherent system of subsection affiliation across the population in the 2000s.

Partly as a result of the changes to subsection affiliation, Mornington Islanders instead 'trace' their relationships to one another through the identification of a common third party (see also Sutton 1998: 9). This was particularly the case for 'foreigners' – visitors from other Aboriginal communities, especially nearby Doomadgee and Normanton. This would often happen even before a visitor had been introduced. In a hypothetical situation someone might ask, for example:

> Person A: Who that un? [gesturing to unfamiliar man walking past]
>
> Person B: He Ralph, Jack Smith's cousin-brother from Doomadgee.
>
> Person A: Oh true. I call Jack 'uncle' so I must be call him uncle too.

The process of tracing or tracking using different third parties within a discontinuous system sometimes resulted in what appeared to be inconsistent or irreconcilable outcomes (see also Sutton 1998: 9). In a particular example, an Aboriginal man born in 1940 reckoned kin relations to a couple in their thirties via two separate third parties, such that he referred to the male spouse as 'uncle' and the female spouse as 'granddaughter'. When I asked the man how this somewhat confusing multi-generation-level relationship had come to pass, he responded, 'I don' know how come girl'.

This was similar to observations by McKnight (2004: 86) from the 1990s, when:

> the situation on Mornington has reached such a state that people often lament to me that they do not know what to call someone. And I too in recent years have been puzzled about how to trace some relationships. Furthermore, I discovered that many people are uncertain about the terminology model. Without a thorough understanding of that model they cannot make a reasonable decision.

The practices of tracing kin relationships highlighted the degree of 'choice' that Mornington Islanders were able to exercise in determining their kinship relationships to one another. There were a number of factors that contributed to decisions to identify a particular person as either close or more distant kin, one of these factors being the desirability of a person as a romantic partner.

Marriage

Marriages between Aboriginal people of different language group affiliations were an important part of the way in which Aboriginal people conceived of one another as family. The terms 'marriage' and 'married-up' had two meanings on Mornington Island during the 2000s, the most obvious being to refer to those persons who were in a relationship as recognized by the Queensland Births Deaths and Marriages registry, and thus in a 'registered marriage'. Another way in which the terms were used was to refer to socially recognized de facto couples, often those whose members had been in a relationship for an extended period of time (usually years) and had children. Data collected by the Australian Bureau of Statistics as part of the Census in 2016 indicates that among Gununa residents, over 30 per cent reported being in de facto marriages, 10 per cent were in registered marriages and over 55 per cent were 'not married'. The largest cohort of Gununa residents who were married were those aged 55–64 years, that is those born between 1952 and 1961 (ABS 2016: Table G06). One explanation for the prevalence of registered marriages in this age group was that most in this age bracket would have reached a marriageable age (i.e. 18

years old) at a time when Mornington Island was run as a Presbyterian mission, i.e. pre-1978.

With the cessation of initiation as widespread practice and the loss of extensive knowledge about Aboriginal kinship also came a reduction in the number of (and a lack of awareness about) 'straight-head' marriages as designated by Aboriginal kinship, with many instead choosing their partner based on love and attraction (McKnight 2002: 64; 2004: 86). During the 2000s, two Aboriginal men aged in their thirties, who had both gone through initiation, commented on their own de facto relationships. In an interview in 2007, one man described to me how he had 'married straight':

> So my missus is my cousin. Ah she's supposed to be mine, but she's my cousin from my mother's side.
>
> *So your missus is your mother's brother's daughter?*
>
> Yep. Like my mother is not actually her like full blood, but they're from different father and mother, but their fathers are brothers.

The man was describing how his partner was in fact a 'distant' cross-cousin, several generations removed from being related by what Mornington Islanders called 'full blood' (see Figure 3.1).

The other man had not married straight: 'I never. I broke the law, me. Oh Aboriginal ways, they just call us law breaking buggers you know'. The man also noted that because he had not married straight, and as his brothers-in-law had not gone through initiation, he was able to disregard the practice where Aboriginal people, both men and women, avoided their in-laws. In 'avoidance relationships', individuals eschewed close contact, including eye contact, and avoided direct speaking and sharing close physical space. Some examples of these relationships included between different gender siblings and in-law relations of different genders. As the man explained, 'for me I got a woman there [his partner] and her brothers never went through law, I still talk to them'. The man, however, did observe an avoidance relationship with those men who were in a skin group for which his sister was marriageable. As he described: 'Main brother-in-law is the person like through law, comes down. You don't talk to your brother-in-law, it's our custom. You can leave, you can go to Mount Isa, walk along the street and he still won't talk to me, no matter where in the world we go'.

Although he had not followed the practice himself, the man remained convinced that straight marriages were socially important: 'but it's good to have it like that [marry straight] too cause your kids

Contemporary Aboriginal Family • 101

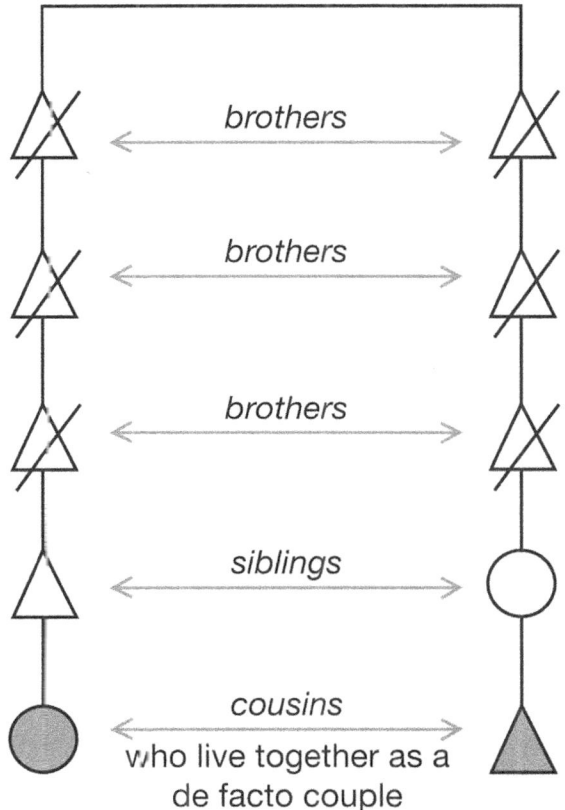

Figure 3.1. Genealogy showing the relationship between a man and his de facto partner (in grey) identified in a 'straight' subsection relationship (figure created by the author).

come down through skin and that. They know where they stand sort of thing'. Some young people were aware of who their potential straight-head marriage partners were, even if they had chosen to form a relationship with another person. During a drinking session at the local Pub in 2007, a man aged in his late thirties approached an Aboriginal woman aged in her early twenties that I was sitting with. After the man left the young woman told me that the man was classified as her 'father-in-law' and that it was inappropriate for her to talk to him. She explained that she was a suitable marriage partner for the man's sons, and that even though she was the de facto partner of another man, the intended relationship (father-in-law/daughter-in-law) remained.

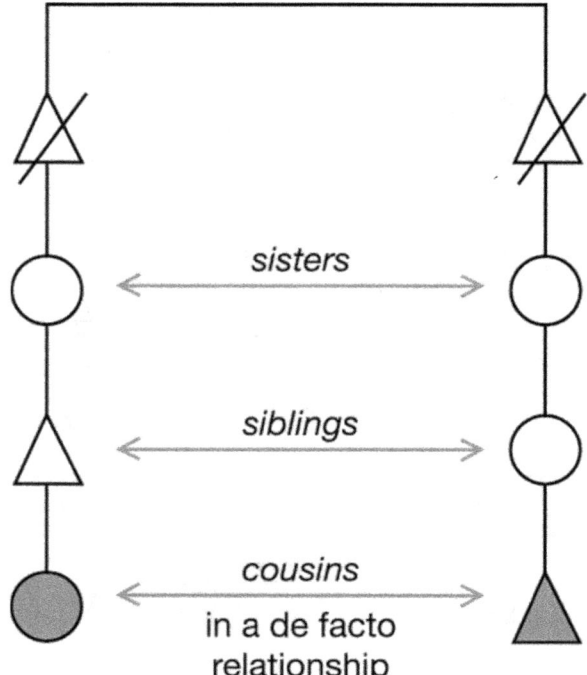

Figure 3.2. Genealogy showing the relationship between a teenage couple (marked in grey) described as 'too close' (figure created by the author).

In March 2009, I was told about a teenage girl who had started 'goin with' (i.e. being in a relationship with) a teenage boy classed as her cousin on account of their great-grandfathers being brothers (see Figure 3.2). Both the teenagers' parents and extended families bemoaned the union, and the couple had reportedly been heavily criticized by the girl's brothers for entering into the relationship. Although I tried a number of times to elicit the nature of concern about the relationship, be it for genetic, subsection or social reasons, most responded that the couple were just 'too close'. After a period of time elapsed and the couple showed no diminishment in their affection for one another, there appeared to have been a begrudging acceptance of the relationship as another example of the ways in which younger people were transgressing social norms, and thus failing to live up to the expectations of those of older generations.

In describing the propensity of young people to form relationships with incorrect marriage partners, an Aboriginal man in his thirties described how 'some of them they married into the wrong skin group', which he acknowledged made it difficult for those involved to discern appropriate relationships based on the subsection and kinship systems. As a way of emphasizing the potential for marriage to create continuity, however, the man also noted, 'but they [are] all still family' Relationships between individuals deemed inappropriate partners were one of a number of other ways in which the continuity of family was challenged.

Children and 'Stolen Ones'

Among young Mornington Islanders, there were few examples where couples remained in long-term de facto relationships. Instead, from their teenage years onwards, young women often had children born as a result of casual or short-term relationships. At the 2006 Census, approximately 65 per cent of women aged 15–24 years had one child, with a proportion having as many as four (ABS 2006: Table B23). This contrasts to the statistic of the same age bracket that only 25 per cent considered themselves to be in a de facto relationship (none were in a registered married), with the remaining 75 per cent being neither de facto nor in a registered marriage (ibid.: Table B06). That the Census only counted mothers aged 15 years and older potentially underestimates the number of young parents, as in 2007 local health workers reported that six Mornington Island girls aged 14–16 years were pregnant (Koch 2007: 13).

Partly as a result of the housing shortage, and in order to care for their babies, teenage girls would often remain living in a household with their maternal relations, and it was common for a child's maternal grandmother in particular to take a very active role in the nurturance of the child. In a survey that I conducted in 2009 (see Appendix One), instances where three or more generations were resident in a single dwelling accounted for approximately 33 per cent of total dwellings, some of which included young mothers and children living with their maternal relations. My observations were that it was not uncommon in these instances for the biological father of the child to be unknown by the general community, and for gossip (among women in particular) to hypothesize about likely paternity based on the traits of the child. In some cases, the secrecy about a child's biological father may have been to obscure the identity of a man who was already in a relationship with another woman.

On Mornington Island, a child born as the result of an extramarital affair was often described as a 'stolen one' (McKnight 2004: 29). A 'stolen' child was one that was conceived while either the mother and/or father was in a married or de facto relationship with another person. As McKnight (ibid.: 29, 81) noted, and I observed during the 2000s, the relationships between parties involved with stolen children varied greatly and appeared to be dependent on a range of factors. Once, while waiting in line at the local store, I saw a middle-aged man kiss and cuddle a toddler, buying her an ice cream along with others who I already knew (through prior introduction) to be his biological children. During the encounter, the toddler's mother waited off in the distance, with her head turned away and body language downcast so as not to meet the gaze of the man. When I queried the Aboriginal woman that I was with as to the relationship between the man and the toddler she mouthed the words 'stolen one'.

In other situations, I was told that stolen children were not made aware of their biological paternity, sometimes never in any overt way and at other times not until they had reached young adulthood. Whether or not overt mention was made, doubts over a child's paternity undoubtedly impacted the way that parents, mothers especially, socialized their children to ensure that biologically close kin were not conceived of as potential marriage partners. Although such situations were not often discussed openly, in one unusually candid interview a man born in the 1960s explained his experiences. The man identified his 'real father' and also another man, who 'adopted' him and 'grew' him up 'from small'. During the interview I asked the man to clarify his use of the terms 'real' and 'adoptive':

What do you mean by 'real'?

Like my full father, like full blood.

Who did you call father or both?

Well, both. Both of them.

And was that something that everyone else knew about? Or was that a secret?

Yeah, they all knew about that … but they didn't tell me until I was little boy because my mother and [adoptive] father, they got married.

The man went on to explain that his mother had fallen pregnant during mission times, when the prevailing ethic was that pregnant women should be formally married and children not born out of wedlock. As the man got older, when he was a 'little boy', he became aware that his adoptive father was not his biological father, and later in his life his 'adoptive' father's family respected his wish to spend time with his biological father and family. As our conversation continued, I asked:

Has that made it hard for you in the way that you ...?

Ah not really. Didn't make it all that hard.

So other people respected that and everything?

Ah yeah, now.

Now?

Now, they're respecting that, yeah. Like the [adoptive father's] family, they knew.

So it wasn't sort of a shame thing or anything?

Not really.

Part of the reason that the situation was treated with respect, the man noted, was because his biological and adoptive fathers were 'brothers, like how you say it, through their skin'. As a result of their shared 'skin' (subsection), the man's 'half' brothers through his biological father were also classified as his brothers through subsection, as they too shared the same skin. Throughout the 2000s, the man lived in a house with his (biological half) brothers, their partners, children and his biological father's wife, who he also called 'mum'.

On other occasions, Aboriginal people[6] (confidentially) mentioned that they held doubts over their own biological paternity, or that of one of their close relatives, often a niece or nephew or classificatory son or daughter. In these instances, there was usually an alternate hypothesis for the child's paternity based on their physical characteristics being dissimilar to their siblings and/or more like those of another man's children. Common traits identified as such were the child's skin tone (fair or dark), facial features (especially the nose), hair (curly or straight) and the shape and rise of the foot (McKnight 1999: 17). While it is impossible to quantify the number of children who might have fitted into this category, I would agree with McKnight's (2005: 139) conclusion that 'there were many stolen children', such that the reputed illegitimate paternity of children was a ubiquitous feature of community gossip and a common cause of tension and fights. In at least one instance, primary school-aged children 'carrying yarns' (i.e. gossiping) about another child's paternity precipitated a fight between two adult women.

Nomenclature for Family

As has been observed in other situations (Babidge 2010; Birdsall 1988; Yanagisako 1979), on Mornington Island, 'family' was a term used in a variety of different contexts and to enact a variety of meanings. As Finlayson (1991: 197) found for Aboriginal people in Kuranda, the term was 'used to refer to the nuclear family; a kin network beyond the nuclear family; or as an umbrella term for a political group united by a common interest'. The performative nature of kinship and family in Aboriginal contexts, as noted elsewhere, makes it nearly impossible to discuss without reference to specific examples. Mornington Islanders, though, used a range of terms, including 'family' but also 'gang' and 'mob', to refer to a range of groupings of kin who came together, either actually or hypothetically, for a particular event or to perform a specific task.

When describing the size of a group of people, Mornington Islanders used adjectives that loosely quantified the number of people present. In contexts where a significant portion, perhaps over one third, of the community were in attendance, such as the dance festival, football games, a large funeral or at the local Pub, a person might refer to 'all the mob' or 'all the families'. On occasions when a lesser number of persons were present, for example on a trip out bush, a common description might be 'the usual gang' or the 'family mob' or simply, 'the family'. This group might consist of some close cognates and their affines, with all able to trace their relationships to each other. Unlike in the Kuranda case, Mornington Islanders seldom referred to their nuclear family, such was the infrequency with which such a group was solely involved in a particular activity. In situations where smaller groups of kin were being referenced – for example, the immediate relatives of a particular woman (her de facto, her mother and her children) – a person might refer to 'just me an my little gang' or 'just us mob'.

The collective terms 'family', 'mob' and 'gang' were often evoked in particular situations as a way of recognizing that everyone was kin. For example, a mother once described how she had used it to discourage her daughters from fighting with children at the local primary school: 'they all your family', she said, 'you can't [i.e. should not] fight with them' (see also McKnight 2005: 121). Similarly, in 2009 a man aged in his thirties contextualized his disapproval of domestic disputes (i.e. between couples) being taken up by other kin. As he pointed out: 'we all families now, we all intermarried, we all neighbours now too'.

Invoking 'family' to encourage harmony is yet another example of the interplay between structure and fluidity in Aboriginal kinship on Mornington Island. On the one hand, there were historically defined social structures, namely subsections and repertoires of kin terms that previously defined kinds of relationships between Aboriginal persons. Intricate knowledge of these structures, and the deference to them to guide social interactions, has been replaced by a fracturing or narrowing of understandings of the systems in previous decades, and a consolidation of kin terms and relationships regularly observed. These changes have led to less rigid expressions of relatedness, particularly among younger generations, and more generalized statements by residents that they were all 'related' or 'family'.

Sutton (1998: 54), though, cautioned against what he saw as a tendency to emphasize fluidity as the guiding principle in the constitution of Aboriginal family. In reflecting on patterns across Aboriginal Australia, he noted that 'fluidity' and other 'freedom-connoting concepts' sometimes formed 'a handy cover for our difficulty in reaching systematic accounts of phenomena' (ibid.). In response to this tendency, Sutton argued that: 'the ethnography required to describe such cases needs to be fine-grained and systematic, but it also needs to be informed by the rigour of anthropological theory, if areas of indeterminacy and enduring structures are to be demonstrated convincingly' (ibid.).

One of the more important factors in understanding the ways in which family was established and reproduced was via the distribution of kin across dwellings. This was predominately in free-standing houses but also a small number of one-bedroom apartments and single room 'studio' apartments. In order to provide some baseline data about dwellings, in 2010 I interviewed two Aboriginal women aged in their thirties about the residents of housing managed by the local Council in Gununa (i.e. excluding dwellings occupied only by Whitefellas). Although an account of the methodology appears in Appendix One, a number of points are worthwhile to make here. In separate interviews with the two women, for each house the names and relationships of all residents were recorded using aerial photographs of the community. At the completion of the two interviews, a joint interview was held with both women, and where the information about a particular resident had been inconsistent, a consensus opinion was formed. In was invariably the case that Aboriginal people, and women in particular, were extremely knowledgeable about such matters, as the daily comings and goings of residents was the source of continuous gossip and social production.

At the time of the interviews, 180 dwellings were occupied by a total of 886 Aboriginal residents,[7] an average of 4.92 residents per house. In terms of the number of generation levels resident in one dwelling, 39.4 per cent (n=71) were occupied by two generations of the same family and 33.0 per cent (n=59) of dwellings were occupied by three or more generations of the same family. Of the remaining dwellings, some were sole-occupancy (1.0 per cent, n=19) while others were couples or multiple siblings living together. Of all dwellings, 23.3 per cent (n=42) were occupied solely by a 'nuclear family', i.e. mother, father and their biological and/or adopted children. Though these data provide hints of the relationship between notions of family and dwelling (or house), taken in isolation they do not account for either the way these dwellings were used or the particular ways in which Aboriginal people interacted with kin nearby. In order to explore these aspects of family, I now introduce two case studies, the Middle families and Neil and Clare, before exploring the ways in which family was constructed.

Case Study I: Middle Families

This case study is of an interconnected network of kin (see Figure 3.4) who resided in a number of houses in two parallel streets in the middle part of Gununa (see Figure 3.3). In order to understand the complexity of the ways in which the network operated, two residences are used as a focus. The first residence (House 1) was a two-bedroom house occupied by Jean and Tom, a couple aged in their early thirties, and their five children, born between 1998 and 2010. A number of Jean and Tom's close kin lived in houses on the same street and adjacent, as shown in Figure 3.3 and Figure 3.4. For example, Jean's maternal grandmother, mother and a number of Jeans' siblings and their children lived in House 6. Jean's mother's sister (a classificatory mother) lived with her husband and children in House 5. As Tom explained: '… most of my in-laws[8] up this street. Everyone down this street, they all relations'. Tom also had family nearby, with his elder brother Zack and his de facto partner Anne and their two young children across the street in House 2..

Jean and Tom's house was a focal point in the local neighbourhood, particularly for women and children, and in the late afternoon people from the nearby houses often congregated in the front yard to eat, gossip and make plans for trips 'out bush' on the upcoming weekend. In the late 2000s, Tom worked full-time as a Ranger; he and Jean had been able to afford to purchase two second-hand four-wheel-drive vehicles, and often took family from nearby residences out with them on weekends. Another regular feature of such afternoons was what I once described as 'the stream of kids that came and went', mostly those from nearby houses, who played up and down the street on the road and kerbside.

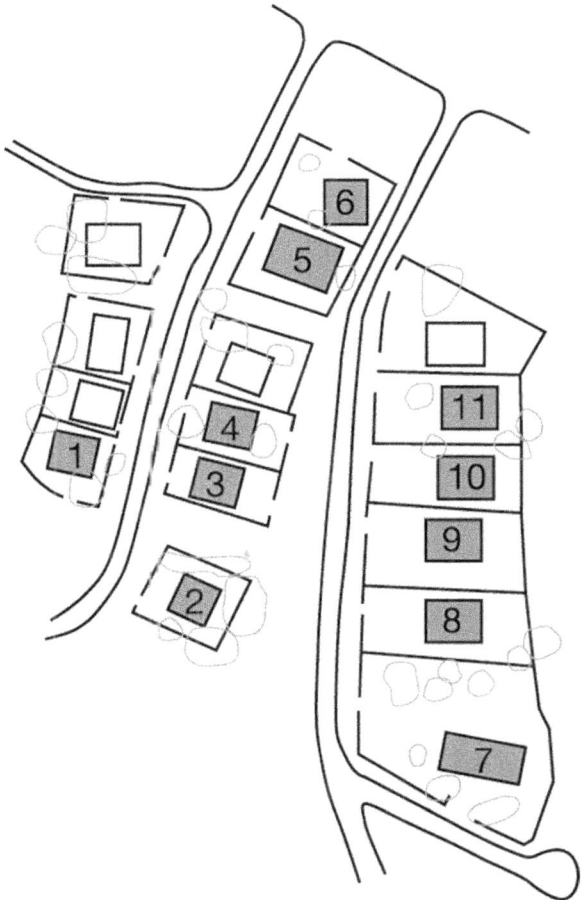

Figure 3.3. Houses of the Middle families, February 2010 (figure created by the author).

The second focal house located within this network was Ian and his de facto partner Sue in House 4, as shown in Figure 3.3. Ian and Sue were aged in their fifties and were 'willed' their 3-bedroom house by Sue's sister, who, Ian explained, had moved to the Aboriginal community of Doomadgee on the mainland. The residency of Ian and Sue's house fluctuated between 2007 and 2010, but generally consisted of Ian and Sue, up to four of their five children and their de facto partners, and two of Ian's and Sue's grandchildren. The potential occupancy of the house was approximately ten people, but because of the high mobility of some occupants, it was rarely more than six or seven at any

110 • *What Now*

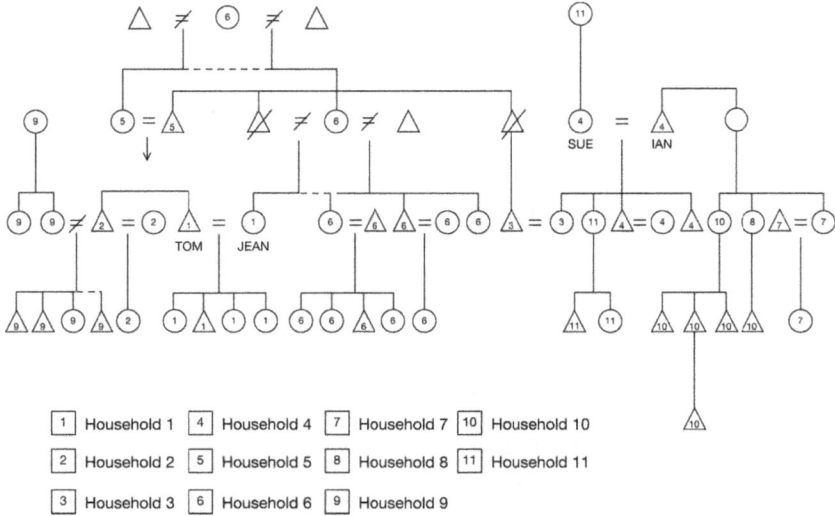

Figure 3.4. Genealogy showing the distributions of residences for the Middle families in February 2010. Two couples, Tom and Jean and Sue and Ian, are used as exemplars and focal points to describe interactions within the broader extended network (figure created by the author).

particular time. Both Ian and Sue had close kin, including classificatory relations, living in the surrounding houses, many of whom were regular visitors to their house, as Ian described to me in 2007:

> I stay in an area where there's my second [eldest] daughter living next door. And then I got my nieces [sister's daughters] staying across the road. And then there's Sue's mother just up the road … then next door, that's her sister, her younger sister … across from her house there's her father's second, her second eldest father [father's brother] stays … family and in-laws, yeah.

On some afternoons between 2008 and 2010, a 'gambling school',[9] a place where Aboriginal people came to bet money on card games that they played, was held in Ian's and Sue's yard. The gambling school attracted a range of kin from the nearby houses, especially women, while at other times, particularly on Council pay days, gamblers drove to the house from other parts of the community.

An almost inevitable part of spending time at any of the houses of the Middle families was the perpetual activity of highly communal lives. At any point in time there were numerous activities going on: women gossiping, men working together to fix a car or build something, the borrowing and return of items such as money, CDs, iPods, and phone chargers, trips to the store and the Council office, and children going backwards and forwards between different houses, seeking out food, toys and playmates. It was the constant ebb and flow, and the highly interconnected manner in which these activities occurred, which defined life for these families.

Case Study II: Neil and Clare

Between 2006 and 2009, Neil and Clare, an Aboriginal couple aged in their thirties, lived in a two-bedroom house towards the 'bottom end'[10] of Gununa with their two children. Many of both Neil and Clare's close kin lived on the mainland, in the regional centres of Mount Isa, Cairns and Townsville, including the majority of Clare and Neil's siblings and both their fathers. Despite their mothers both growing up on Mornington Island, Clare's father was an Aboriginal man traditionally connected to the Mount Isa region, while Neil's father was a Whitefella. As a result of this, both Neil and Clare had themselves spent periods living on the mainland and attending high school in Mount Isa, where Neil spent the majority of his youth growing up with his father. In later years, the couple managed to secure a house on Mornington Island while Neil worked as an apprentice electrician at a large zinc mine on the adjacent mainland.

In 2004 the couple moved back to Mornington Island to be closer to their maternal relatives, in particular Clare's mother, who stayed with the couple during her scheduled days off from her job in administration at the same mine where Neil had been working. Neil signed his apprenticeship indentures over to the Mornington Shire Council and began working on the Island as a third year apprentice electrician, making him the only local Aboriginal person employed locally with a trade at that time. The couple's house was on one of the back streets of the community, which was less densely occupied than other parts and further away from the main services, such as the store and post office. According to Clare and Neil, this meant that there was little incidental traffic or visitation to the house by Aboriginal people passing by. For this reason, Clare and Neil were pleased with the location of the house, as it ensured them a degree of independence from their family members. As Clare explained to me in 2009: 'We're not living here for family, we like our space. We like it. It is quite good this little area because you don't see much people, don't hear much, right out of the way and its always been'.

On several visits to the couple's house between 2007 and 2010, including a six-week period in 2007 when I was staying in a house next door, I found that this was generally true; it was unusual for anyone to be at the house other than the couple, their children and Clare's mother. This changed somewhat in 2008 and 2009 when Clare began a small business (as described in Chapter 1), a shop, in the front patio of the couple's house. The store sold home wares, clothes, toys, plants and other bric-a-brac, and it was one of few private enterprises being run by an Aboriginal person on Mornington Island at that time.

A number of aspects of the couple's perspectives and life experiences set them apart from others on Mornington Island, perhaps particularly Neil's experiences growing up with a Whitefella father and the couple both attending school in regional centres on the mainland. Though attending school on the mainland was not an unusual experience for Mornington Islanders, who since at least 1966 had attended boarding schools on the mainland (Memmott 1979: 301), it seemed less common for such children to live in those centres with close or extended family members. A formative aspect of these experiences for Neil and Clare had been the development of the desire and drive to work in whatever capacity they could manage. As Neil himself pointed out, 'I have had a lot of work outside. I've worked underground, I've worked on electric shovels, in Kmart, Coles, open [mine] pits, all over the place', while Clare had 'worked at the preschool [in Mount Isa] for ages'.

Perhaps more than anything else, it seemed that these experiences afforded both Neil and Clare the ability to critically reflect on the lives of Mornington Islanders and contrast them to those living elsewhere. Illustrative of this critical perspective were comments made by Neil in a discussion of the reliance of Mornington Islanders on one another: 'a lot of the times the problem is that you depend on them that have got, depend on them for using their car, bit of sugar and you can never really do things in the community clear minded when you're living out of somebody else people's pocket. Your judgement, your vote, you've gotta run with them people'. This indebtedness contrasted, Neil said, to those in the 'mainstream' and on the mainland, including those of mixed-descent and Whitefellas, who 'you don't owe them anything because they're your friend … they got nothing to gain from you'.

These feelings contributed to the couple's decision to relocate to the mainland city of Cairns in late 2009. Another deciding factor was that Clare was pregnant with the couple's third child and that their eldest son had reached primary school age. Clare identified her children's education and her and Neil's own education experiences as important motivators for the move: 'Yeah well want to try an' move for our boys' sake. Got to go out for school soon, school is alright up here but just need to have a look at the big wide world I suppose. I went to school in Mount Isa and Neil went to school in Mount Isa too. [It is a] big thing taking them out for school even though they going to miss Mornington'. After the couple left the Island, Clare's mother took over tenancy of their house and began running her daughter's small business.

Constituting Residence and Household

Between 2006 and 2010, all housing on Mornington Island occupied by Aboriginal people was part of the 'One Social Housing' system provided by the Queensland State Government and administered by the Mornington Shire Council ('the Council') under a Local Indigenous Partnership Agreement (LIPA) (Queensland Department of Housing 2008: 3,6). Rent for these houses was paid weekly via a levy set at AUD 40.00 per week for those employed full-time and AUD 37.00 per week for all others earning an income, including welfare payments (ibid.: 14). That the levy was tied to individual people (rather than dwellings) meant that the arrangements remained in place even when people moved house or when individuals were mobile between houses. It also meant, for example, that a person living alone in a house (which accounted for 1 per cent (n=19) of dwellings in 2010) paid the same amount as a person living with nine others (which accounted for 0.6 per cent (n=11) of dwellings in 2010). In spite of this, as in other parts of Australia (Musharbash 2001: 4), houses were said locally to be 'owned' by particular individuals or couples.

From 2006 to 2010, the Council maintained a 'waitlist' of housing applicants, which in 2008 had a total of forty-four pending applications. In August 2007, an advertisement was placed in a community newsletter reminding residents of the process of applying for a house.

> If you wish to be considered for a house it is a requirement that you place your name on the housing list. The Housing Officer ... has housing application forms. Once you have filled in an application, your name will be placed on the Waiting List and when a house becomes available you will be notified.

In 2008, the Queensland Department of Housing (2008: 12) noted that: 'the longest period an applicant [has been] on the waitlist is since 1997. Many of these applicants are living off the Island. The long wait time is due to larger families taking priority over smaller families'.

There were ways, however, to circumvent the formal waitlist process. Neil and Clare, for example, were allocated their house in 2004 via a private arrangement with the Council. As part of the arrangement, Neil described how he had signed his electrical apprenticeship indentures over to the Council and had paid two years of the housing levy in advance.[11] As Neil described it: 'I didn't get this house because I was on the list or because of family or anything. I paid two years. Nobody on Mornington does that, pays two years' rent. Sometimes you gotta think outside the circle'. Neil was also unique in the sense of being one of few local Aboriginal people working full-time for the Council, and was thus perhaps in a better position to use his employment as a negotiation tactic to secure housing.

Many changes to house occupancy, however, occurred informally, through the transfer or succession of houses between family members, a process described by Aboriginal people as 'inheriting' or being 'willed' a house. The transfer of houses in this way occurred for a number of reasons, sometimes when the dwelling 'owner' died, but more commonly when the 'owner' moved elsewhere, to the Aged Persons' Hostel, the mainland or to another house within the community (Queensland Department of Housing 2008: 13). During an interview in 2007, for example, Ian explained how he and Sue had acquired their residence:

> I was living down the bottom end, before, me and Sue had a house way down the bottom end. Then we moved up there and got that house off Sue's sister, left that house for us, Gabrielle.
>
> *Did she pass away?*
>
> Nah she ... [laughs].
>
> *Sorry!*
>
> She went out [off the Island] working and she ended up staying out Doomadgee, living it up with one fella there.

In instances where an arrangement was made between family members, a caretaker occupant was sometimes called upon to carry out tasks or duties. Ian and Sue, for example, cared for Gabrielle's young daughter until Gabrielle had settled permanently in Doomadgee and asked for her daughter to be sent over to live with her. Asking close kin to act as caretakers while they went off the Island reduced the likelihood that the Council would reassign the house through the formal housing system. Jean and Tom had gained their three-bedroom house in a similarly informal manner through Jean's classificatory mother (her mother's sister), who they had been living with. When Jean had her first child, her mother's sister 'willed' the house to her and Tom, and the couple and their children had lived there ever since. Historically, these kinds of succession arrangements appear to have been accepted by the Council, who had 'no formal process for reviewing tenancies to ensure appropriate utilization of housing stock to meet the housing needs of the community' (Queensland Department of Housing 2008: 13). During my housing survey I found instances in which, for example, fourteen people lived in a three-bedroom home while elsewhere a single resident lived alone in a four-bedroom home.

As well as the practice of willing houses, periodically other types of informal arrangements were made between Gununa residents in order to obtain a house more proximal to close kin. For example, in early 2008, Ian's niece Iris was living in a large, relatively new house at the bottom end of the community when an opportunity arose for her to swap houses with a Council employee living across the road from Ian and Sue. The move suited Iris because the house was situated amongst her immediate family – her sisters in House 7 and House 10 and (Iris' uncle) Ian in House 4. The house was also much closer to the main services such as the hospital, store and post office, which was particularly useful as Iris did not own a car. The Council employee, an older Aboriginal man from the mainland who had lived in the community for many years, was reportedly pleased with the swap as the newer house was in a quieter part of town. Although the house was located further from basic services, the man had access to a car as part of his employment.

The informal processes of constituting residences allowed close kin to reconfigure distributions of occupancy such that they were located near one another. In an interview in 2008, Jean described this residential proximity in that it 'makes us stronger, to be family'. As in other parts of the community, the Middle families referred to the proximate area around their houses as 'our area' and noted that when 'strangers' – Aboriginal people from other parts of the community – came to 'visit', they 'won't feel comfortable' because they were aware that it was 'not their area'. When I asked residents if they would like a newly constructed house in Gununa, they would often note that while they desired a new house, they were not prepared to move out of 'their area' in order to obtain one. As an Aboriginal woman aged in her 50s explained: 'Oh no I wouldn't live nowhere else, I'd rather live where I am now. If that house going to be knocked down then I rather see a new one built in that same spot'. A variety of reasons were given for this, but most often it was because the house where they were already living was near their close kin.

Sentiments such as these were regularly expressed in 2009 and 2010 when the Queensland State Government was undertaking the construction of fifteen new residences (Queensland Department of Housing 2008: 20). The new houses were being built at the 'bottom end' of the community, which had only recently been opened up for development. Although some families aged in their thirties were being offered the new houses, at least one couple in the Middle families had declined, electing to remain 'in their area'. Remaining in one's area, nearby to close kin, was seen as more contiguous with ethics of sharing and more consistent with the kinds of spatial proximity with which Aboriginal Mornington Islanders were most familiar. As Cyril Moon, for example, lamented in 2007: 'No more, no more like before, families used to live together. Today all separate. They live long, long way. 'Nother [another] countryman that 'ay [way] sit down, sleep la long way, 'nother one back this 'ay [way], 'nother one that 'ay'. Despite this, he also noted: 'But 'e all still meet up, come see one another and come say "hello"'. An obvious benefit of remaining close to existing networks of kin was that it facilitated resource sharing, a key feature of Aboriginal family on Mornington Island.

Kin, Sharing and Resources

As research has demonstrated, the ethic of sharing, and particularly demand sharing, is integral to the constitution of Aboriginal 'family' across a range of contexts. Sharing as the Middle families practised it accorded with Diane Smith's (2005: 180) summary that 'linked households are instrumental in the economic survival of many families, and serve to reinforce patterns of relatedness at the heart of extended family identity'. For the Middle families, the 'extended family identity' was reinforced via the continual activation of sharing, especially with those living nearby. As a particular node in this extended network, during an exercise that I undertook with Ian and Sue in 2008 the couple explained which other households and people they most frequently visited (and were visited by) to borrow household items, food and cash.

The most common kind of transaction (in either direction) was with their closest kin: their second-eldest daughter living next door in House 3 and Sue's mother who lived across the street in House 11. Ian often visited his nieces (S+D) at Houses 7, 8 and 10 to borrow household items such as a lawn mower. Sue often visited her mother's house to use her washing machine, as Ian and Sue did not have their own. In 2008, Sue's mother also owned an aluminium dinghy and motor that Ian occasionally borrowed to go fishing or hunting for dugong and (sea) turtle. On his return from such a trip, Ian shared out part of his catch with kin living nearby. The first part of this distribution went to Sue's mother in exchange for the use of her boat. Other shares of the catch went to Ian and Sue's daughter next door at House 3, Ian's nieces and their children living across the road and others who would happen to drop in at the time of his return.

The sharing of cuts of locally hunted dugong and turtle, often just referred to as 'meat', was an important and regularly cited example of a person's commitment to the demonstration of family, or performing a kind of relatedness. As one man aged in his thirties who hunted dugong and turtle explained: 'Oh yeah, I share my meat out with my family. When my family come home, come up to the Pub and they say "you been go hunting?" and I say "yeah", and they say "you got any meat?", I might just tell them "yeah, I got some meat, you come home, pick em up" and they come home, pick em up. Either that or I give them out the next day'. Elsewhere I have detailed how modern practices and expressions relating to the sharing of meat among kin were related historically to more prescribed rules about butchering and distribution, where particular cuts of each animal were assigned to individuals (Dalley 2012). Phrases often heard in transactions relating to meat, such as 'we share our meat' and 'it's not about greed', emphasized what Martin (1993: 32) described for the Wik as 'a powerful ethos of equivalence and balance'.

There were factors which impacted on the balance of resource-sharing practices: what Myers (1986: 170) referred to as the 'expectation of reciprocated help, the image of things flowing back and forth'. For Mornington Islanders, though, the idea of reciprocation, where giving was equitably balanced with receiving, was notional, as in reality there was a much greater onus placed on the 'giver', or the person that had a resource (see also Peterson 1993: 870). Macdonald (2000: 91), for example, noted generally that 'demand sharing sets up a system of social obligation on the part of those who control resources rather than indebtedness on the part of those that receive them'. Illustrative of this dynamic were Neil and Clare, who believed that their success in seeking reciprocity had been somewhat frustrated by their own economic prosperity.

In a specific example Neil gave a 'deep freeze' (free-standing freezer) to a classificatory brother (his mother's sister's son, also referred to as a cousin-brother. When Neil gave his cousin-brother the freezer, he reportedly asked that in exchange he be provided with cuts of dugong or turtle when his cousin-brother returned from hunting: 'you take it [the freezer] as long as you give me some meat'. Despite the request (or perhaps more accurately quid pro quo) and Neil's anticipation of a return, it was apparently several years before any such transaction transpired.

Neil explained his cousin-brother's behaviour by saying, 'he's got a lot of people to feed and he probably knows that I've got food'.

Another key resource with particular expectations among kin was lifts in cars around the Gununa community and out bush (including boat trips). Though I discuss trips out bush in more detail in Chapter 5, within the community, transport was particularly important given the dispersed nature of residential housing and the low rates of motor vehicle ownership[12] (ABS 2016: Table G30). Most of the basic services – the supermarket, post office, school and hospital – were located in the centre of the community, while the Council offices were located on the foreshore away from the main residential part of the community. For residents living at the fringes of the community, particularly at the 'bottom end', a visit to any of these places entailed a journey of approximately 2 km. Residents found this journey particularly difficult when carrying children and groceries and during the hotter months of the year from September to April, when the daily mean maximum temperature averaged over 30 degrees Celsius (Australian Bureau of Meteorology 2010).

Those who did not own a car were mostly dependent on kin for lifts in these situations. As a resident in House 10 (in the Middle families), aged in her fifties, explained, 'if I have to go shopping or to the Council, my daughter-in-law is on hand. She is a great help to me'. The woman's daughter-in-law, aged in her thirties, who owned her own car, explained that the pressures placed on her by family for lifts was one of the reasons why she chose to live elsewhere in the community: 'that's the only reason why I like to stay [live] separate from them, humbug!' 'Humbug' is a term used to refer to the persistent requests made by kin for goods or services. Despite living separately, the daughter-in-law had not been able to deny her family's requests entirely: 'if any of them wants help, wants to go here, wants to go there then they'll just ring up'. The woman worked full-time in administration at the local hospital, making her one of about twenty local Aboriginal women working full-time during the 2000s.[13]

Men and women working full-time, either currently or in the past, were often the target of intensive demands from kin. In a conversation in 2009, Neil and Clare described being regularly approached for large cash loans and for Neil to use his skills as an electrician to fix home appliances. As Clare explained: 'We've still got people coming here to fix stuff, lights, antennas, microwaves, stereos, TVs and he [Neil] doesn't even work for the Council anymore. He hasn't worked there for ages'. Neil acknowledged that in these instances he often agreed to help his kin because it was 'very hard for me to say "no". My mum was like that [too]. I feel really guilty, like I've let someone down'. The frustrations that the couple sometimes felt at the lack of reciprocity in their relationships with kin was characterized by a comment made to Neil by his Whitefella father: 'Neil, the trouble with your mob is they like to give, they like to share, but most times Neil it's you giving and they got nothing to share'.

Though Neil remembered reacting to his father's comments by feeling 'pretty hurt at the time', later in life he had begun to think there were times when the obligations placed on him by his Aboriginal family were excessive. This perceived inequality, and the subsequent desire not to share, was described by Martin (1993: 36) among the Wik of western Cape York as a 'denial of relatedness, of one's rights and interests in that relatedness, and a denial of a set of norms and values understood and represented as axiomatic'. Denying relatedness by refusing to share, or at least making attempts to avoid it, created social and economic imbalances that challenged the maintenance of extended and interconnected Aboriginal family in established forms. Thus, in such situations the high (or higher) value placed on autonomy over the demonstration of relatedness accords with Peterson and Taylor's (2003: 107) discussion on the emergence of the 'more inwardly focused household' as part of a 'modernizing of the domestic moral economy'. This 'inward focus' referred not only to Neil and Clare's economic situation, but also to their social and spatial position in the community in a 'quiet' area away from other kin and Clare's comment that they were 'not here for family'. Resources and the location of housing were not the only ways that Aboriginal people expressed relationships to one another; this also happened via 'distributions of care'.

Distributions of Care: Women and Children

As well as the sharing and distribution of material goods, the distribution of care, particularly of young children, was an important component in the cultivation of relatedness among kin and the formations of family identity. Childcare arrangements were of particular importance on Mornington Island because of the proportion of young children as a percentage of the total population. In addition, for many years Mornington Island lacked a formal childcare facility. In 2016, 34 per cent (n=333) of the Aboriginal population of Gununa were under the age of 14 years (ABS 2016: Table G07). Of this group, those aged 5–9 years and 10–14 years formed 25 per cent (n=245) of the total population and were the two largest cohorts of any demographic group living on the Island at the time. This demographic profile, of a young and growing population, has already played a defining role in crafting social relations, particularly for women, who were identified as the primary caregivers. Partly, this reflects Yanagasiko's (1979: 166) observation that 'domestic activities' or 'those pertaining to food production and consumption and those pertaining to social reproduction, including child-bearing and child-rearing' dominate much of daily life.

The role that gender plays in the formation of identity and in relations between Aboriginal people continues to be dismissed, as McKnight (2005: xvi–xix) did, as a 'feminist' perspective (as also noted by Martin 2007: 110). While I share McKnight's (ibid.: xvii) general view that 'it is possible for a male or female anthropologist to do research with both sexes and obtain a balanced account of the society', there are, and have been, continual biases in accounts of the normative features of relations, which gloss over gendered inequalities. Though 'child rearing' and the 'domestic roles' of men and women on Mornington Island have been discussed elsewhere by Huffer (1980) and McKnight (especially 2002: Chapter 5, Chapter 10; 2004: Chapter 3), there appears scant reference to the gendered nature of such allocated tasks and responsibilities. Though McKnight (2005: xvii) counters this by saying that he 'never found it difficult to discuss all manner of things with Aboriginal women', it may be that research inattentiveness reflect the a priori and ingrained inequalities, which influence the types of questions posed and issues explored.

To make what may seem an obvious point and one made previously by Birdsall (1988) and Finlayson (1991: Chapter 7) elsewhere, mothers and maternal kin undertook, and were expected by others to be responsible for, the vast majority of care for children. By 'care', I mean tasks such as feeding, bathing, nursing, playing with, watching and being attentive to the needs of children throughout the day. While a father and male relatives often took a keen interest in children, their role was to oversee the care provided by the child's mother and other maternal kin. Male kin (especially a mother's brother) were often sought out by mothers to punish children for misbehaviour, or to allow children to accompany them on a particular task in order to give their mother a 'break'. The normalization of these roles was reflected in the use of parenting payments (social security) assigned to women. In two instances in which the parenting payment was claimed by a woman in a de facto relationship, the payment was used to pay for the all of the mother and children's financial needs, including food, clothes and toys, while the father's income was used at his own discretion.[14] If in these instances a woman needed additional assistance to meet an extraordinary expense, such as a trip off the Island, she might 'try ask' (i.e. request) her partner for cash.

In 2010, announcing the birth of their fifth child, a man referring to his partner of over ten years told me (via text message) that she 'just had her baby boy'. The normativity of these kinds of statements, where a child was referred to as belonging particularly to a woman, was such that they were non-noteworthy. There were also some situations where Aboriginal fathers and grandfathers did take a far more active role in parenting, one of them being in the case of Neil and Clare. While I was in their company, Neil often took charge of the couple's children, feeding them, putting them to bed, intervening in squabbles and playing with them. In one case, in 2009, Neil entertained the children so that I could record an interview with Clare without interruption. A contributing factor in Neil's involvement may have been that there were few other kin nearby to provide Clare the kinds of communal care which were so frequently seen elsewhere. As I briefly mentioned earlier, the care of children from the Middle families was an example of this shared style of care.

Children from the Middle families often played together in a large group somewhere in the proximity of houses within the network. This meant that any of the adults or older children living within the network, but especially women, took on the responsibility for watching and monitoring the behaviour of children playing nearby. In one situation, when a man was seen driving down the street erratically, Jean's mother stood on the street outside House 6 where she lived and shouted down to Ian's and Sue's house (House 4), alerting them to get children off the road: 'Get those children off the road!' Once the message reached Ian's and Sue's house, it was then transmitted to the other houses nearby, and parents shouted for any children nearby to get off the road.

This kind of neighbourhood surveillance among the Middle families meant that if children were seen fighting or a child was injured, or if an adult saw children acting in a way that they considered inappropriate, they could report such behaviour back to the child's parents. As well as providing information to other households, these types of situations meant that later, in more intimate social settings, women revisited events and incidents through repetitious retelling. These kinds of storytelling offered an alternative to an atmosphere that Mornington Islanders often referred to as 'slack' or 'too slack', which generally meant that there was little happening in the way of noteworthy social interaction.

As most women were not engaged in employment, they spent large portions of their time interacting with their own close kin in domestic settings, usually close to their home residence. Prime amongst this group were a woman's mother, her sisters and sometimes her sisters-in-law. The closeness of maternal relations was exemplified in a number of situations. Classificatory mothers (especially mothers' sisters) would often develop a close relationship with their sisters' children, and would regularly nurse a sister's baby for hours on end. Indicative of the importance of mothers was that the most serious of provocations on Mornington Island was to tell another person (especially a man) to 'fuck your mother', or to call someone a *ngumbuldaan*, a Lardil word literally meaning a person who has sexual intercourse with their mother (see also McKnight 2004: 42). When said in earnest, the term was likely to precipitate serious violence or fights between protagonists.

Caring for children on Mornington Island was both practical and a reflection of the reality that children are 'born into a web of connectedness with many people having interests in them that entail reciprocal obligations for the child' (Peterson and Taylor 2003: 109). The first enactment of this connectedness occurred when the child was named. Aboriginal children on Mornington Island were often given multiple Christian names, and more often than not, a child would be given at least one name from close kin or affine. For example, Tom and Jean's son born in 2010 was given the middle name of Jean's classificatory brother, who lived in House 3 adjacent to Tom and Jean. This naming was a tacit recognition of the potential relationship between the child and his uncle, one of the most important social relationships for Mornington Islanders. On another occasion, three Aboriginal men in their thirties explained that a nephew could expect their uncle to 'take it easy' on them, whereas a father was very 'bossy' and 'cheeky'. Another way kin could perform connectedness was to purchase gifts for a baby, especially toys and clothes. In instances in which the relative could not afford their intended gift at the time of the birth, they would sometimes inform the parents of their intention beforehand and request that no other kin purchase the same gift.

For the small number of mothers who were engaged in full-time employment, a maternal or paternal grandmother often provided childcare during work hours. In one family, a single woman aged in her thirties, who worked full-time and had four children, lived in a house with her mother, aged in her fifties. In 2009, the grandmother acted as a carer for the two youngest children, as the children's mother explained: 'She claims for my two younger ones'. This 'claiming' referred to the 'parenting payment', an Australian Government welfare payment made to those on low incomes, generally without full-time employment. In this instance, the attribution of carer status to the grandmother (rather than the mother) ensured that the payments were not discontinued on account of the mother's income. At the same time, the payment reflected the amount of time that the grandmother spent with the two children and ensured that the mother had an almost undeniable right to childcare. In other words, for this family, the reassignment of welfare payments enmeshed the grandmother, mother and her children into important reciprocal relationships.

Conclusion

In this chapter I have focused on a particular aspect of Aboriginal life, and one which has dominated anthropological studies of Aboriginal people in Australia. Interpreting contemporary forms of social organization and manifestations of sociality is vital to understanding the intensity of relations. As others have noted, the enduring importance of family is a critical component of contemporary indigeneity in Australia, and is part of Aboriginal people's relational ontologies. On Mornington Island, the elaborate production and reproduction of social relations is consuming and pervasive, and a guiding ethic that underpins all social action in daily life. Low levels of participation in formal employment had two particular outcomes: as a proportion of any day, almost all time was spent among family, and also, for many the sharing of resources was a means of grappling with systemic impoverishment brought about by reliance on meagre government welfare.

In exploring changes to kinship structures, Sutton (1998: 54) cautioned against interpretations of social forms that emphasize fluidity merely as 'a handy cover for our difficulty in reaching systemic accounts'. In the case of Mornington Island sociality, such caution is warranted, as during the 2000s there remained a basis of structural elements, namely relations between kin as defined by birth, marriage (registered or de facto partnerships) and descent group affiliations, which were often relied upon as the basis for defining relationships between individuals.

At the same time, these structures – the building blocks of sociality – have undergone considerable change brought about as a result of demographic changes, such as population growth and the co-residence of Aboriginal people from diverse groups in a single settlement. Thus, the relatively autonomous but related Lardil, Yangkaal and Kaiadilt kinship systems defined by McKnight (1999) and Memmott (1979) for the pre-contact period have coalesced into a series of ideas which underpin the ways in which residents in Gununa construct their relationships to one another. In relation to these systems, there are now notable discontinuities, such as the inconsistent practice of male initiation, the diminishment of knowledge about subsection affiliation and the associated proliferation of 'wrong-head' marriages. While such discontinuities might be seen to destabilize the more established kinship polities of Lardil, Yangkaal or Kaiadilt people, the desire for identity based on shared affiliations has nevertheless supported the application of systems that recognize particular bonds of relatedness. The key point to be made here is that in spite of quite dramatic changes over time, the locally persistent nature of relational ideologies continues to be the defining ethic of daily life.

In this continuously evolving kinship polity, Aboriginal people trace their connections to one another in order to determine those who might be 'close' kin, classificatory or otherwise, and those who are more 'distant', but still 'family'. When it came to defining particular models of family and household, the examples of the Middle families and Clare and Neil represent two ends of a spectrum of Aboriginal social relations operating on Mornington Island. The case of the Middle families represents an example of the extensive and overlapping networks of relatedness within which the daily lives of residents were highly interconnected. This interconnectedness was exemplified by the interrelated kinship bonds between residents, which were in turn demonstrated through the close spatial proximity of dwellings, the patterns of sharing resources between dwellings and the distributions of care, particularly for children. In contrast was an example of the model of what Peterson and Taylor (2003: 119) described as the 'more inwardly focused household'; a more autonomous, smaller family unit, typified on Mornington Island by the example of Neil and Clare. For Neil and Clare, and other young families like them, their identity was defined by their expressions of social and economic autonomy, which influenced their interactions with Aboriginal kin. A number of factors were seen to give rise to this autonomy, including seminal time spent living with family on the mainland. While they did attempt to share with kin, their experiences of sharing were unsatisfying and were ultimately one of a number of factors which contributed to their decision to leave the community.

Notes

1. Aboriginal people often describe individuals as 'carrying' a particular name, either first name or surname. It may be inferred that the use of this verb (to 'carry') is more purposive than simply 'having' a name. Carrying a name also reflects the common practice among Aboriginal people of naming a child after a forebear. In this sense a person only ever 'carries' a name to pass it on to another generation.

2. Initials are commonly used in the literature to denote kinship relations. M=mother, F=father, Z=sister, B=brother, S=son, D=daughter, W=wife, H=husband, with '+' meaning older and '–' meaning younger (Sutton 1998: 15). For example, an older sister would be Z+ and mother's younger brother (i.e. an uncle) would be MB–.
3. This accords with McKnight's (2004: 18) observation that: 'in 1966 … people in their thirties and forties [i.e. born between 1917 and 1936] spoke English (and very good English when they chose to do so) but they had a general understanding of Lardil'.
4. This ideal marriage partner being a second cross-cousin was also true for the Kaiadilt, even though they did not observe a subsection system at the point of removal to Mornington Island.
5. An estimate of the proportion of surviving men to have undergone initiation is difficult to obtain for a variety of reasons, including a general reluctance to discuss such issues with a female anthropologist, and also because there appeared to be great variation in its prevalence between men in different age groups. At the time of his research, Memmott (1979: 117) recorded there being ten living initiated men.
6. In my experience, such matters were discussed far more often by women than men, but this may also reflect that women felt more comfortable discussing such matters with me.
7. This is likely to be an underenumeration. See Appendix 1 for further discussion.
8. Though Tom and Jean were not legally married, Tom still referred to his partner's family as his 'in-laws'.
9. It is unclear why these compilations of gamblers are referred to as 'schools'; however, the term was in common use on Mornington Island, and in Aboriginal Australia more broadly (see also McKnight 2002: 75; Trigger 1992: 99, 202).
10. Gununa had three spatial divisions: 'top end', the older part of the community close to the airstrip and council offices; the 'middle part', close to the supermarket, school and hospital; and the 'bottom end', the furthest from all services and the most recently developed part of the community.
11. In 2008, the housing levy was AUD 37.00 per person per week for those who received pay through the Mornington Shire Council. I estimate the amount that Neil paid the Council upfront as approximately AUD 4,000.
12. The ABS (2016: Table G30) Census figures suggest that in 2016, the number of motor vehicles per dwelling was 47 per cent no motor vehicle, 33 per cent one motor vehicle and 17 per cent two or more motor vehicles. These figures include all residents, Aboriginal and non-Aboriginal. Such high rates of reported ownership are difficult to reconcile with my own (albeit anecdotal) observations of many fewer cars. It is possible, however, that Aboriginal people may have answered in the affirmative for cars they used during the day but were owned by the local Council and CDEP, and for cars not in drivable condition.
13. The Census (ABS 2006: Table B41) lists the total number of women working full-time in Gununa as thirty-three, including both Indigenous and non-Indigenous women. Owing to the high levels of non-Indigenous female employment at the hospital and school, I estimate that local Aboriginal women accounted for half this number.
14. It seemed to be the case that few men paid child support to former partners to assist with the care of their children, women sometimes telling me that they 'didn't worry about it' (i.e. that they didn't ask for it). The inference in these situations was that the social difficulties in securing payments outweighed the potential benefits, especially when the father's income was already very small.

 4

Alcohol Management and Violence

In 2010, a 28-year-old Aboriginal man stole and crashed Mornington Island's only ambulance, which had been on a callout to attend to a sick patient. Images that surfaced on social media showed the abandoned ambulance impaled on the fence of the local Uniting Church, a palm tree's fronds covering the car bonnet. As was reported at the time, the joyrider was found to have a blood alcohol level almost three times the legal driving limit and had travelled only a short distance before crashing. That the man was reported as being 'inebriated' was noteworthy for the fact that under an Alcohol Management Plan (AMP), the community had been designated as 'dry' for over twelve months. That is to say that since January 2008, it has been illegal to possess or manufacture alcohol on Mornington Island. The management of alcohol availability in remote Aboriginal communities in Australia has been contentious, in that most strategies involve either the establishment of differential (reduced) access or (attempts at) prohibition, both of which rely on discriminatory policies that impinge on 'rights'. Yet the known impacts of excessive consumption, a common problem in many Australian Indigenous communities, include hugely detrimental effects on wellbeing, not just on drinkers but also on their communities as a whole.

Mornington Island is an archetypal location to consider the ways in which the state, in this case the Queensland Government, attempts 'harm minimization' through policies that further criminalize Aboriginal people. Of all areas of policy, on Mornington Island prohibition has been the most significant example of the failure of Government's own stated intentions: to reduce the harm caused by excessive alcohol consumption. In this chapter I describe the history of alcohol management and the ways in which alcohol is embedded in social praxis. The years that I spent the most time on Mornington Island, between 2007 and 2009, corresponded to a locally significant epoch in the availability of alcohol. When I first visited Mornington Island in 2006, and also in 2007, alcohol was available for consumption at a pub, but in early 2008 the community was declared 'dry' and total prohibition came into place. As the crashed ambulance example indicates, however, alcohol continues to be illegally sourced and consumed, albeit within realigned legal and social parameters. So, while the government mantra has been 'harm reduction' and 'harm minimization', what has actually taken place is the introduction of new forms of harm with far less manageable consequences. In this sense, prohibition has become an example of what Lea (2012) has called the 'fantasy of regulation', where the Government's actions, or more precisely inactions, continue to rely on a façade of considered policy development while actually obscuring deep uncertainty about how to manage alcohol.

Mornington Island is one of nineteen Indigenous communities subject to specific alcohol management regimes in Queensland. For many of these communities, alcohol is now unavailable to purchase, a reality made possible by their designation as within a particular zone, and the refusal of the Queensland Government to issue liquor licences within those zones. In many of these locations, the declarations came as a specific intervention in response to dramatically declining circumstances, often publicly reported instances of violence involving alcohol. A study of perspectives on these processes, garnered from 'key service providers and community leaders', found that at the time of their introduction (at different times in each community), AMPs provided an 'abrupt reduction in violence along with seemingly dramatic improvements in quality of life in communities' (Clough et al. 2016: 70). While drastic policy change may have provided an important turning point in building momentum for change, what has become apparent in the intervening period is how short lived and unevenly distributed these benefits have been. This is particularly evident in the Queensland Government's own statistical analysis of rates of violence (offences against the person), school attendance, and child protection orders along with convictions for breaches of the locally operating AMP (Queensland Department of Aboriginal and Torres Strait Islander Partnerships 2014, 2015, 2016). A study conducted in 2014–15 surveyed over 1200 residents of ten mainland (i.e. not including Mornington Island) Aboriginal and Torres Strait communities in Queensland about their impressions of the impacts of the AMPs (Clough et al. 2017). The survey tested fourteen propositions (seven positive and seven negative) to understand how the residents of the communities perceived the impacts of the AMPs.

According to the study, 'participants recognized overall the 'favourable' impacts of AMPs on reducing violence, improving the safety of women and children, improved school attendance and community amenity' (ibid.: 55). However, these opinions were not uniformly held. The study also highlighted the unintended consequences of AMPs, most notably the 'failure of AMPS to reduce alcohol availability and consumption', alongside related issues of criminalization and discrimination.

What stands out from the Government's data and the findings from the residents' survey is the limited success of the AMPs in preventing access to alcohol or its consumption. Arguably, part of the reason for this has been stagnation in the policy which directly addresses alcohol availability, given that it has now been over ten years since the AMPs were introduced in most communities. In the context of the state's numerous interventions into Aboriginal people's lives, alcohol management is one area where government has no definable strategy post-prohibition.

In the first half of this chapter I describe the Pub on Mornington Island, and the kinds of social interaction that occurred within its grounds in 2007, its final year of operation. I discuss the spatial use of the venue and demonstrations of 'family', the sharing of cash and beer among kin. This is contrasted with the gradual disintegration of order that occurred over the period of drinking and the chaos and violence which ensued, particularly at closing time. In the latter part of the chapter I consider drinking which occurred after the permanent closure of the Pub in 2008, including the illegal consumption of alcohol and the strategies, including off-Island travel, that Mornington Islanders implemented in order to access and consume alcohol. In both the Pub and post-Pub settings, I discuss the types of surveillance enacted by police and the impacts that this had on social interaction, especially violence, and the drinking practice of Mornington Islanders.

Alcohol and Aboriginal People

Studies of Aboriginal drinking emerged in Australia from the 1960s, when anthropologists were becoming increasingly aware of the impact of heavy drinking on the transmission of cultural knowledge (Beckett 1964; Sackett 1977: 97–98). These accounts associated Aboriginal drinking with a 1964 legislative amendment that conferred Aboriginal people's right to purchase and consume alcohol legally (Brady 1990: 201; Rowse 1993: 394; Sansom 1980: 75). Both at this time and more recently, Aboriginal people have sometimes mobilized 'equal rights' discourses as a means of legally and ideologically contesting alcohol restrictions in their own communities (CMC 2009: 120; Martin and Brady 2004: 1282; McKnight 2002: 109). This contrasts to much of the health-driven alcohol management mantra, which focuses on 'harm minimization' or 'reducing harm' caused by excessive alcohol consumption and its associated social ills.

Another type of analysis of Aboriginal drinking, and the one on which I draw primarily here, is of the degree to which social behaviours around heavy drinking have become integrated into Aboriginal social life (Brady 1988; Brady and Palmer 1984; Martin 1993: 183–99; Sansom 1980: 53). Collmann (1979: 209), for example, described the 'consumption and sharing of liquor' as part of a broader set of norms within which 'Aborigines construct their social world'. In such studies more broadly, alcohol consumption was also a way that Aboriginal people defined their own social identity, sometimes as a particular kind of drinker or as distinct from non-drinkers (Sansom 1980: 63). Sansom (ibid.: 70), for example, discussed the 'controlled' drinking style of 'masterful men' and the autonomy of 'solo drinking', two of a range of drinking personas adopted amongst Aboriginal drinkers in the fringes of the northern Australian city of Darwin. In the way that Collmann and Sansom discussed it, drinking behaviour was conceived of as productive of social identities, particularly between groups.

The anthropologist Maggie Brady conducted the best-known research on alcohol consumption by Aboriginal people in remote settings in the 1980s (1988, 2007; Brady and Palmer 1984; Martin and Brady 2004). Brady's (1992: 700) approach was to focus on the uses, meaning and social controls enacted by Aboriginal people surrounding drinking, though she has increasingly written about the efficacy of alcohol management policies (particularly prohibition) and the success of personal interventions with alcoholics (e.g. Martin and Brady 2004; Brady 2007). Another aspect of investigations has been the commoditization of alcohol, particularly cans of beer, as an item of exchange amongst Aboriginal people (Brady 1990: 203). In some places, including historically on Mornington Island as McKnight (2002: 75) recorded, the commoditization of alcohol has extended into gambling, with unopened cans of beer used as a form of currency in card games. The integration of alcohol into local informal economies supports Bain's (1972: 48) description of alcohol as having 'two functions, as a material asset and as the basis for a group activity', or put another way, as 'alcohol, the thing; and drinking alcohol, the activity'.

Investigations of drinking which focus primarily on the social or cultural incorporation of alcohol, however, have been critiqued, including by those in fields such as public health and epidemiology (Lex 1986;

Room [with comments] 1984). Room (ibid.: 172), for example, described a 'problem deflation'; what he saw as anthropologists' propensity to downplay or downgrade the seriousness of problem drinking, as ethnographic fieldwork and methods were 'better attuned to measuring the pleasures'. Though it remains to be seen if this 'deflation' can accurately be seen as emanating from methodological issues, critiques about the failures of anthropologists to consider the negative impacts of alcohol consumption are relatively common (e.g. Rowse 1990: 187; Sutton 2001a: 141–42; Trigger 2011: 237).

One of the best known of these critiques came from Peter Sutton (2001a, 2009), who abandoned any 'capitulation to identity politics' (Austin-Broos 2010: 137) and published an account which focused on the negative impacts of certain types of behaviour in Indigenous communities. One of the critiques raised against Sutton was that in disavowing the 'silence' on issues such as violence and excessive alcohol consumption, his writing ventured too far into the epidemiological realm, and thus that he 'pathologized' Aboriginal people and culture (Cowlishaw 2003: 3; Lattas and Morris 2010: 72). Yet Sutton's work is not unique in this regard. Rather, there have been an (albeit limited) number of anthropological studies which have attested to the ways in which Aboriginal patterns of drinking are destructive to normalized social interaction and contribute to higher than average rates of alcoholism, antisocial behaviour, interpersonal violence and child neglect (e.g. Brady 1992; Martin 1993: Chapter 4; Memmott et al. 2001). Indigenous scholars have themselves been vocal on these issues (e.g. Langton 2010; Wright 1997).

In Australia, this approach is typified by David McKnight's (2002) most prominent literary work about Mornington Island, *From Hunting to Drinking: The Devastating Effects of Alcohol on an Australian Aboriginal Community*. Anthropologists and commentators on Aboriginal affairs often refer to this book to exemplify the negative impacts of alcohol on Aboriginal communities (e.g. Austin-Broos 2011: 134; Langton 2010: 99; Sutton 2009: 40). McKnight argued that the excessive consumption of alcohol was responsible for the irrevocable disintegration of Mornington Island culture and sociality, a change that he characterized with the phrase 'from hunting to drinking'[1]. Of all his conclusions about Mornington Islanders, the most damning was that:

> the individual body is a person's social identity and not only his or her individual identity. By controlling people's bodies they have been left without a social identity. Mornington Island now consists of a community of individuals who are bereft of a social identity except in negative terms: they used to

have this or that, they used to be this or the other, but now they have nothing and are no one. (McKnight 2002: 2)

McKnight pointed to alcohol as the single most influential cause in the damage that was being done to the bodies of Mornington Islanders.

Though published in 2002, the majority of the experiences McKnight details in *From Hunting to Drinking* occurred in the late 1970s through to the mid-1980s, the period immediately following the opening of a local 'canteen'[2] in 1976 (ibid.). McKnight's analysis positioned drinking as oppositional to social practice, rather than embedded within it. His approach was critiqued by Sackett (2004: 241), also known for his research on Aboriginal alcohol consumption (see Sackett 1977, 1988), who said of McKnight: 'he all too often and readily tosses off remarks and opinions in lieu of analysing situations and contexts'. One of the contexts that eluded McKnight's detailed consideration was the canteen venue itself, the only premises licensed to sell alcohol in the community (as distinct from alcohol 'taken away' and consumed elsewhere).[3] It is an ethnographic examination of the canteen, now referred to as the 'Pub', in 2007 (which was to become its final year of operation), which forms the basis of part of this chapter.

In 2003, the Queensland Government's concern with the impact that alcohol was having in the community led to the introduction of an Alcohol Management Plan (AMP) (Queensland Government 2003). The AMP was reportedly devised by the Island's community Justice Group (Junkuri Laka Justice Group), 'who put the local AMP together' and were 'backed by' the Queensland Government (ibid.). At the time, the Justice Group Board was comprised mostly of older Christian non-drinkers, a minority of the larger Mornington Island population (McKnight 2002: 204). As an Aboriginal man explained in 2008, it was 'mostly all the old ladies were in that [the Justice Group]. They're trying to go back to their ways of living when they were young. Trying to change young people'. The major change instigated by the AMP was to limit the sale and consumption of alcohol to within grounds of the local canteen ('Pub') and only between 3pm and 7pm, Monday to Friday (Queensland Government 2003).

At the time that the change was instigated, the Queensland Government publicly commended the Justice Group for navigating 'the right way forward for the community', noting that the amendments were geared towards 'reducing harm caused by alcohol abuse and associated violence' (Minister Judy Spence, quoted in Queensland Government 2003). However, a week after the restrictions came into place, a new 'pro-alcohol' board was elected at the Justice Group annual general meeting and 'demanded' that the AMP be amended to include the sale of take-away alcohol (Koch 2003: 27). The then Queensland Minister for Aboriginal and Torres Strait Islander Policy responded 'angrily', saying that 'the reforms would not be relaxed' (Minister Judy Spence, quoted in ibid.).

In spite of Aboriginal people's objections, from its instigation the Queensland Government used incremental changes to the AMP to gradually stem both the strength and amount of alcohol available for sale to Mornington Islanders. Despite this, the Pub remained the key social venue on the Island, including during the lead-up to its closure in 2008. As the Whitefella Manager of the Justice Group noted shortly after its closure: 'it was *the* place socially. There was no other place where people could all get together' (her emphasis). Similarly, as an Aboriginal man aged in his fifties described: 'the main place that we mix with people is at the Pub'. As was explored in Chapters 1 and 2, in the community context, the spatial arrangement of individuals in particular residential areas and the people (kin) that they spent time with within those areas were powerful indicators of a person's affiliations and identity. When in the Pub grounds, a venue where social activity was constrained in both time and space, these patterns were a highly concentrated instantiation of the social interactions that Mornington Islanders experienced elsewhere in the community. This description is similar to the situation with Wik people at Aurukun from the mid-1980s to the early 1990s. As David Martin (1993: 231) described:

> The struggle over the appropriation of space by Wik did not concern just the houses per se, because the flux of Wik social life was not, and could not be, contained by such boundedness ... Even where people sat within the beer canteen was the subject of watchful monitoring. The fluid use of geographical space and the mapping onto it of social groupings continued to be reproduced.

The strongly delineated spatial distributions of people at the Pub on Mornington Island, however, disintegrated as the evening of drinking progressed. As an Aboriginal man aged in his forties (speaking in Hearn 2007) explained, the Pub conditions 'actually encouraged binge drinking' and 'took away the afternoon hours, that you could be spending time with family at home'. The intense social interaction and violence which occurred in and around the Pub was heavily monitored by the police and the Pub licensee, who were all required to enforce the restrictions of the AMP. When breaches of the AMP occurred, Aboriginal drinkers came into contact with the local police and often the criminal justice system (Queensland Government Department of Communities 2011: 42). The embeddedness of drinking within social life resulted in marked changes to Mornington Island sociality when the Pub was shut down in early 2008.

In early 2008, the Pub's liquor licence was suspended indefinitely in response to what the then Queensland Premier Anna Bligh described as 'a series of incidents surrounding binge drinking, alcohol related violence and poor management' (Premier Anna Bligh, quoted in Queensland Government 2008b). The Queensland Government was also concerned that the local Mornington Shire Council, as the holder of the liquor licence, had a conflict of interest which prevented it from implementing necessary reductions in the sales (and therefore profits) being made by the Pub (see also Brady 2007: 188; Martin and Brady 2004: 1283). Subsequently, the liquor licence was cancelled and the Mornington Shire Council local government area became a 'zero carriage limit', making it illegal to brew, possess or consume alcohol within the designated local government area (Queensland Government Department of Communities 2011: 41). The possession of alcohol, supply of alcohol, implements to brew alcohol and intoxication were all illegal. Thus, drinking, which had been at the heart of Mornington Island social life for over thirty years, was prohibited and criminalized (see also Langton 1993: 196).

Despite this, Mornington Islanders have continued to brew alcohol, known in local parlance as 'homebrew', and smuggle in alcohol from the mainland, known as 'sly grog'. The availability of homebrew and sly grog is illustrated in the rates of convictions recorded for breaches of Section 168B and C of the *Liquor Act (Qld) 1992*, relating to the possession, supply or manufacture of alcohol (Queensland Government Department of Communities 2011: 42). In the twelve-month period immediately following the closure of the Pub, the annual rate of charges resulting in a conviction for alcohol carriage offences was 345.6 per 1,000 persons (March 2008–March 2009) (ibid.). From the inception of the AMP in late 2003 to December 2010, '444 distinct individuals were convicted of 1,121 charges for breaches' (ibid.). These rates are extraordinarily high when considering that the number of people over the legal drinking age (those aged over 18 years) numbered only approximately 600 during this time (ABS 2006: B04; 2011: B04). The illegality of alcohol-related practices defined new relations with police and increasingly, attempts to obscure drinking practice such as drinking 'out bush' or travelling to the mainland to drink in towns and cities unaffected by alcohol restrictions.

The Pub

As with some other remote Aboriginal settlements, the availability of alcohol for purchase and consumption has been a relatively recent phenomenon on Mornington Island. During the late 1960s and early 1970s, alcohol was an issue of increasing concern to the then mission superintendent Reverend Douglas Belcher (McKnight 2002: 78). Though by that stage it was legal for Aboriginal people to purchase and consume alcohol on the mainland, the Wellesley Islands remained an Aboriginal reserve where possession was illegal (Roughsey 1971: 158). In spite of this, the disposable incomes that Mornington Islanders were earning through their employment as domestics and stockmen on the mainland, and the establishment of a regular commercial air service to and from mainland towns including Mount Isa, saw an increase in the amount of alcohol being smuggled onto the Island (Memmott 1979: 410).

The illicit status of alcohol had an impact on the manner of its consumption, and in the period from 1973 to 1975, Memmott (ibid.) observed that, unlike the majority of other social behaviour, 'drinking sprees usually occur indoors' in order to gain 'privacy from passing mission staff and unwanted guests'. In an attempt to stem the kinds of fighting being precipitated by smuggled alcohol and to encourage more social drinking, a wet canteen was opened in 1976. Later renamed the Lelka Murrin Tavern, and known in local parlance more recently as the 'Pub', it has been the only outlet legally selling alcohol in Gununa (McKnight 2002: 2; Memmott 1979: 410). Between 1978 and 2008 the liquor licence was held by the Mornington Shire Council, which used the profits to provide general services for local residents, such as the establishment of a market garden in the 1990s (McKnight 2002: 113).[4] Over its life, the Pub went through a number of iterations involving a series of variations to the quantities and types of alcohol sold, and the opening hours (ibid.: 95–109). At various times, this included the sale of 'takeaway' alcohol, including spirits, and the operation of a social bar where patrons could order meals and listen to live music. During the 1980s, it was also possible to order alcohol from outlets on the mainland and have it delivered to the Island via the weekly barge service that already delivered food and other goods (ibid.: 99). As previously mentioned, in 2003 the Queensland Government introduced an Alcohol Management Plan (AMP) as a means of governing the amount of alcohol available to Mornington Islanders. At the core of this intervention was the premise that alcohol was inextricably linked to violence and ill health, and that greater restriction and surveillance could positively reform socially deviant behaviour and reduce harm.

Figure 4.1. Lelka Murrin Tavern licensing and rules, March 2008 (photograph by the author).

Following the introduction of the AMP, there were a number of changes to the Pub's liquor licence, each amendment further reducing the operating hours and/or the amount and type of alcohol being consumed. The first of these was the prohibition of the sale of 'take-away' alcohol, which restricted consumption to within the Pub grounds. I first visited the Pub in April 2007 with a middle-aged Aboriginal woman who had agreed to 'partner' me. Over the subsequent seven months until November 2007, I estimate that I undertook approximately forty visits, either alone or with Aboriginal and Whitefella drinking partners, and it is these experiences that form the basis of my ethnographic account. In 2007 the Pub was open five nights a week (Monday to Friday) from 4pm to 8pm. As well as weekends, the Pub was also shut on 'community days' when funerals or other local events were being held, such as an annual Aboriginal dance festival.

The Pub's limited opening hours constrained the amount of time available to consume alcohol, which in turn contributed to the formation of a daily routine for some Aboriginal people structured around its operating times. During 2007, this routine began before the 4pm opening time, with those working for the local Mornington Shire Council, either as part of CDEP or on the roadwork gang, for example, structuring work activities so as to ensure that tasks were completed before 'knock-off' time at 3pm. Finishing at 3pm enabled drinkers to go home to prepare for their visit to the Pub. It was obvious from their appearance that most Pub-goers made an effort to look clean and neat before arriving at the Pub, sometimes borrowing clothes from kin. The anticipation of the Pub's opening time built over the course of the day. In 2007, I was working with an Aboriginal ranger group, and during the day, discussion centred on the events at the Pub on the previous night, on which Aboriginal people had been drunk, fighting or implicated in sexual dalliances, and on eager speculation of similar events to come.

Part of the preparation for some drinkers included seeking out loans or calling in repayments to fund their evening of drinking, and seeking out lifts to the Pub from those who were non-drinkers. The Pub was located to the south-west of the community, making it a 1–2 km walk for most residents via a complex of paths and tracks. Most of these tracks were short cuts running in-between houses or along the waterfront of the Appel Channel, and they enabled patrons to make their way to the Pub without being seen from the main residential streets. On arrival, patrons would wait under trees and on the verandas of the nearby council buildings until the doors opened at precisely 4pm. The surreptitious way in which patrons made their way to the Pub meant that it was a surprise to find it full of patrons only five minutes after opening time.

As soon as patrons arrived at the Pub, they would proceed through a narrow entryway, past the security guard and into the indoor service area in the central part of the grounds (see Figure 4.2). On each visit to the service area, patrons could purchase two cans of mid-strength or light beer, priced at AUD 4.20 each in 2007, which were opened by the server to ensure that consumption occurred on the premises.[5] Once patrons had purchased their beers, they proceeded through the Pub doors to a range of outdoor seating, including fixed and moveable benches, picnic tables and clusters of large rocks where Aboriginal people sat. The area where most Mornington Islanders congregated was in the southern part of the Pub overlooking the Appel Channel. A six-foot mesh fence topped with two strings of barbed wire surrounded the Pub grounds (as marked by the dotted line in Figure 4.2), enclosing drinkers in a confined space, clearly designating the area within which alcohol could be consumed.

The numbers of patrons visiting the Pub on any given day was dependent on factors such as the weather,[6] but based on my observations in 2007, I estimate that on average between 300 and 400 people attended

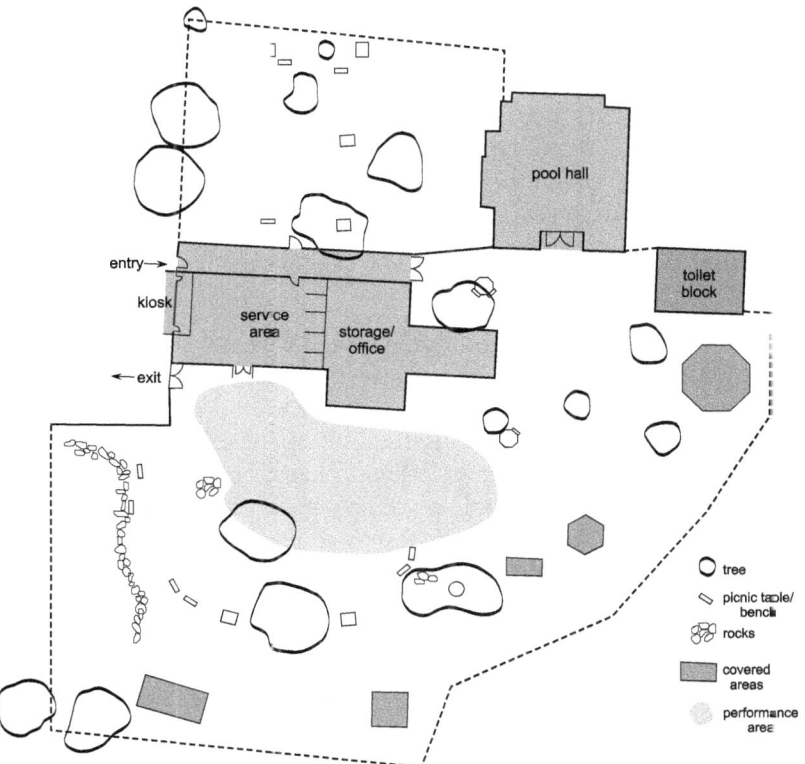

Figure 4.2. Plan of the Pub grounds, March 2008 (figure created by the author).

Monday–Thursday, and up to 500 on Friday.[7] When taken as a proportion of the total legal-age drinking population in 2006 (i.e. those aged over 18 years), this equated to between 50 per cent (Monday–Thursday) and up to 80 per cent (Friday) of those of legal drinking age (ABS 2006: Table B04). There was a slightly larger number of drinkers attending the Pub on a Friday was because it was payday for Council employees and CDEP participants, and was also a day when many casual drinkers attended, including a small number of Whitefellas (McKnight 2002: 103; see similar observances by Sackett 1977: 92 for Wiluna in Western Australia).

Many Aboriginal people were regular drinkers, visiting the Pub four or five nights a week; however, a minority described themselves as 'drinking when I feel like it', visiting the Pub once or twice a week (often including Fridays). Drinking on particular days also allowed them to demonstrate their distinctness from regular drinkers, who they described as 'mad for grog' (see also Bain 1972: 49). Some who drank casually had other responsibilities that influenced their visitation, particularly the care of young children if they were unable to secure child minding from non-drinking kin. This meant that there was a much larger proportion of men than women in the Pub, as was noted by one man: 'yeah I'm sure men go to the Pub more than women'. This gender imbalance seemed particularly sharp among those aged up to their thirties, the bulk of whom had young children.

In separate interviews with one such couple, aged in their late twenties (Jean and Tom, mentioned in Chapter 3), Jean explained that she rarely attended the Pub on account of the couple's four children, all aged less than 10 years in 2007. Jean referred to her non-attendance as 'missing out' and said that during the Pub opening hours she instead sought out non-drinking kin that lived nearby, including her mother's sister (a classificatory mother). Jean's partner Tom was a regular Pub-goer, attending most nights of the week that it was open, such that he (and others) identified a table where he sat, 'me there all the time', along with a group of close kin. It was the consistent identification of particular individuals with areas within the grounds that was a defining feature of the spatial distributions of people within the Pub.

Constituting Family at the Pub

During the first hour of the Pub being open, drinking was a quiet and somewhat tense affair, and those present closely watched the movements of individuals. At this time body language was muted, with people talking quietly, moving slowly and avoiding eye contact until they had reached an area where they were going to sit. As Martin (1993: 193) noted of the canteen at Aurukun: 'rather than there being an air of relaxation and bonhomie, each table or area of ground would be occupied by its own group, and in the early stages before much alcohol had been consumed most people would drink in cautious silence, watchfully monitoring'.

On Mornington Island, patrons joining family in the southern part of the grounds walked out of the service area through the set of double doors and across a wide grassed area, talking quietly (see Figure 4.2). Drinkers who had already arrived sat at tables surrounding this area, many of which were oriented so as to be facing the exit doors, thus making this area a focus for attention within the Pub grounds. On occasion, men and women who had arrived at the Pub already drunk from homebrew or sly grog would dance suggestively in this area, doing what was known as the 'doggie dance',[8] a provocative swaying of hips backward and forwards in a highly sexualized manner. As this would happen, men and women already sitting down, often family members of the person dancing, would whistle loudly and shout out in recognition and encouragement of the person's bravado.

Given the ways in which Mornington Islanders observed one another, the positioning of bodies in the Pub was a powerful demonstration of individual allegiances to particular groups. In a paper exploring Yolngu Aboriginal people's connections to land, the anthropologist Franca Tamisari (1998: 250) emphasized the importance of the body as the core of human experience, and that in this way 'land becomes place through being in-the-world, that is by being experienced through the body'. By placing phenomenological experiences at the heart of 'being in-the-world', Tamisari (ibid.: 251) described the importance of 'visibility' and of public demonstrations in crafting shared identities. As she described it, 'the act of making visible social and emotional relationships and political links is central to the fashioning and negotiation of group and individual identities' (ibid.). In a similar way, the collective positioning of bodies in certain parts of the Pub grounds meant that those areas came to be associated with groups of kin, who were often families.

One way that 'family' was articulated by Mornington Islanders was through the expression of collectively held surnames, as exemplified by the ability to identify the predominant surnames of those who sat in particular areas. The predominance of 'surnamed family groups' has been recorded elsewhere in Australia (e.g. Babidge 2010: Chapter 4) and was described by Peter Sutton (1998: 65) as a shorthand way of referring to a cognatic descent group. A cognatic descent group is those able to trace a relationship to one another through a common shared ancestor (ibid.). In one example on Mornington Island, a man described how surnamed family groups were distributed across a particular part of the Pub grounds. As he put it, 'you got all the Robinsons, Kings sitting down behind. Then the band plays in front, playing their little instrument and then on the side you got them Browns and Johnsons'. In much the same way that Babidge (2010: 117) and Sutton (1998: 49) explained it, this was not to say that each of the people in these groupings had the same surnames, though many did. Rather, they were descended, generally by only one generation, or affiliated by registered marriage or de facto relationship, from a person who did carry that name.

In other examples, areas were associated with kin whose connection was derived via a particular estate or what was referred to locally as a 'country', being an estate. The notion of countries will be dealt with in further detail in Chapter 5, but for reference, each country was an estate a geographic area on Mornington Island or the surrounding Wellesley Islands, including large tracts of sea country, to which a group of kin claimed an identity affiliation (Memmott and Trigger 1998). When at the Pub, these land and sea-derived connections were sometimes reproduced in the names that people ascribed to those who sat in particular areas, such as the 'Birri mob', Birri being a country estate on the northern side of Mornington Island.

The most discrete example of the country-affiliated Pub grouping was two picnic tables known as the '*Kanba* tables', or where the '*Kanba* mob' sat. *Kanba* is a Lardil word for the name of a country on the south-eastern side of Mornington Island, claimed by the descendants of four brothers who were historically connected to the area (McKnight 1999: 98). One man, aged in his late thirties, explained where he sat at the Pub, saying: 'sometime I sit down with the *Kanba* mob ... I got a part in *Kanba* because [of] my grandfather, he's my mum's dad'. Although the descendants of the four brothers lived in various parts of the community, many of them sat together at the Pub. Most of the *Kanba* mob had one of three surnames, the Whites, Stewarts and Taylors, though there were others who had different surnames but were still identified as part of the family group.

Such was the connection between families, their country areas and seating at the Pub that places within the grounds were sometimes described as signifying features of the associated country. For example, a man who described himself as a 'full-blood Kaiadilt' (traditionally affiliated to the South Wellesley Islands) explained how he and other people from Oak Tree Point on Bentinck Island sat on and around three large rocks in the southern part of the Pub grounds. When I showed the man a photograph of the rocks during an interview he exclaimed: 'that's Oak Tree Point! Yeah, see the rock?' Although Oak Tree Point was not a particularly rocky place, in fact being more noteworthy for its high sand dunes,[9] the landscape feature was seen as a marker which symbolized and triggered a recognition of the connection to the place. In another instance, a family that sat in a part of the Pub grounds that was particularly exposed to south-east winds was seen as congruent with them as Windward[10] people from the southern coast of Mornington Island. As one of the group explained: 'yeah, most of the time there's one table where they like to go sit down ... They like to sit against the wind cause they're Windward people'.

In discussions about the ways in which certain families commandeered moveable seating within the Pub into their own particular areas, one man aged in his fifties described this as being when 'they steal from another tribe what there, they take from other country'. The same man contextualized the reproduction of country affiliations as a demonstration of the continuity of 'traditional' socio-spatial distributions. As he described it: 'how we sit at the Pub, I think we sit in tribal way again, how we sit in the Pub'. Younger people aged in their twenties and thirties, though, sometimes emphasized other connections as explanations for the clustering of individuals into particular areas. A particular example of this was that some areas in the Pub were occupied by networks of kin who lived in residentially proximate areas in the community. For example, one part of the Pub grounds was described by a man aged in his late twenties as being the regular haunt of 'all the little middle bit of town you know, [sit] in that little spot there'. Although some of these kin shared traditional country affiliations and considered one another as family, it was their occupancy of residences in close proximity which was identified as the basis of their communal drinking.

Such was the observance of individuals' drinking and socializing habits that when someone went to see a person at a table other than where they usually sat, they were described as a 'visitor' and would rarely assume a seat at the table, often standing until the interaction was complete.[11] These behaviours, and the maintenance of the spaces between groups, defined the contours of drinking groups. In an ethnography of Aboriginal people at Wallaby Cross outside Darwin, Sansom (1980: 57) observed that in the socio-spatial patterning of drinkers, 'maintaining a boundary about any exclusive drinking set is required activity'. One of the important distinctions between the Wallaby Cross example and the Pub on Mornington Island was the contained nature of the spatial groupings, being confined to within the boundary fence. This boundary fence was also an important delineation of those who drank and those who did not, as non-drinkers rarely entered the Pub grounds. When non-drinkers needed to get a message to someone who was drinking, they would stand at the fence until the person that they were waiting for came over to meet them. Although children were not allowed in the Pub grounds, a small take-away kiosk that sold hot food, chips, lollies and non-alcoholic drinks was located in the same building as the Pub service area and non-drinking kin and children could often be seen visiting the kiosk in the afternoon and early evening. The circulations of cash and the expenditure on alcohol was another defining feature of the socio-spatial use of the Pub grounds, as the location of kin near one another in the Pub grounds also facilitated sharing, another important aspect of kin relations.

Sharing Behaviour and Whitefellas at the Pub

As well as a clear demonstration of the connections between kin, sitting together at the Pub was an opportunity to practice what some consider the quintessential aspect of Aboriginal family life: sharing. Accounts of sharing, including in Chapter 3, sometimes focus on the distributions of basic needs such as food, shelter and care. However, as Peterson (1993: 870) explained, Aboriginal models of sharing represent 'complex behaviour not predicated simply on need' (see also Macdonald 2000: 89). The Pub on Mornington Island was one of the most concentrated examples of what might be conceptualized as non-need-based sharing. In 2007, a single can of beer cost AUD 4.20, and thus, for those drinking large volumes of alcohol, say for example between ten and twenty cans, a single visit to the Pub could cost anywhere between AUD 45.00 and AUD 85.00. Given that the weekly median individual income of Mornington Islanders was AUD 209.00 in 2006 (ABS 2006: Table B02), a single night could account for between a quarter and a half of a drinker's weekly income. As a result, for many who drank four or five nights per week, part of their time at the Pub was spent borrowing money from family, sometimes described as 'cadging', 'loafering', 'couching' or 'bludging' (see also McKnight 2002: 69), or calling in loans previously given out.

In my experience, the diversity of types of sharing on Mornington Island was demonstrated by the use of particular types of language, dependant on the expectation of return. Requests with little or no anticipation of refusal were framed in demanding language, often 'gimmie some' or 'ont some' (shorthand for 'I want some', often used by children) or simply the name of the item, 'smoke' or 'meat', for example. These demands were made between 'close' kin, such as among siblings, children, parents, grandparents and other close classificatory kin. If the person posing the request, however, believed that they might be refused, they might 'try ask' (see also McKnight 2002: 66). The language and intonation of 'try ask' was open ended, often beginning with a qualifier – commonly 'any', hence 'any smoke?' or 'any meat?' Even more tenuous requests were delivered with further embellishment, sometimes implicating present or absent third parties: 'Albert was wondering if you could possibly give us lift, cause we asked all them other mob but they say they got no fuel, please my daughter-in-law?' Naming the kin relationship was a way of reminding the potential giver of their relationship, placing additional pressure on them to respond positively.

Thus, more than simply a financial transaction, sharing beer or money to buy beer on Mornington Island cultivated relationships of proximity to kin. A man aged in his late thirties, for example, described the Pub scene one afternoon: 'ah well you can see there's a different lot of families sitting around, sharing with one another like they always do and ... like if anyone haven't got money they come along and sing out to their family and they like to share with one another'. As this quote suggests, sharing was more than a transaction between those who had beer or cash and those who did not. Rather, it reflected that people 'like to share', not only because it created a reciprocity which could be relied upon in the future, but also because it contributed to the convivial drinking atmosphere. In this way, sharing practices around the Pub were an element within the broader systems of reciprocity operating among Aboriginal kin. The universality of these systems of sharing was recognized by Mornington Islanders as underpinning all Aboriginal social praxis, with one man described sharing as 'what all Aboriginal people do, even out in the mainland'. Similar sentiments regarding the universality of sharing practices have been recorded by anthropologists conducting research with Aboriginal people in other parts of Australia (e.g. Macdonald 2000: 88).

There were parts of the Pub grounds specifically identified with sharing behaviours, where people 'stood up' with their 'hand out' or where they 'fight [argued] with family' to buy them beer. The least discriminate of this group, those described as being 'hard-up' (i.e. having no money), would approach others, close or distant kin, for money. Likewise, there were other areas, such as a large shed in the south-east of the Pub grounds, which were described as places where drinkers would go to get away or 'dodge' the intensity of demands. One of these areas was described by the same men mentioned above as a place where: 'some people just sit there to get away from other people, couchers', and 'sometime they wanna get away from their family. Some family wanna get away from them cause, they ask for money'.

As in sharing behaviour practised elsewhere in the community, denying or subverting the demands of kin was interpreted by some Aboriginal people as a denial of relatedness. One way to practise relatedness while minimizing the economic burden was the provision of 'silvers', coins of up to fifty-cent value. It was partly Aboriginal people's demands for money that discouraged some Whitefellas from visiting the Pub. A young White doctor, who visited the Pub once a week when he was working on the Island in 2007, explained that while he had 'no problems saying "no" [to Aboriginal people] ... a lot of people [Whitefellas] find that quite confronting'. Thus, while the demands to share were something that Aboriginal people expected from a visit to the Pub, some Whitefellas found the demands for money unfamiliar and overbearing. The same doctor noted that in the context of their roles in service delivery, drinking in a small community presented challenges for Whitefellas: 'I mean really it was only health [medical] people [that went there], certainly the police wouldn't go there. I mean, I wouldn't think that they could go there and operate effectively in their jobs. And I never saw school teachers go there much'. Contrary to McKnight's (2002: 95) interpretation of a 'changed morality' of Whitefellas living on the Island in the post-mission period, in more recent times not attending the Pub was articulated by some as part of their responsibility in maintaining their professionalism. A government employee made a similar observation of his decision never (in eighteen months living on the Island) to drink at the Pub: 'As a government representative, I felt that responsibility'.

This notion of 'responsibility', or more accurately the performance of responsibility, was also noted by those Whitefellas that did visit the Pub, with an emphasis on a sense of duty to model good drinking practice. A woman aged in her forties who worked for the local Council explained, 'you certainly didn't want to stay there long enough so that you were under the influence. You feel responsible for setting an example to the community'. The woman was like most of the very few Whitefellas that visited the Pub, having 'one or two [cans of beer] at the most', but rarely staying longer than a couple of hours, almost always departing before it got dark (as explained in at least another two interviews with Whitefellas). Another middle-aged White woman explained why she never stayed at the Pub after 7pm:

> I never saw anyone really drunk until later on but I was never there late in the evening. I made sure that I left by 7 o'clock because I didn't want to see it. I know that sounds strange. In my head I wanted to keep that idea [of the Pub] being all the families, in their areas enjoying a drink in a beautiful place, ra la la, rather than [seeing people] beating someone up.

For this woman, drinking in the early hours of the Pub allowed her to maintain an (acknowledged) ideal of convivial drinking: that it was simply people 'enjoying a drink in a beautiful place'.

Comments made to me while the Pub was open suggested that other White women, and even some Aboriginal women, were concerned about risks to their safety while at the Pub, especially on their journey home (usually on foot). This concern was evidently shared by many Aboriginal people, who often insisted that I have a reliable person to accompany me on the 500m walk between the Pub and my home. Perceptions of safety among the non-Aboriginal population were largely fed by statistics and accounts of violence related by others who had previously worked on the Island. A 2009 review into policing in Queensland

Indigenous communities noted that from 2004 to 2006, Mornington Island had a nominally high rate (32 per cent) of non-Indigenous victims for offences against the person (CMC 2009: 55). This rate is particularly high given that in 2006 at least, non-Indigenous people constituted less than 10 per cent of the total Mornington Island population (ABS 2006: Table B07). Though this period was prior to my regular visits to the Island, this figure is much higher than I would have anticipated. One explanation may be that the figure includes assaults against (Whitefella) police, notably when executing searches and arrests on Aboriginal people. Aboriginal people reported that these situations were tense affairs in which physical struggles sometimes ensued with police.

While these kinds of statistics are responsible for generating perceptions in both the non-Aboriginal and Aboriginal populations, understanding the nuanced contexts that generate them may shed light on perceptions of violence versus the actual threat posed by violence. Regardless of the authenticity of the threat, the perception of danger and the decision of most Whitefellas to leave the Pub before closing time meant that it was very much an Aboriginal domain, dominated by the social and economic activities of Aboriginal people, especially once it had become dark.

After Dark: The Emergence of Chaos

The sense of order and of rigid boundaries between groups, which was evident in the first couple of hours after the Pub opened, gradually dissolved as more alcohol was consumed and the sun began to set. On my first trip to the Pub in April 2007, for example, I noted how 'as [it] got darker, drunker, groups moved closer together (moveable seats – benches) and people moved more freely between groups, people filled the lawn areas more, some sitting on [the] grass'. It was not unusual for men in particular to have drunk more than ten cans of beer over the preceding hours, and most patrons varied from slightly to visibly inebriated. Drunkenness brought about a reduction in inhibitions and emotions usually concealed: intimacy, acrimony, bereavement, desire and wrath all spilled out among kin, creating a heady social atmosphere.

By 7pm, the pool hall was closed and the outer areas of the Pub grounds became shrouded in darkness, and patrons moved into the lawn area near the exit gate. As well as being close to the serving area, the lawn was the only part of the grounds that was well lit, with floodlights that were mounted on the side of the building. Thus, a swelling mass of people formed on the lawn area, talking, dancing and shouting out to friends and family. Different family groups mixed more readily, as people more intently sought out cash and beer through their extended kin networks. In anticipation of closing time at 8pm, the desire for alcohol and the growing lines at the bar meant that the service area became clogged with people. At 7.45pm a loud siren sounded, indicating that the sale of alcohol had ceased and that patrons had fifteen minutes to finish their beers and leave the premises.

The process of departing the Pub contrasted starkly with the surreptitious means of arrival some hours earlier. Patrons would spill out of the exit gates, usually loitering in the car park outside, waiting for kin to emerge. The sheer number of people exiting the Pub at this time, many in a drunken state, made it difficult for kin to see each other, and verbal confrontations would sometimes begin in this area. Groups of kin with arms or shoulders interlinked would begin walking home along the back streets towards the community. From 8.30pm, the main street was awash with people, many very drunk, standing or staggering, or walking along the road, sometimes fighting or arguing. The sheer numbers of people on the streets made it risky to drive through the community at this time.

Though a regular feature of closing time at clubs and pubs in major cities, this scene was made more conspicuous by the small size of the community and the high proportion of drinkers among the adult population (McKnight 2002: 204). A Whitefella aged in his forties living in the community, who had at one time been a drug and alcohol counsellor, described it: 'It wasn't like other places that have a pub, non-Aboriginal places. White people have problems with alcohol too, it's true. But [this was] hundreds of people getting blind rotten drunk every day and going back to the same streets and houses every day'. In another situation, in Wiluna in Western Australia, Sackett (1977: 92) noted how the arrival of drinkers at an Aboriginal camp caused a deal of 'commotion' and 'disturbance' associated with drunken arguing and fighting. On Mornington Island, on returning home, drinkers would often play loud music and drink homebrew or sly grog in small gatherings. These parties were often invitation-only, hosted by the people who had procured the alcohol or brewed it themselves.[12] The combined noise of drinkers returning home of an evening and those 'chargin up' (i.e. getting drunk) at parties could be heard through the community for hours after the Pub had closed. As a middle-aged White woman who had lived on Mornington Island for eighteen months, including when the Pub was open, recalled:

the continual noise at night ... people drunk, yelling at night, I presume bashing each other up, screaming and yelling ... at first that was quite disconcerting and something that I wasn't use to, I had to get used to it cause I hadn't experienced that sort of stuff before ... never that sort of loudness and what appeared to be violence going on at all hours of the night. I wasn't used to women, particularly, women yelling really, really loudly.

Also during this time, some of the children who had been asleep in their homes also spilled out onto the streets, either to seek out their parents or because they had been woken by drunken kin arriving home. This mirrored what O'Connor (1984: 174) recorded in Central Australia, where: 'Nocturnal violence among parents and older siblings after drinking bouts often leads to younger children fleeing in fear to grandparents or neighbours – or indeed to any camp or house where they can find refuge from the chaos'. In trips to Mornington Island in 2008 and 2009 after the Pub ceased operation, it was the absence of these nighttime scenes and sounds that struck me as the most notable change to the community.

Monitoring and Being 'Barred Off'

While some of the conditions of drinking on Mornington Island were similar to the conditions imposed at pubs and venues in other parts of Australia, there was in operation a particular kind of punitive surveillance where individuals were identified and 'barred off' for varying periods of time. Each night, the behaviour of patrons was monitored and recorded by video cameras mounted on the side of the Pub building (see Figure 4.3) and each day the Pub manager, sometimes aided by Mornington Islanders, would view the footage to identify individuals who had broken the Pub rules. Breaches included abusing pub staff, spitting, pushing in on queues, fighting, failing to exit the premises by the designated closing time and removing alcohol from the premises (see Figure 4.3). Although cans of beer were supposed to be opened at the time of purchase, it was sometimes possible to get intact cans when an Aboriginal family member was working at the counter: 'some people got mob what behind the counter, they pass it, they don't bother to open it'. Getting unopened cans of beer made it possible to smuggle them out of the Pub grounds undetected in a bag, under a coat, or down a person's pants to be consumed at home or during the walk home.

The list of people barred for offences committed in the Pub was supplemented by court orders relating to offences in which alcohol was

Figure 4.3. Front entrance to the Pub (entrance door at left) with notice board listing those 'barred off'. Note the security camera at top right pointed towards the exit gate (photograph by the author).

involved but which were not necessarily related to the Pub. As part of a sentence, a magistrate could include a direction that an offender should not attend the Pub, or they would be found to be in breach of their bail conditions or a good behaviour bond. Offences attracting this punishment were at the discretion of the presiding magistrate, but could include those identified as being associated with consumption or addiction. Although not a common occurrence, police did attend the Pub periodically to locate and arrest those breaching these orders. Those who had been barred would first become aware of their ban the following day when a list was posted outside the Pub (see Figure 4.3). At one time during 2007, over thirty people were 'barred off' for a period of one week as a result of remaining in the Pub grounds after closing time, determined using the time signature on the security camera.

Those barred off would sometimes drink at Birri Fishing Lodge, a small resort on the northern side of Mornington Island, about thirty minutes' drive from Gununa. From the 1980s to the mid-2010s, Birri was operated by a middle-aged Whitefella couple though a tenancy agreement with the local Mornington Shire Council. Although Birri catered primarily for clients flown in on a charter plane for fishing holidays, up to approximately twenty-five local people (Aboriginal people and Whitefellas) could book in to drink there provided that they also purchased a meal. Birri was a preferred drinking place for many Whitefellas living on the Island, as Whites generally thought of it as having a more convivial drinking atmosphere than the Pub, as it was somewhere they could 'get away' from the community for a short period of time. In May 2007, a young Aboriginal man was killed and three men injured in a single-vehicle drink-driving accident after leaving the Lodge (*Cairns Post* 2007: 9). At the time, Aboriginal people suggested that the men had been speeding back to Gununa so that they could attend the Pub before it closed for the evening. After the accident, the Birri operators made it a requirement that Mornington Islanders nominate and sign in a 'sober bob' (i.e. a person who would abstain from drinking alcohol) that would drive them out to Birri and home to Gununa at the end of the night. An Aboriginal man aged in his fifties, who had been barred off from the Pub in Gununa for three months, reflected on the difference between Birri and the Pub, noting that as fewer Aboriginal people drank at Birri, there was less pressure to share. He pondered: 'I might go back in the Pub, I don't know. I'm thinking about still going back out Birri, having a drink. It's more better out there. You don't have people coming round loafering for money. Drink better out there'.

Like the Pub, Birri also had a system for barring unruly patrons, though the fewer number of patrons allowed entry meant that there were greater controls over the amounts of alcohol sold and consumed. When the Pub was shut down in 2008, Birri continued to operate and sell alcohol with meals, and Aboriginal people often booked in for birthdays and other special occasions. The closure of Birri in the mid-2010s signalled the end of an era, as it was the last venue on the entire island selling alcohol. Though the local Council had plans to turn the remaining infrastructure into a rehabilitation facility for Aboriginal people, these were eventually quashed when they were unable to reach land-use agreement with the local Traditional Owners.

Homebrew, Sly Grog and Going 'Bush' to Drink

As the vignette at the beginning of this chapter suggested, the closure of the Pub in January 2008 did not result in abstinence from alcohol consumption. Rather, it was the beginning of a new period of alcohol consumption dominated by 'homebrew' and 'sly grog', which had both been illegal under the Alcohol Management Plan (AMP) since 2003. Rather than referring to homebrewed beer, 'homebrew' was actually an unrefined spirit made using common household ingredients, usually fruit juice, yeast and sugar left to ferment in large containers. It is its 'unrefined' quality that makes homebrew so alcoholic and so dangerous to health, particularly kidney and liver function. At times, homebrew would be mixed with methylated spirits, further increasing its alcoholic content. In order to avoid detection, homebrew stills were often kept at outstations in the more remote parts of Mornington Island and smaller nearby islands. Such was the demand and risk of being caught that in 2010, a 20-litre 'paint tin' of homebrew could reportedly sell for AUD 500.00 (*Townsville Bulletin* 2010: 4). The term 'sly grog' referred to commercially brewed beer and spirits, purchased on the mainland and smuggled (hence 'sly') to the Island. As previously mentioned, this method of procuring alcohol had precedent on Mornington Island towards the end of the mission era (c.1970s), when: 'liquor was smuggled into the settlement by Aborigines returning from trips to mainland towns. Loaves of bread and watermelons provided ideal means of concealment. Flasks of spirits were taped to the body under one's clothes' (Memmott 1979: 330).

That alcohol remained available on Mornington Island was implied in the Queensland Government's reporting of key statistics relating to the AMP. As previously mentioned, in the twelve-month period immediately following the closure of the Pub, the equivalent of 20 per cent of the Mornington Island population aged over eighteen years was convicted for breaches of the AMP (Queensland Government Department of Communities 2010a: 49). In the following year, the rate for conviction skyrocketed from 69.8 to 346.6 per thousand persons in 2008/2009, and has remained high since that time, with the most recent rate reported as 284.1 per thousand persons in 2015/2016 (Queensland Government Department of Aboriginal and Torres Strait Islander Partnerships 2016: 6). Although rates of conviction convey only part of the story of what was occurring on the Island at the time, what it does indicate is the failure of policy to successfully achieve or maintain prohibition.

Part of the difficulty was that the size of Mornington and nearby islands made it almost impossible to enforce prohibition effectively, even with growing allocations of police from six officers in June 2007 to ten in July 2009[13] (CMC 2009: 374). Brady (2007: 186) made a similar observation of Aboriginal communities in the Northern Territory, where 'illegal trade' was 'inherent in general prohibition' and that 'governments in general have more control over legal trade'. An anecdotal flourishing of cannabis use, especially among younger men, was also said to have followed the Pub's closure. The increase in police numbers resulted in a ratio of approximately one officer per hundred residents, putting the daily lives of Mornington Islanders under heavy surveillance. One of the ways that this surveillance was enacted was through searches, known locally as 'raids', conducted in Aboriginal people's houses. Under special measures introduced in 2008 as an amendment to the *Police Powers and Responsibilities Act 2000*, police were given the power to search a house or a person without a warrant 'if they reasonably suspect that they are carrying illicit alcohol' (Queensland Government Department of Communities 2008: 2).

As part of the AMP, travellers arriving on Mornington Island by plane also had their bags 'randomly' searched by police. Aboriginal people frequently expressed irritation at the infringement by police of their right to privacy and their belief that police targeted certain people unfairly for searches (CMC 2009: 120). In one particular incident, members of a children's basketball team returning from a carnival in Cairns had their bags searched, causing resentment among some of the community (Australian Broadcasting Corporation 2008). This incident and others like it heightened tensions between Aboriginal people and police, fuelling Aboriginal community perceptions of police as 'the enemy' (CMC 2009: 87).

In reality, though, it seemed a greater volume of sly grog was brought to Mornington Island by trips via boats than that which came with individuals by plane. Aboriginal relatives or family living on the mainland, at Doomadgee or Burketown, would drive to the coast with prearranged orders of alcohol. These trips, generally undertaken by men, were also an occasion for transfer of other goods between Mornington Islanders and their mainland neighbours. Often, these exchanges included meat, especially dugong and turtle from around the Wellesley Islands, for 'clean-skin'[14] bullock meat from the mainland.[15] Exchanges such as these maintained a sense of regional connectedness and reciprocity with Aboriginal families living in Doomadgee and Burketown.

Boats returning to Mornington from the mainland tended to travel at night to avoid detection, sometimes landing at an outstation where alcohol could be buried for consumption at a later date. Outstation programs were developed around Australia during the 1980s to facilitate Aboriginal people spending time in their traditional country. In 2010 and 2011, a smaller island not permanently inhabited became a known drinking spot for Aboriginal people. Aboriginal people reportedly drank sitting on the beach, enjoying sunsets across the Gulf of Carpentaria, which led the location to be called the 'Sunset Tavern'. As well as their attractive surrounds, outstations were an ideal place to store and consume grog out of the sight of police, an important factor given the illegality of possessing and consuming alcohol and being intoxicated. During this period, it was well known that police seldom worked outside the 'grid', the streets of the community, and did not conduct searches of outstations.[16] A police officer indicated that outside the community itself, Mornington Island had 'blind spots' in radio reception and that for safety reasons it was against policy for officers to be outside reception. In any case, the task of tracking and following Aboriginal people who were engaging in illegal activity and were potentially inebriated posed further risks to police safety.

Concealing and consuming alcohol in outstations also reduced the pressure to share grog with kin or others in the community, and allowed those who had procured the alcohol to be more selective with who they invited to drink. This situation appeared unchanged from that of the mid-1970s, when Memmott (1979: 330) observed how: 'When such group drinking bouts occurred, the sharing ethic prevailed. As many as 40 or 50 relatives might arrive at a residence to participate. Rum was consumed quickly and sometimes secretly so as to obtain the maximum share, before others arrived to exploit their kinsman's [sic] resource'. In the contemporary community, drinking sessions were often said to be in honour of a particular event – a person's birthday, even that of a young child or baby, or the anniversary of a relative's death – and could extend well into the following day. In one instance in 2010, an Aboriginal woman aged in her late twenties explained her drunken behaviour to me as drinking for her own birthday and that of her baby son, both on the forthcoming weekend.

Avoiding Surveillance: Drinking and Off-Island Mobility

The closure of the Pub also contributed to the kinds of travel that Mornington Islanders undertook off-Island. Since the advent of regular air services in the 1960s, the majority of off-Island travel has been undertaken to destinations within the immediate region (McKnight 2002: 83; Memmott 1979: 441). Over the last ten years, a number of different regional airlines have operated flights approximately six days per week from Mornington Island in two directions, to the mainland town of Mount Isa (via Doomadgee) and to the coastal city of Cairns (via Normanton). The main reasons for off-Island mobility are shown in Table 4.1[17].

The travel costs for such trips were often borne by the Queensland State Government, which was responsible for providing access to some of the services not available on Mornington Island itself. Trips off the

Table 4.1. Reasons for off-Island mobility, based on author observations.

Category of travel	Activities	Destinations
Training and meetings	AGMs, board meetings etc. as organized by government and non-government agencies	Burketown, Cairns, Century Mine, Normanton
Healthcare	Access to health services not available on Mornington Island	Mount Isa (basic surgery and birthing), Townsville (major surgery, dialysis), Brisbane (heart surgery)
Visiting family/ Events	Funerals, weddings, shows, birthdays, rodeos	Doomadgee, Mount Isa, Normanton, Aurukun, Weipa
Prison[18]	Incarceration	Townsville Correctional Centre (high security), Townsville Women's Correctional Centre (high security), Lotus Glen Correctional Facility (low security outside Mareeba)
Secondary Education	Attending boarding school	Cape York, Townsville, Brisbane
Holiday	Shopping, drinking, visiting family, purchasing a car	Cairns, Mount Isa, Normanton

Note: Multiple categories of travel were often combined on a single trip.

Island, especially those to destinations where Mornington Islanders were permanently resident, were sometimes combined with sessions of heavy drinking, as had been the case during the 1970s (McKnight 2002: 83; Memmott 1979: 440–41).

One of the towns most impacted by short-term mobility was Normanton, approximately 300 km south-east from Mornington Island on the mainland, and a short plane trip on the regular route. In an interview in February 2010, Councillor Fred Pascoe, the Mayor of the Shire of Carpentaria (which included the town of Normanton), discussed how the implementation of AMPs in the communities of Mornington Island, Pormpuraaw and Kowanyama had impacted Normanton. He described how in the period immediately following the closure of the Pub on Mornington Island in 2008, a large number of people had arrived in Normanton to drink. He also noted that the high cost of air travel from Mornington Island to Normanton, approximately AUD 150.00–250.00 per person one way, made it difficult for Mornington Islanders to afford to return home. Specifically, he observed that Mornington Islanders spent longer periods of time in Normanton compared to those from other Aboriginal communities such as Pormpuraaw and Kowanyama, who could travel to Normanton by car.

Pascoe also suggested that during this period, there had been an anecdotal increase in petty thefts and violence, the latter of which he associated with disputes between Mornington Islanders[19] and Normanton residents over illicit sexual relationships. Certainly, during this time Normanton had a reputation as a party destination for Mornington Islanders. It was the combination of these factors, the association of the place with indiscriminate sexual liaisons (i.e. like dogs) that led to Normanton being referred to as 'Dogtown' by Mornington Islanders.

Another destination that Mornington Islanders often visited was the regional centre of Mount Isa, also on a regular flight route. In 2010, the Mount Isa Shire Council Mayor, Councillor John Molony, was quoted as characterizing people from the Northern Territory and Gulf communities who visited Mount Isa as follows: 'they come here and drink and create social problems' (Molony, quoted in Andersen 2010: 9). Between 2008 and 2011, Molony was regularly quoted in Australian mainstream media discussing 'grog refugees', a term he used to describe Aboriginal people who travelled to Mount Isa from communities where alcohol restrictions had been implemented. The arrival of grog refugees in Mount Isa was reportedly associated with impacts such as homelessness, increased violence and child neglect (Michael 2008; Strutton 2009; Watson 2011). At the same time, negative impacts were somewhat tempered by the existence of close social ties, partly through intermarriage, between Mornington Islanders and residents of regional towns. These connections meant that Mornington Islanders could often rely on extended kin to provide accommodation and food during their stay.

In the years immediately after the Pub shut down, although the amount of travel undertaken by Mornington Islanders appeared to increase, few remained off the Island for more than one or two months at a time. A contributing factor in this mobility appeared to be that while not in their place of primary residence, Mornington Islanders either ran out of money to drink or exhausted the social networks that were supporting them. The desire to drink in familiar social cohorts was what O'Connor (1984: 180) described in Central Australia as 'contingent drunkenness', that is, 'a group dependence ... contingent in that it depends for its occurrence or character upon some prior occurrence or condition: the correct physical and social environment'. Remaining away from Mornington Island placed a great burden on kin networks in these locations. In one situation in February 2010, a Mornington Island woman who lived permanently in Mount Isa arranged for a sign to be posted on a public notice board on Mornington Island. The sign advised that 'visitors' (as distinct from 'family') would no longer be able to stay at her house while in Mount Isa.

As well as those who travelled and drank for short periods, after Mornington Island went 'dry' there was also a smaller number of people who relocated permanently to regional centres. Though there was a complex interplay of factors which contributed to decisions to relocate, for a least a proportion, and especially those that moved soon after the Pub shut down, the need to consume alcohol outweighed any desire to drink with Mornington Island family or friends, or in particular surrounds. The permanency of their dislocation from the Mornington Island community suggested that their desire to enact relatedness to kin on Mornington Island was subservient to their alcohol addiction.

Another example of the impacts of the interplay between the closure of the Pub and increasing regional mobility was on Mornington Islanders' preference for particular government welfare schemes. In September 2008, a former Community Development Employment Project (CDEP) Coordinator reported that over the nine-month period following the Pub being shut down, the number of CDEP participants' had dropped from 270 (in 2007) to 140 (in 2008). CDEP was an Australian Government-funded program that employed Aboriginal people to complete work around the community in order to receive a basic amount of income. Although people gaining employment outside CDEP may have contributed to the decline in the number of participants from 2007 to 2008, there was also a reported increase in the number of people claiming other forms of unemployment benefits. One reason for the preference of unemployment benefits in favour of CDEP was that they allowed for flexibility of residence, enabling people to travel between Mornington Island and other centres without financial penalty. CDEP participation, on the other hand, was dependent on the participant being resident on the Island in order to complete the designated number of participation days (generally two per week). At the same time, however, mobility removed Mornington Islanders from the comparatively contained drinking contexts with kin to centres where they had fewer networks to provide basic needs, particularly food and shelter. These less familiar contexts and socially unregulated drinking also exposed a number of other potential problems for drinkers, especially issues of violence.

Drinking and Violence

Ethnographies that examine the sociality of Aboriginal drinking rarely do so without paying attention to the interconnectedness of alcohol consumption and violence, sometimes as designated as 'fighting'

(Memmott 1979: 330). As was discussed in the Introduction, over the last decade sustained debate has considered the role of anthropologists in describing, analysing and interpreting violence and dysfunction in Aboriginal communities (for instance, see papers in Altman and Hinkson 2007, 2010; Merlan 2009). Austin-Broos (2010), for example, critiqued the process of 'quarantining violence' by which anthropologists addressed violence separate from their more general ethnography. At the same time, she cautioned against stressing violence in ethnography: 'Ethnography need not always go to violence ... Yet good anthropology should be *consistent* with these contexts where they exist. It should provide an analysis that, if called upon, can address these conditions – not simply shut them out and close them down for the sake of stressing continuity' (ibid.: 142, emphasis in original).

Likewise, Hinkson (2009: 9) argued that ethnography should consider 'the extent to which such violence or suffering can be said to dominate social life in such places'. Mornington Island could be considered as such a context, as both when the Pub was operating and in the period following, it was regularly reported as having one of the highest rates of violence (measured as per capita 'offences against the person'[20]) of all Queensland communities (CMC 2009: 42,59; Queensland Government Department of Communities 2010a: 91)[21]. This measure, together with hospital admissions for assault-related conditions, child protection orders, school attendance and convictions for breaches of alcohol restrictions, has been regularly published by the Queensland Government as a means of reporting conditions in remote communities where AMPs have been implemented. While there has been some indication of downward trends in some of the primary indicators relating to violence on Mornington Island from 2000–2001 to 2013–2014, over the period it remained the case that residents were exposed to much higher degrees of violence than the general Queensland population (Queensland Government Department of Aboriginal and Torres Strait Islander Partnerships 2014: 2–5, 109).

There has been some suggestion by anthropologists that an 'abnormal enculturation of violence' (Martin 2009: 52) in some Aboriginal communities is at least partially derived from an historical past which included some degree of normalized violent behaviour (Sutton 2009: 91). Historical reviews of the causality of alcohol in the disintegration of Aboriginal sociality are sometimes fraught by a failure to grasp the concurrent and compounding impacts of poverty, the concentration of settlements, the coming together of a range of previously disparate cultural groups and escalating population growth on such normalized behaviours (McKnight 2004: 130). The associative impacts of sustained alcohol misuse through a population are nevertheless more complex and embedded than violence alone. Saggers and Gray (1998: 18), for example, list job loss, financial costs, detrimental effects on children, sickness and early death and effects on culture as five of the major categories of 'harm' which demonstrate the negative flow-on effects of alcohol abuse. At the same time, violence was not always alcohol-related and, as Sutton (2009: 3) pointed out, 'alcohol alone cannot carry anything like a full explanation for the dramatic deterioration in the people's quality of life'.

In spite of the complexity of the factors that contribute to high rates of violence in a population, others have identified alcohol abuse as the root cause of the deterioration in quality of life (e.g. CMC 2009: 42; Langton 2010: 99). McKnight's (2005: 112) conclusion that 'with very rare exceptions all the violence was alcohol related' was strongly supported by my own observations. In a non-identified remote community in Cape York, David Martin (1998: 8) found that alcohol was implicated in 88 per cent of assault injuries which occurred over a twelve-month period in 1995/1996. Even fights between sober persons on Mornington Island often related to prior incidents that had taken place while under the influence of alcohol.[22]

A complex relationship between alcohol and violence on Mornington Island was suggested by quantitative data collected by the Queensland Government to monitor the success of the AMP. Two of the (linked) key indicators were reported offences against the person and rates of hospital admissions for assault-related conditions. Over the period that data has been collected, from 2002/03 to 2010/2011 and from 2014/15 and 2015/16 (i.e. excluding the years 2011/12, 2012/13 and 2013/14) hospital admissions for assault-related conditions[23] were relatively steady and surprisingly showed no clear correlation to the rates of reported assaults. The reported rates of offences against the person were much more volatile, with the most noteworthy rise being a 50 per cent increase from 100.8 per 1,000 persons in 2007/2008 to 152.6 per 1,000 persons in 2008/2009, which corresponded to the period immediately following the closure of the Pub (Queensland Government Department of Communities 2011: 42). In subsequent years, rates remained relatively low until 2014/15, when they again began to rise (Queensland Government Department of Aboriginal and Torres Strait Islander Partnerships 2016: 42).

Caution must be exercised in the interpretation of such statistics, and consideration given to the range of factors beyond alcohol availability in influencing rates and statistics of harm. Some of these considerations include the numbers and approaches of police and hospital staff to recording such incidences, and Aboriginal people's hesitancy to self-report. Nevertheless, even at their lowest points taken over the period, the rates for reported offences against the person and rates of hospital admissions for assault-related conditions were consistently over ten times the average rates for the rest of Queensland, indicating exceptionally high rates of violence (Queensland Government Department of Communities 2011: 41–42). Arguably, the sustained high rates of violence are at least partially indicative of the continued availability of alcohol through illicit channels[24] (as I have previously discussed in this chapter). What these data do not necessarily show, however, are the changes to the types of contexts in which drinking occurred.

After the Pub closed, drinking took place in smaller, more intimate contexts 'out bush' or at parties at houses, which were markedly different social contexts to that described at the Pub, namely for the lack of social regulation by kin and the police. This changed drinking atmosphere, and the lack of interventions that it fostered, also meant that people were much more likely to drink to excess, and that volatility could escalate unabated into situations where people injured themselves and others. The illegality of alcohol consumption was compounded by the social conditioning not to report to the police incidences of violence involving alcohol. It was noteworthy that even some of those who had been in total support of the decision to close down the Pub in the initial stages, particularly Whitefellas that lived on the Island, had later become more circumspect about its success in 'reducing harm'. Three reasons for this change in opinion were anecdotal increases in youth suicide (which I do not explicitly address here), the reporting of serious injuries among those who had previously been described as 'good drinkers' and three deaths that occurred on the Island between July 2010 and October 2011.

The first death occurred in July 2010, when a 19-year-old woman died following an 'all-night drinking session' at a house on Mornington Island (Johnson 2010: 6; Michael 2010: 10). Initial reports suggested that the woman had died as a result of drinking homebrew; however, her 'drinking partner' at the time of her death was later convicted of her manslaughter (Healy 2013: 17; Johnson 2010: 6; Michael 2010: 10). Another woman, aged 35 years, died in similar circumstances in June 2011, following a drinking session with a 21-year-old man who was subsequently charged with her manslaughter (*Townsville Bulletin* 2011: 7). Both the media accounts and reports from Mornington Islanders suggested that in both deaths the women were brutalized, each dying as a result of the injuries inflicted. In October 2011, a 29-year-old man died after sustaining injuries reportedly associated with being speared by a 15-year-old boy (Elks 2011:

7). The deaths of these three young people, all in shocking circumstances, reverberated through the community, particularly given that all three of the deceased were the parents of young children.

Drunken violence that occurred in public contexts was not the kind of 'traditional' fighting described by Bain (1972: 49) where 'there was socially accepted control or attempted control, by certain kin or by ritual leaders and elders'. Partly this was because the reason(s) for the fight were often judged as insufficient in magnitude to warrant the intervention of others (cf. Sackett 1977: 92). These fights were different to sober fights, as people placed less weight on their outcome, sometimes brushing them off as 'just drunken fight', as McKnight (2005: 126) also recorded in the 1970s. Memmott (1979: 409) made a similar observation of drunken fights at Gununa during the 1970s, where 'assisting kin in these fights is not always the rule' and 'seldom are any codes of fighting adhered to in drunken fights'. In one instance in August 2010, I noted how:

> When we arrived there was a fight across the road from us – two men both drunk with their shirts off wearing jeans and punching one another. No one was very worried – lots of cars were driving past from the airport. A little while later when we drove past there was a paddy wagon [vehicle equipped to carry persons taken into police custody] putting at least one of the men in the back.

Perhaps just as noteworthy, though I did not bother to comment on at the time because I was so accustomed to seeing it, was that both of the men were visibly intoxicated at a time when the Island was supposed to be 'dry'. This supported MacAndrew and Edgerton's (1969: 83) suggestion that drunken behaviour, albeit within limits, provided 'time out' from the usual societal expectations. On Mornington Island, while there were sometimes repercussions from drunken fights, especially injuries and police charges, it was generally true among the Aboriginal protagonists that, as Sackett (1977: 93) described it for the Western Desert community of Wiluna, 'the day following such a fight all is forgiven and forgotten'. On Mornington Island, though, fights were followed by intense social politicking and gossip, particularly among women, who analysed the details of each fight.

Conclusion: 'I Don't Drink Any More Black Fella Sayin'

This phrase came to me via a text message from an Aboriginal man aged in his thirties on Mornington Island in 2010. I had asked the man via (mobile-phone) text message if he was drinking alcohol and watching a highly anticipated Australian Rugby League match between his favoured Brisbane Broncos and another North Queensland team, the Cowboys. The man's response was an often-heard phrase on Mornington Island, sometimes expressed sincerely but more often with a sense of ironic humour, that despite their assertions and perhaps intentions otherwise, local Aboriginal people rarely gave up drinking. The main reason for this was that drinking was at the core of much of the social interaction that occurred on the Island.

This research straddled an important period in the local availability of alcohol, including the final year of the operation of the local Pub, 2007, and the years following its closure when the community was supposedly 'dry'. When the Pub was operating it provided a means through which Mornington Islanders could visibly demonstrate their affinity and allegiances to kin by sitting and drinking in groups. These were not trivial expressions and were derived from particular aspects of social life: family groups, surnames and traditional lands. Such was the social investment in group-drinking behaviour that, as Sansom (1980) suggested for those at Wallaby Cross, and as Bain (1972: 49) concluded of Aboriginal society more generally, 'drinking alcohol has become an activity positive enough to distinguish one group from another'. While the closure of the Pub in 2008 may have given the impression of the discontinuation of drinking practice, the reality was that 'homebrew' and 'sly grog' continued to be consumed. The ongoing presence of alcohol in the community from 2008 onwards is reflected in the high occurrence of the possession, consumption and supply of alcohol, recorded as breaches to the relevant legislation (Queensland Government Department of Communities 2011: 42). The illegality of these practices means that while alcohol consumption continues to occur, it is conditioned more heavily by attempts to subvert surveillance and monitoring, by increased off-Island mobility and drinking out bush or within a person's home.

The reproduction of social knowledge and surveillance surrounding drinking, both before and after the closure of the Pub, was one of the most important components in the broader Mornington Island social milieu. Much of daily life revolved around gaining access to alcohol, getting drunk, being drunk, being 'grog sick' and dealing with all of the social implications of drunken behaviour. It both drove and destroyed social interaction. While early ethnographies of Aboriginal drinking contextualized it as a performance of citizenship rights, Sackett maintained that 'while this appears to adequately account for the situation as it was then, it does not explain the present level and pattern of Aboriginal drinking.' (Sackett 1988: 75). Yet McKnight's (2002: 2) assertion that drinking had rendered Mornington Islanders 'bereft of a social identity' simplifies more complex renderings of the kinds of social interaction that surrounded drinking.

While excessive alcohol consumption had serious negative impacts, particularly as a major contributor to levels of violence, it did occur in a richly elaborated social context. While these aspects relate to the social conditions under which alcohol consumption occurred, it was also the role that drinking played in crafting kinds of identity that made its negative impacts so pervasive. The primacy of alcohol has become clear over the last few years. Almost every year since the Island went dry, councillors and the local justice group have petitioned the Queensland State Government, seeking various changes to the structure of alcohol management on the Island. Yet very little has changed.[25] A Whitefella who at one time worked on the Island as a drug and alcohol counsellor described this situation: 'Alcohol will remain the critical issue. It is *the* critical issue, the be all and end all of this place' (emphasis in original).

Notes

1. At times, Mornington Islanders used this metaphor ironically as an explanation for their own tendency to drink: 'well you know, we all from hunting to drinking or whatever they say'.
2. The 'canteen' was the Lelka Murrin Tavern. Although some older Mornington Islanders still refer to it as the canteen, to most it was simply the 'Pub'.
3. It is difficult to ascertain whether McKnight ever actually went to the canteen itself, as his ethnography does not relate to goings-on in the canteen venue.
4. It was partly this conflict of interest between providing services for the well-being of residents and receiving Pub profits that led the State Government to demand the transfer of the liquor licence. This transfer became a moot point when the licence was revoked on other grounds.
5. The alcohol content of the majority-favoured brand XXXX Gold was 3.5 per cent (alcohol by volume). It was unusual to see persons in the Pub grounds consuming non-alcoholic drinks, and I am unaware if they were available for purchase in the service area. They were, however, most definitely for sale from the kiosk, though the entrance was located outside the designated drinking area.
6. I never attended the Pub during the wet season (December–February) and thus my observations are confined to the periods of the year when the weather was congruent with sitting outside.
7. This estimation is consistent with McKnight's observations in an earlier period, and the number of legal-age drinkers from the 2006 ABS Census. Although he did not record numbers at the time of his fieldwork, in 2002 McKnight (2002: 105, 108) made (retrospective) estimations of the number of drinkers in the town during the period 1989–1999 as 400.
8. The action might be thought of as replicating intercourse, and the term may also have been a reference to the association of dogs as being sexually promiscuous or

162 • *What Now*

    indiscriminate. In other cases, women referred to men who were sexually unfaithful as 'dogs'.
9. I visited this estate with some of the Kaiadilt Traditional Owners, including this man, in August 2007 and again in April 2008.
10. In pre-mission settlement times, Mornington Island had a number of important forms of social division, the remnants of which continue to form an important part of contemporary sociality. One of these divisions was a distinction between two moieties, Windward and Leeward, which corresponded to those associated with country estates on the two sides of the Island.
11. I can recall an instance of drinking with a particular family, and of some Aboriginal people being introduced to me simply as 'visitors' (being from another table). As is discussed in Chapter 5, this behaviour was also observed around cooking fires 'out-bush'. In one instance, a woman stood holding her baby in the sun for 15 minutes while talking to a couple cooking at their fire. She was not offered to sit (in the shade) and she did not request it.
12. I attended approximately half a dozen of these gatherings in 2007. Based on these experiences, I formed the opinion that such parties were 'social', rather than familial gatherings. They tended to be drinkers of a similar age, who shared some historical or recent connection such as being in the same grade year at school or being in the same CDEP work gang.
13. Periodically, additional officers were also brought to Mornington Island from the mainland town of Mount Isa to undertake specific raids and execute warrants, often in the days prior to scheduled court sessions. This often resulted in large numbers of people being held in the Mornington Island watch-house overnight.
14. An animal without a mark (usually a brand on the rump, a plastic ear tag or cuts in the ear) to identify its owner.
15. Despite historically being coastal dwellers, it appeared that residents of Doomadgee seldom hunted for dugong or turtle, perhaps owing to a low level of boat ownership and the distance from the coast, contributing to the loss of the customary habit of hunting in the sea (David Trigger, pers. comm. 2011).
16. A police officer once informed me that this was because police radios had unreliable reception outside the 'grid', creating a safety risk. In any case, police were insufficiently knowledgeable to attempt to track or chase people in the unfamiliar terrain. In 2011, I heard that this situation had changed somewhat; however, I did not have the chance to substantiate this.
17. These reasons had changed little from Memmott's (1979: 434) observations in the mid-1970s, although it appears that travel to access employment is now less common.
18. McKnight (2002: 147) estimated that 10 per cent of the adult male population of Mornington Island was 'in gaol, or in prison, or detained at any one time'.
19. One of the issues that Pascoe identified with these increases was a failure of police and hospital staff to accurately record the home residence of those involved in such incidences.
20. 'Offences against the person' include 'Murder and Attempted Murder, Grievous Assault, Rape and Attempted Rape, Serious Assault, Serious Assault (Other), Armed Robbery. 'Other' offences include: Common Assault, Driving Causing Death, Kidnapping and Abduction, Life Endangering Acts, Other Sexual Offences, Stalking, Extortion' (Queensland Government 2010: 99).
21. Often alongside the communities of Aurukun and Woorabinda (CMC 2009: 42,59).

22. It appeared to me, anecdotally at least, that women and especially teenage girls fought sober more often than men. This may have reflected the fact that more women were non-drinkers than men (as discussed earlier in the chapter).
23. In 2014/2015 the description was amended slightly from 'hospital admissions for assault related conditions' to 'episodes of care for assault related conditions' (Queensland Government Department of Aboriginal and Torres Strait Islander Partnerships 2015: 1). In 2015/16 no hospital data was published, apparently 'due to unavailability of data' (Department of Aboriginal and Torres Strait Islander Partnerships 2016: 1).
24. This was also supported by the large volumes of people charged with alcohol offences (see Queensland Government Department of Communities 2011: 42).
25. One incremental change in 2018 was the instigation of a once-a-month 'Tavern Night' or 'Community Liquor Night' from 4:30–9:30pm. I have not attended any of these events, and it is too early to determine how they impact broader consumption patterns.

5

CONNECTIONS TO LAND AND SEA

The majority of this book has focused on the social interactions of Mornington Islanders in the residential community. The community was the primary backdrop for most of the day-to-day activities of Mornington Islanders: where they played, cried, loved, fought, worked, laughed, died and were ultimately buried in the graveyard overlooking the sea. Thus, the residential community was an intensely socialized landscape. At the same time, however, Mornington Islanders retained an enduring sense of connectedness to other places in the Wellesley Islands, which they referred to as their 'country'. For Mornington Islanders, their country, more so than the community, was the interlocker between themselves, their ancestors and their culture. As one man aged in his thirties explained, as country affiliations were inherited (that is, transmitted through kin connections) they were in a sense inalienable: 'know that's your mob's land and they been there for generations and no one can take that off you'. It is the transmitted nature of country between various generations of people living in a particular area that has been the defining characteristic of Aboriginal landed identities in Australia (Sutton 1998: 33).

Much has been written about the connections of Aboriginal people to sea country, and the notion of coastal Aboriginal people, particularly in northern Australia, as 'saltwater people' (Bradley 2010; Memmott and Trigger 1998: 112; Sharp 2002). Likewise, Mornington Islanders were intimately connected to the seas surrounding the Wellesley Islands, and also to the creeks, rivers and waterholes that engraved the islands. During the wet season, lakes formed on the vast inland saltpans, joining brackish watercourses to the sea. Sea country throughout the Wellesley Islands is intensely animate; brimming with animals and with constantly shifting tides and currents. It is also from sea country that many forces originate, wind and weather and the vast multitude of curios, natural and otherwise, that wash up along the beaches. In the historical past, the sea also brought visitors: Aboriginal people and Macassans, followed by missionaries and traders and, in the contemporary period, kin from the mainland communities of Burketown and Doomadgee (Dalley and Memmott 2010: 115; Trigger 1992: 26).

The journeys of these visitors mimicked those of Lardil, Yangkaal and Kaiadilt ancestor beings, spirits who had moved through country leaving tangible records of their presence at sites referred to as 'story places', richly encoded with meaning for Aboriginal people (Memmott 1979: 123–26). As it defined types of appropriate behaviour while in country, knowledge of story places was a vital part of the way that Aboriginal people related to country. Story places were interspersed with other types of places formed in the more recent past, where generations of Aboriginal relatives had themselves inscribed the landscape with meaning. Thus, the landscape was also a record of these events through time: the birthplace of an important person, a cattle-mustering camp, a place where a four-wheel-drive vehicle had been bogged, the sighting of an albino crocodile or the place where someone had planted a mango tree many years previously.

Not only was country imbued with the features of spirit ancestors and relatives through sites and places, but it was also where contemporary Mornington Islanders carried out practices and embodied knowledge that were part of their culture. As with most aspects of identity, individual and family connections to country were part of a broader social milieu, intensely politicked and contested. Connections to country took on particular meaning in the context of social relations, in part of what Trigger (1997a) described as an 'emergent politics of identity' in the Gulf country. As Trigger (ibid.: 87) explained for the nearby mainland Aboriginal community of Doomadgee, 'the politics of personal worth and reputation among Aboriginal people rests partly on the importance of inherited links to indigenous linguistic identities, areas of country and groups of kin'. Such was the gravity of country in identity politics that it loomed large in almost every discussion about what it meant to be a Mornington Islander, both in the contemporary period and previously (McKnight 1999: 81).

These connections were partly conceived of by Aboriginal people as what Sutton (2001b: 17) called 'one of essences, arising from their bodily nature, usually their bodily descent'. Mornington Islanders often expressed sentiments that emphasized the singularity or uniqueness of their connection to land. For Mornington Islanders, country has remained as a defining, persistent and pervasive idiom in the expression of personhood. For example, an Aboriginal man aged in his thirties, who was recognized as a primary owner (in the Lardil language, '*dulmada*'[1]) of an estate at the top end of Mornington Island, explained: 'Me and [my country], I just feel for it, I know the whole country up there. It'll never ever let me down ... Yeah, it just accepted me'. Another Aboriginal man aged in his thirties explained the feelings that he and other Mornington Islanders associated with going out on country: 'I reckon a lot of people, when they go to their country, they get the same feeling. It's cleansing to get on your country. I got to get home for recharge. I need to get back to land. That's important to us'. It was also the strength of these relationships, the coalescing of inherited and demonstrated links, that Mornington Islanders perceived as differentiating them from others, including other Aboriginal people whose connections to landed identities and specific language-group affiliations have become attenuated (Paradies 2006). As the Mornington Island man above described, 'that's why I feel sorry for the east coast mob because they can [only] claim Kmart'.[2] The sense of competitiveness evident in this statement was echoed in references to country by other Mornington Islanders, who derived a sense of pride, not only in their knowledge of country, but also that the land and seas around the Wellesley Islands have remained free from the kinds of development common elsewhere.

In other parts of Australia, anthropologists have explained how country and related knowledge becomes a kind of 'capital' claimed and counter-claimed by Aboriginal people (Finlayson 1997: 147; Merlan 1998: 169). Just as sharing was conceived of as a quintessentially Aboriginal practice, to claim country was seen as a distinctly Aboriginal trait. Yet the degree to which other Mornington Islanders legitimized such claims among themselves was largely dependent on a person's or a family's active involvement in caring for it. Thus, to be recognized as legitimately having country meant more than simply 'owning' it or being entitled to it, it also required knowledge of it: how to get there, where to fish, the story places contained within it and so on. This system of authority created disparities between older and younger living generations who had markedly differing experiences, and therefore knowledge, of country. These kinds of disparities were also emerging when David McKnight (2002: Chapter 5) and Paul Memmott (1979: 333) conducted anthropological research on Mornington Island, especially between the late 1960s and late 1970s.

In this chapter I explore a range of Mornington Islanders' relationships to country, and how their experiences were mediated by factors such as access to transport, which in turn contributed to their capacity to be recognized as legitimate owners by others. I also explain how as a result of being firmly embedded in social relations, country sometimes became the site of conflicts and tensions expressed verbally as relating to the proper management of country. I also elaborate on how land and sea were at the heart of some Mornington Islanders' hopes for the future, expressed through 'aspirational statements', most commonly the desire to relocate permanently to a particular area of country.

Claiming Country, Native Title and 'Localism'

As has been described in previous chapters, Mornington Islanders derived and asserted connections to specific linguistic territories within the Wellesley Islands. At a broad level, these linguistic groups were Lardil from Mornington Island,[3] Yangkaal from the North Wellesley Islands between Mornington Island and the mainland (Denham, Andrew, Forsyth, Pains and Robert Islands) and Kaiadilt from the South Wellesley Islands. Together with Ganggalida Aboriginal people of the adjacent Australian mainland, it was this ownership, based on identification with broad linguistic groups, that was claimed and recognized under the relevant Federal legislation, the *Native Title Act 1993 (Cth)*. The claim process commenced in the late 1990s and became known locally as the 'Sea Claim' (The Lardil Peoples v State of Queensland 2004 FCA 298).

The Sea Claim covered waters in and around the Wellesley Islands and adjacent mainland coast up to the high-tide mark (National Native Title Tribunal [NNTT] 2004: 19). The boundaries of the area claimed (see Figure 5.1) were set out as being 'as far as the eye could see' from high points of land on the various islands (ibid.: 21). In the 2004 determination, non-exclusive rights were recognized over a lesser area of sea country than in the original claim, partly as a result of the presiding judge's conclusion that the area under claim was at the extreme of what portion of sea might have generally been visible from frontal dunes or beaches (ibid.). Subsequently, a claim over 121,775 hectares of land on the Wellesley Islands was resolved through the negotiation of a consent determination (i.e. without proceeding through a trial) in December 2008 (NNTT 2009: 1). Unlike for the Sea Claim, Aboriginal applicants were granted exclusive rights over the vast majority of land that they had applied for (ibid.)

A newspaper article described a ceremony held to mark the land determination at a hall on Mornington Island, noting that the presiding

168 • *What Now*

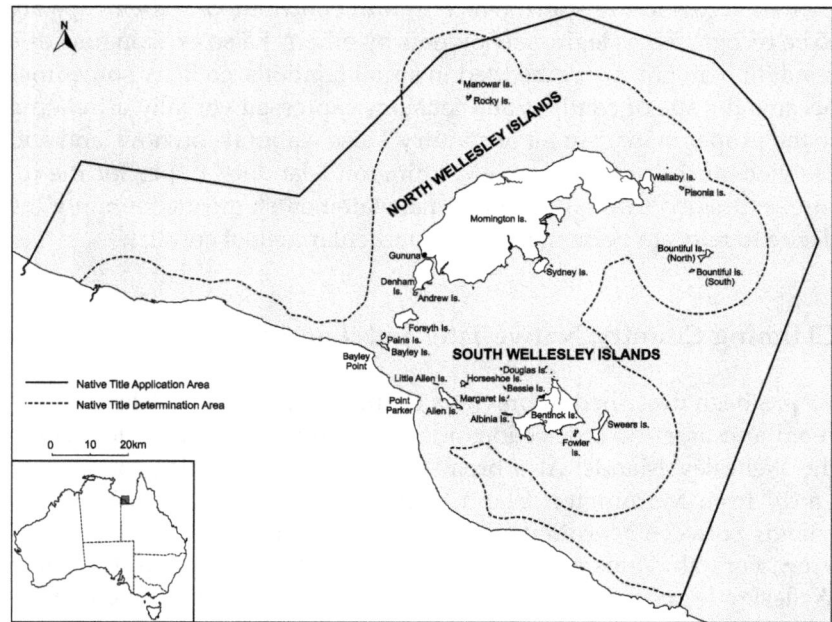

Figure 5.1. Map showing the area of sea claimed (inside the continuous line) and granted (inside the dotted line) during the Wellesley Sea Claim (author-adapted version of a map reproduced with the kind permission of the National Native Title Tribunal 2005).

judge, 'a berobed Federal Court Justice', had entered the hall 'dodging a snoozing dog' (Wenham 2008: 11). Such was the lack of fanfare associated with the land determination that during a visit in 2009, when I mentioned the ceremony, many Mornington Islanders were either unaware that the determination had been made or, more commonly, assumed that they had always held such rights. This situation suggests a different engagement with and experience of the notions about ownership conferred by native title than has been recorded in other parts of Australia (Babidge 2010; Smith 2003, 2008; Vincent 2017). For Aboriginal people living in Charters Towers and Coen (both in north Queensland), for example, Babidge (2010) and Smith (2003, 2008) explored the ways in which Aboriginal people formed and (re)formed connections to country and to kin through the processes and mechanisms of claiming native title. In those locations, Aboriginal people were sometimes permanently resident at a distance from their traditional country, and the claim process was a means through which they sought to activate and claim (or reclaim) landed identities (Babidge 2010: 163; Smith 2008:

211). Also, in those locations, privately held land tenure, including large pastoral holdings, sometimes reduced the ready access that Aboriginal people had to their country (Babidge 2010: 2), especially since the 'huge decline' of Aboriginal participation in the pastoral workforce from the 1970s (Smith 2003: 28). In Ceduna, in South Australia, Vincent (2017: 24) describes how native title processes have resulted in re-identification with dormant linguistic affiliations, creating 'revelatory and empowering opportunities for self-discovery'. In the context of the town itself, Vincent describes how the native title era heralded a period of division between groups of resident Aboriginal people, including a significant population of Kothaka people who were said to have historically migrated to Ceduna from the Western Desert. The production and reproduction of identities around native title processes featured prominently in these and other contemporary Indigenous communities.

In the Wellesley Islands, however, a different experience emerges. The majority of the resident population is located on or close to their traditional country, and have unfettered access (though mediated by other factors) to it on account of it being an Aboriginal reserve. Another factor that might be seen to contribute to the lack of knowledge about the legal recognition of native title rights among contemporary Mornington Islanders was that those involved in the process tended to be older persons. As Trigger (1997a: 92) noted for a different land claim on the mainland, most of the Aboriginal people who contributed evidence during the Sea Claim process were elderly, and although the claim was determined relatively recently, of the forty-four Aboriginal residents of Mornington Island who gave witness affidavits in the process, that more than half have passed away.[4] Tragically, some of these deaths occurred in November 1999 when a chartered light plane, the passengers of which had been on their way to a meeting to discuss native-title matters, crashed into the sea near Bentinck Island (Meade 1999: 3). The diminished number of living persons who had been involved in the Sea Claim might be seen to have contributed to a lack of knowledge of the formal legal processes of native title among younger persons.

Another important factor in understanding the role of native title discourses in informing discussion about country was that Mornington Island, and the Wellesley Islands more broadly, were free of the large-scale development projects, especially mining, which are often found in remote regions of Australia. Elsewhere, these projects, and the negotiation of associated royalty and compensation packages for Aboriginal people, have sometimes required the (ongoing) articulation of group compositions in order to access benefits (e.g. B.R. Smith 2005: 228). Thus, in some parts of Australia, including on the adjacent mainland as discussed by Trigger (1997b, 2005), these processes have precipitated fracturing among impacted Aboriginal groups, with issues often surrounding the assertion and refuting of various claims to be included in the group identified for royalties or compensation. In the Wellesley Islands, however, the Aboriginal administrative organization empowered through the native title determinations (the Registered Native Title Body Corporate) has only been required to determine land ownership in a small number of incidences, such as the construction of a new rubbish dump on Mornington Island in 2010 and the small-scale mining of sand for construction projects on the Island. These projects were of limited scope and financial reward, meaning that their outcomes were not considered noteworthy.

This situation meant that native title did not figure prominently in discussions about ownership and the descent of country, particularly among younger generations. On Mornington Island, all of these factors heightened something similar to what Finlayson (1997: 146, citing Martin 1996) referred to as a kind of 'localism', described in the following terms: 'issues specific to the local situation not only form a focus for interest groups, but have precedence over wider, regional or even national concerns'. Though Finlayson used the term to explore the operation of various kinds of Native Title Representative Bodies (or 'NTRBs'), groups with responsibilities established under native title legislation, the concept also has application more broadly in understanding the framing of interests by Aboriginal people in particular settings. On Mornington Island, localism was iteratively created and supported by the concentrated and contained nature of the Island as a remote physical place of residence, and as a relatively closed social world. The somewhat laissez-faire attitude of Mornington Islanders, especially younger people, towards the recognition of native title and its subsequent apparatus contrasted with intensely politicked debates relating to land filiations among Mornington Islanders themselves. This politicking related to the descent of land and sea ownership over particular units or estates, referred to as 'countries' (Memmott 1979: 71).

The Descent of Country in the North Wellesley Islands

Extensive research into the nature of Lardil and Yangkaal connections to land and sea was undertaken by David McKnight (1999) and Paul Memmott (1979), based primarily on fieldwork conducted during the 1960s and 1970s. McKnight (1999: Chapter 5) and Memmott (1979: Chapter 4) mapped Lardil and Yangkaal countries around the North

Wellesley Islands, describing each estate as including land and sea with 'clear boundaries that run roughly at right angles to the coast' (Memmott 1979: 74).[5] In the Wellesley Sea Claim, a Ganggalida man and long-time resident of Mornington Island noted that for local Aboriginal people land and sea were interpreted as relatively seamless in regards to ownership: 'That sea belongs to that country' (Sewter 1999: paragraph 22). Each of these countries was claimed and 'owned' by a particular group or groups of kin, determined nominally through patrilineal descent, that is, through one's father (Memmott and Trigger 1998: 118). Key persons within each patriclan group were the *dulmadas*, a Lardil word denoting senior men responsible for making decisions about a particular country (Memmott 1979: 72).

The notion of 'owning' was a means of denoting those with 'primary' rights, as distinct from those who may have interests derived from other affiliations such as by birth. Thus, a descent group, or 'patriclan', those with primary rights in a particular country, was notionally composed of patrilineally related men and their children (ibid.: 71)[6]. Rather than being a prescriptive system, patriclan affiliation served an ethic or 'ideology' that was subject to interpretation and reinterpretation (Memmott and Trigger 1998: 118). There were numerous examples in the current and recent history of Lardil and Yangkaal people where the recognized principle of descent deviated[7] from a patrilineal path. One case that illustrates this is at a country at the north-eastern end of Mornington Island. Though it was unclear if there was more than one recognized *dulmada* for the country, at the beginning of the twentieth century the senior *dulmada* was recorded as a man named Gammon (McKnight 1999: 96). Gammon had only one child, a daughter named Gertie, who took responsibility for the country after Gammon's death, eventually passing that responsibility on to her eldest son (ibid.). The deviation to a daughter in one generation, though, appeared to be viewed as acceptable because it was then followed by two successive generations of patrifiliation.

Primary rights derived through patrilineal descent, however, were only one of a number of ways that Mornington Islanders derived rights in country. In the past, Lardil and Yangkaal women married into patriclans (other than their own) and came to identify with their husband's country while still retaining interests in their own father's country (Memmott 1979: 71). Other types of secondary rights for Lardil and Yangkaal included those derived from being born and being 'signed', or spiritually conceived, in an area of country. The key distinction between those with 'primary' and those with 'secondary' rights, and an issue which was discussed by Aboriginal witnesses in the Wellesley

Sea Claim, was the need to 'ask permission' from a *dulmada* in order to access or visit country (e.g. Roughsey 1999: paragraph 30; Jacob 1999: paragraphs 8, 30, 31).

In other cases, country inheritance occurred when a man who had no male children of his own willed or gifted his country to a younger man, usually not his actual descendant. For example, a Lardil man aged in his forties (indicated in grey in Figure 5.2) described how his classificatory mothers (his mother's mother's sister's daughters) had passed on their father's (i.e. his classificatory grandfather's) country to him and an older classificatory sister:

> Through my grandfather gave me and my eldest sister. I was the only eldest grandson that they ever had and the girls, well they were just girls. Yeah, I was the only eldest grandson in the whole family ... his daughters never had any eldest kids and I growed up with them like half my life an that. They looked after me like I was one of their own and they gave me and my sister this country.

His assertion that his classificatory mother 'never had any eldest kids' referred to the fact that he was the first male grandchild born to his classificatory grandfather.

In other cases, the connection between the country giver and the receiver was affinal, that is a relationship arising from marriage, or through a child having been born in country. These examples were often expressed as being a case of transmission between two parties based on a particular relationship. As one man aged in his thirties explained of his father's country, 'that's my father's birth country. He was born there, was given that country by his old mother in laws, they gave him that country'. In another example, a mainland woman was promised in marriage to a senior man and *dulmada* of a particular country on the southern side of Mornington Island (McKnight 1999: 100). Although the couple had never married or had any children, the mainland woman asserted that the *dulmada* had promised his country to her eldest son (ibid.; McKnight 2002: 174). The son established an outstation on the country during the 1990s, and his sons (i.e. grandsons of the mainland woman) now assert *dulmada* status for the country (McKnight 1999: 100). These kinds of assertions and deviations from patrilineal descent based on gifting were liable to contestation because they relied on understandings reached with a (usually) deceased person at some point in the past (Memmott 1979: 72; McKnight 2002: 173). However, and as Sutton (2001b: 7) explained for Aboriginal land tenure across Australia, 'in time, such acts of individual succession would usually become the basis of the emergence of a replacement group holding country'. For

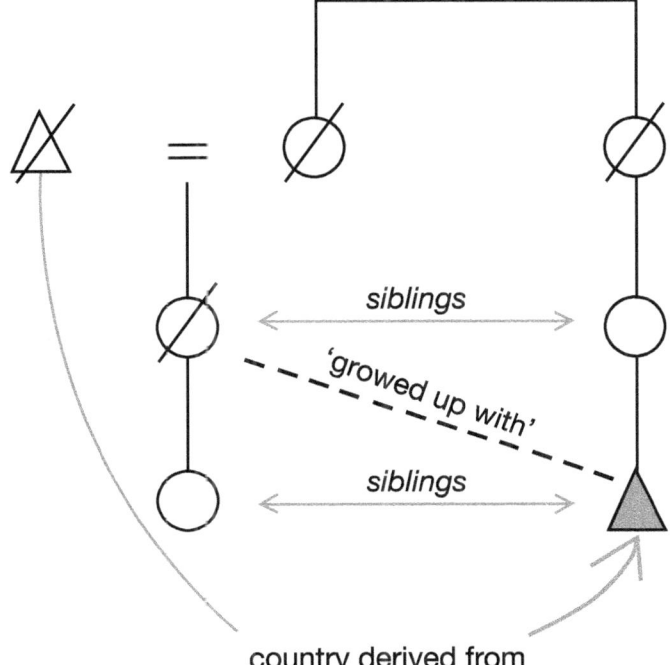

Figure 5.2. Genealogy showing the derivation of country from a classificatory grandfather (figure created by the author).

Lardil and Yangkaal, the 'replacement group' was in any case often related to the original group with primary rights.

Deriving country from one's father became problematic either when children had a White father, when their father was Aboriginal but from the mainland or when there was ambiguity about a child's paternity (Sutton 1998: 68).[8] Having an Aboriginal father from the mainland meant that one's patrilineal country was located a long way from Mornington Island, making it impractical to visit and difficult to remain connected with its ongoing management. In some of these cases, children instead claimed country through their mother's father (maternal grandfather). Although this could be described as matrilineal descent, i.e. through a person's mother, Aboriginal people living on Mornington Island almost always referred to this as being through their grandfather, emphasising male-to-male transmission. Male-to-male country inheritance was more closely matched to the ideal of patrilineal descent and was more readily accepted than if a person claimed country through their mother.

In another example, also referred to in a previous chapter, a man born in the 1960s discussed the implications on the descent of country of having two fathers: his 'biological father' and a man who had married his mother and 'grew him up from small' (see Figure 5.3). When I asked him: 'Who do you call 'father', or both?', he responded: 'Well, both. Both of them. Yeah, they all knew about that … but they didn't tell me, until I was little boy because my mother and father, they got married. That's when I'm born then'. As the man aged, his biological father's wife had begun to treat him as her own son – 'she call me her son' – and in later years, the man lived in a house with the woman and her sons (his biological half-brothers), who called him 'brother'. This relationship was further strengthened by the men all being of a similar age and the same skin group, and that they had similar interests as dancers in a local Aboriginal dance group and often went hunting together.

When it came to deriving rights in country, the man's (social) father was a Yangkaal man whose country was on Forsyth Island, while his (biological) father's country was on the Windward (southern) side of Mornington Island, in relatively close proximity to the community. In his estimation, the demonstration of relationships by his biological father's wife and his biological half-brothers had given him 'a bit' of rights to his biological father's country. At the same time, though, there was some ambiguity as to whether he would 'follow' his biological father or his social father when claiming country: 'Well I'm not really sure cause they never really gave it to me yet. I've just got to wait and see what part of the country I can have'. Partly this refers to the ongo-

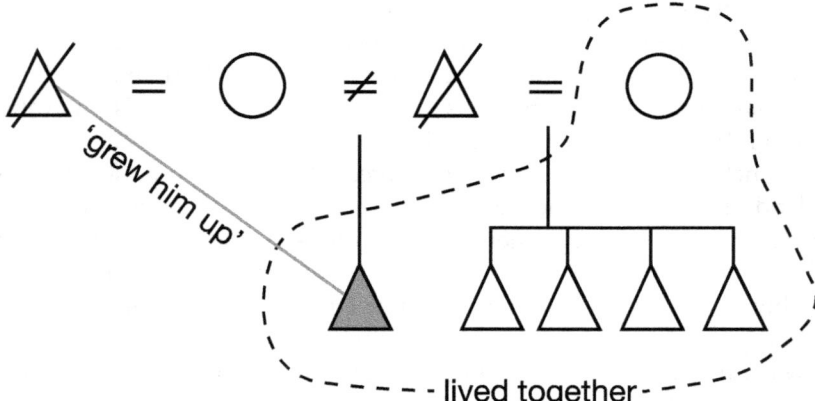

Figure 5.3. Genealogy showing relationships surrounding an Aboriginal man (in grey) (figure created by the author).

ing sifting that occurs in the determination of affiliations to particular estates or countries. At times, Mornington Islanders definitively and unreservedly attached themselves to a particular estate, but then with similar vigour also sought recognition for affiliations to another estate.

It could be argued that the multiple channels of claim used by Lardil and Yangkaal people in the North Wellesley Islands in the way that they derived ownership and rights to country represented a generalized shift away from patrilineal descent and toward cognatic descent. Yet there remained a gendered ideology that privileged transmission between closely related men, especially father to son and grandfather to grandson. The role of patrilineal descent, both in pre-contact times and during the 2000s, was a point of difference with the Kaiadilt of the South Wellesley Islands, who had a system of tenure and inheritance historically based on a person's place of birth.

Kaiadilt and the South Wellesley Islands

Unlike Lardil and Yangkaal people, at the time of their move to the Mornington Island Mission in 1948, Kaiadilt people claimed country based primarily on their place of birth. This system of country descent was defined by the linguist Nicholas Evans (1998: 4–5) as a response to the relatively small population of Kaiadilt people, estimated at 120 in 1948, and the limited land size of the South Wellesley Islands. Evans (ibid.: 5) suggested that these factors led to the formation of a 'more flexible land-holding system that lacks closed clan-group affiliations'. The focus on birth-affiliated connection to land meant that, unlike the Lardil and Yangkaal, Kaiadilt siblings with the same biological parents, often referred to as 'one mother, one father', did not necessarily share a primary affiliated country. This system was exemplified by two sisters with the same father but different mothers, born at different countries on Bentinck Island during the 1940s. One described how her grandmother (her mother's mother) purposefully chose the location of her birth: 'Me, I was born on the hillside … looking out to the sea … my grandmother took my mother to that place so I could claim that area, our great-grandfather's land and I own that land'. In the case of the other sister, the woman noted that despite her mother's intentions to give birth to her on the western side of Bentinck Island, she had ended up being born near a river on the eastern side:

> Well for me, my mother, she supposed to have me over there [on the western side of Bentinck Island] country, but family wanted to keep moving. Maybe

she had [labour] pains then, so we went to my country where my father was, and some other family went to the river to take fish, and my mother stayed up [awake] and then she had me where my birthplace is now.

Such was the link between place of birth and an individual's identity that a person's birthplace was one of the Kaiadilt language names given to them (Evans 2008: 57). For example, a child born at the place called *Rukuthi* would be called *Rukuthingathi*, or *Thuundi* would be named *Thuundingathi*, with the suffix *ngathi* meaning 'person of' (Evans 1998: 25). As Evans (ibid.: 24) described it, these names gave 'an instant index of affiliation to country'. Being born in country also gave a person[9] the role of *dulmarra dangka*, which prescribed much the same roles and responsibilities as the Lardil and Yangkaal *dulmada*. The relocation of Kaiadilt people to the Mornington Island Mission had particular implications (Evans 2016). As Kaiadilt people no longer had the opportunity to be born in country, the descent of rights was determined using other processes. An unusual event in country, for example, often involving animal encounters, presaged a woman's pregnancy and thus connected a child to the country where the event occurred (Evans 1998: 25). This process of being 'signed' in Kaiadilt country, however, also became more uncommon over time, as people spent the majority of their time on Mornington Island.

During an interview in 2008, five Kaiadilt women born between 1937 and 1946, who were among the last of those born in the South Wellesley Islands, emphasized the increasing role of cognatic descent in country transmission. That is, younger Kaiadilt who were neither born nor signed in the South Wellesleys claimed country affiliation via their descent from a relative who had been born there. As one of these women explained: 'They are descendants of us … we share'. In evidence given as part of the Wellesley Sea Claim, a senior Kaiadilt man (now deceased) noted that the transmission of country to younger generations was 'the right thing to do' (Bentinck 1999: paragraph 34). In some cases, this descent was cognatic in that it was traced variously through male and female ancestors until reaching a person who had been born in country. Thus, over a relatively short period of time, Kaiadilt people transitioned from a country inheritance system based primarily on the individual's place of birth to the formation of cognatic descent groups.

In addition to cognatic descent, willing or gifting country was an important part of the system (Evans 2016) and a recognition that, as a woman who had been born in country in 1942 explained, 'Every place needs to have someone to look after it … Where there are too many owners, they promise places to others' (N. Loogatha 1999: paragraph 80). This was partly explained as a way of ensuring that all places

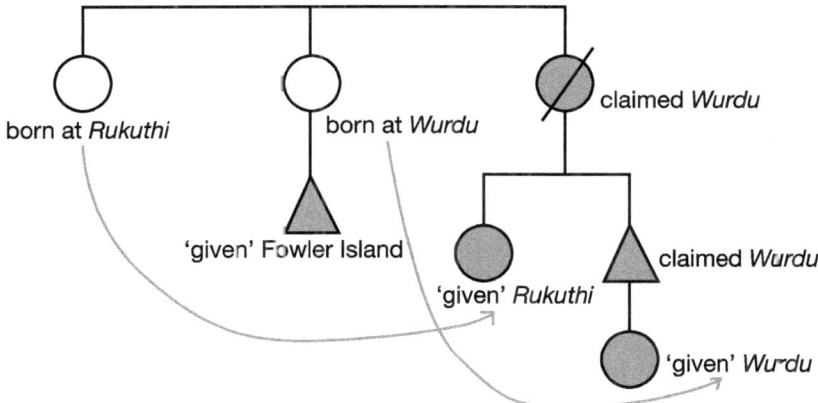

Figure 5.4. Genealogy showing the transmission of country affiliations among a close group of kin. Those in grey were born in places other than traditional Kaiadilt country (figure created by the author).

had someone to 'look after' them, but perhaps also a way of reducing the potential for disputes between those claiming a particular country. In some cases, the intermingling of cognatic descent and gifting resulted in seemingly complex derivations of country ownership, as was explained by another senior Kaiadilt woman (now deceased) in her affidavit given at the Sea Claim: 'My [eldest] sister, has given [my daughter] Oaktree Point [*Rukuthi*]. My country is *Wurdu*. It is given to [my son's] daughter … It was [my elder sister's] country. She was the second eldest sister. [Her son] … got Fowler Island. So [she] gave it [*Wurdu*] to [my son's] daughter' (O. Loogatha 1999: paragraph 27). These complex gifting and claiming relationships to country have been diagrammatically represented in a genealogy in Figure 5.4.

The efficacy of cognatic descent as a method of determining group identity was reinforced by the fact that most Kaiadilt shared a small number (approximately eight) of common surnames. Of these surnames, at least four were actually poorly translated versions of the place names in Kaiadilt country (Evans 1998: 29). For example, a man who was the *dulmarra dulk* of *Rukuthi*, a country on the northern tip of Bentinck Island, was given the surname 'Loogatha' by the missionary Reverend Robert Wilson. At least some of the man's descendants also carried this surname, and claim *Rukuthi* as their country as a result of their descent from the man. Although many Kaiadilt are no longer ascribed *ngathi* names, as those who had been born in country did, there was, for some at least, an ongoing connection between their surname and their country affiliation.

Choice and Continuity

As has been previously discussed, Mornington Islanders were not bound by single Aboriginal language group affiliations. Rather, the intermarriage of Lardil, Yangkaal and Kaiadilt people, and also with Aboriginal people from elsewhere (including Mainlanders) and Whitefellas, had become a ubiquitous feature of social relations in the contemporary context. This partnering also presented opportunities for multiple associations with country. A particular example of the complexity of country associations was a couple, Ian and Sue, both aged in their fifties, and their five children, ranging from teenagers to those aged in their late twenties, who lived on Mornington Island. The relationships described in this example are shown in Figure 5.5. Ian referred to himself as a 'full blood Kaiadilt' and claimed country at the northern end of Bentinck Island through his father and grandfather who had both been born in that country. One of Ian's older sisters, being 'from the same mother and father', had also been born in the same country, and they both carried the surname which was an English translation of the name of the country. Despite having been signed at a country on Mornington Island, Ian noted that he 'don't claim it'.

According to Sue, her father was Lardil and her mother was mixed-descent Lardil/Waanyi through Sue's Waanyi maternal grandmother. Sue claimed country on the Windward (southern) side of Mornington Island through her maternal grandfather, but also had rights to her father's country on the Leeward (northern) side. Ian explained that his children could claim country 'through their mother or my side'. In addition, Ian and Sue's youngest daughter was signed by a dugong in the channel between Bentinck and Sweers Island, and she subsequently retained rights there as well; however, her father Ian asserted that her claims to his country were 'more stronger'.

Despite the complexity of the derivations in this example, country identification was not entirely 'fluid' or solely a matter of choice among potentially endless possibilities. Rather, relationships with close kin, often those arising from what Sutton (1998: 68) described in the broader Australian context as 'consanguineal (blood) descent from antecedent landowners', provided a set of potential country affiliations, or multiple pathways through which each person could legitimately claim country. For each individual, there were connections which were considered 'more stronger' than others. In the North Wellesley Islands, there remained a potent ideology of male-to-male descent, while in

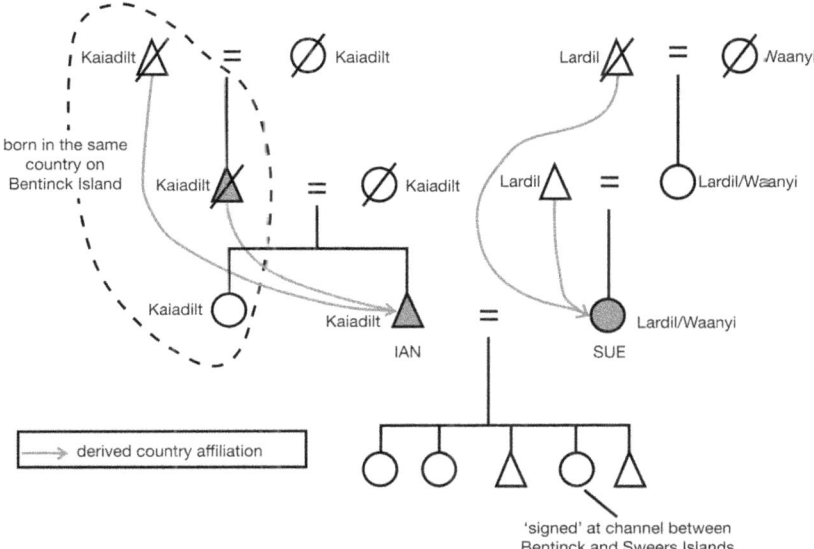

Figure 5.5. Genealogy showing the ways in which Ian, Sue (marked in grey) and their children derived country affiliation (figure created by the author).

the South Wellesleys, cognatic descent had become the primary means through which country was transmitted. In both contexts, the practice of willing or gifting had also given rise to interests in country beyond those inherited genealogically. Across all the various modes of country derivation, more often than not, was a way of cultivating connectedness to others, especially kin.

As Myers (1986: 128) detailed for the Pintupi of Central Australia, 'people view "country" as the objectification of kin networks and as a record of social ties'. One *dulmada* on Mornington Island described this 'record' in the following terms: 'It's important for us because, for our sons and their sons and their sons, all the way down that line ... one day they'll look back and say, "ah smart bastards, they're dead now but yeah, he done a good job"'. In this way, people were entwined with others, both living and deceased, through their affiliations to country. At the same time, such desires were in continual flux, balanced against those of personal autonomy (ibid.: 129) and a range of practical considerations that related to contemporary life in a very remote context. In the remainder of this chapter I consider some of these factors, starting with an exploration of authority as it varied between generations.

Authority and Country

Although I have already discussed the inherited nature of claims to country, the success or otherwise of individuals' or groups' assertions to country was also dependent on other factors. For example, the desirability of the place and the number of competing claims also impacted the success of those wishing to identify with a particular country. The potential for negotiation surrounding this process reflected Myers' (1986: 128) finding for the Pintupi Aboriginal people of the Western Desert that: 'Identification is an ongoing process, subject to claim and counterclaim, dependent on validation and acceptance or invalidation and nonacceptance'. Thus, while historical inheritance and kin connections provided pathways to ownership by establishing connections to particular counties, it remained up to the individual to maximize what Martin (1993: 247) called their 'personal qualities', specifically the assertion of authority, in such a way as to be recognized by others. In this regard, and as Chris Anderson (1988) titled a paper on Aboriginal authority at Bloomfield River in Cape York Peninsula, 'all bosses are not created equal'. Anderson's (ibid.: 508) contribution emphasized the importance of factors beyond those of 'age, sex, and kinship', which he identified as having typified previous studies in identifying those with authority on issues relating to country. However, on Mornington Island these factors did represent a starting point in terms of understanding the establishment of hierarchical relationships.

Broadly, the legitimacy given to claims to country on Mornington Island reflected a gendered hierarchy noted in Aboriginal Australia, with men assuming positions of authority in the public domain. There were situations during the 2000s where Aboriginal women were seen as having the rightful capacity to make decisions about the management of country. Some of these instances, though not all, were as McKnight (1999: 107) described for an earlier period: 'when a woman does not have a man to speak for her, then she may speak out in public and make decisions about her Country on an equal footing with men'. In one such example, the widow of a *dulmada*, herself the daughter of a very senior lawman, was acknowledged by others as (rightfully) making decisions about her husband's country. More generally, though, both men and women (in the latter case sometimes to their own detriment) asserted that it was men who were primarily empowered with authority in matters relating to country. The capacity of particular men to actualize this authority, however, was dependent on recognition by others that they were 'dominant men' (Gerritsen 1982: 21) or 'forceful individuals' (Austin-Broos 2003: 122).[10]

On Mornington Island, the authority of these individuals stemmed from similar traits to those identified by Anderson (1988: 516):[11] 'forcefulness, determination, articulateness and an ability to resolve issues for people, intelligence, political acumen, willingness to be aggressive and, perhaps most importantly, a *self*-conscious or a righteous belief in one's own importance' (emphasis in original). These qualities, although somewhat applicable to leadership in many contexts, were the foundation of assertiveness through which individuals activated claims to country. These traits alone, however, were not the sole determinants of an authoritative country identity. In older living generations, particularly those born in the 1930s and 1940s,[12] authority was grounded in the traditional cultural knowledge that a person held. This knowledge came through experiences of living 'out bush' prior to incorporation into the mission dormitories as a child (McKnight 2002: 52). Living out bush was associated with a genuine Lardil/Yankgaal/Kaiadilt identity:[13] that of knowing language, having gone through initiation and having been alive at the same time as the last generations of people who had lived entirely separate from settlement life (ibid.). Thus, their authority was based predominantly on the depth and complexity of their knowledge of country and of 'traditional culture'.

As Martin (1993: 226) found at Aurukun, it was these older individuals who had worked with anthropologists (on Mornington Island, David McKnight and Paul Memmott) to map important sites in country and record ceremonies. It was also their input that formed the basis of the Lardil and Kayardild language dictionaries by the linguists Ken Hale (Ngakulmungan Kangka Leman Language Projects Steering Committee 1997) and Nicholas Evans (1992) respectively. Some of these Aboriginal men, and a smaller number of Aboriginal women, had also acted in the past as cultural mediators between Whitefellas and Aboriginal people, through the export of their 'culture' to a wider Australian audience through dance, art and film (Memmott 1979: 307–10).

When discussing their country, those of the older generation often began by sequentially reciting the individual places within their country. When I asked Cyril Moon, for example, where his country was, he responded:

Lelka Murrin, Gununwukaun. Right up la *Dadgigbigun* right lung *Nunguwa*. *Gununjaddi*. *Mirrahgud*. From *Mirrahgud* to *Mudbunthundbah*. *Mudbunthundbah*, *Lingkale*, *Lingkale*, *Juwi*, *Lingkale*, *Juwi*, *Dedrangkun*, what this place? *Minalgun*. *Whadhidguhn*. *Wradidguhn*. All that country. *Bilmudgun*, *Dulgenberra*, *Dulgenbudda*, *Neyithalan*, *Wirrajerra*. *Wirrajerra*, that far.[14]

Although recitals of place names in local Aboriginal languages (here in Lardil) were a relatively frequent occurrence among those of Cyril's generation, those of the younger generation tended to respond to such questions with one or two language names in their country, usually the location of an outstation or major story place. Often these place names had been anglicized, a particular example being the place recorded by McKnight and in the Lardil dictionary as *Kanba*, now usually pronounced as 'Gun Bar' by many Aboriginal people. A man born in 1970, whose father had been a pivotal leader in regional initiation ceremonies, reflected on the loss of detail in country knowledge among those of his own and subsequent generations. He explained:

> See some of these young fellas on this Island they don't know nothing about their history, like where they're really family from and what part of the land they own, some of them young fellas miss out and they don't know. They just only know the places but they don't know where their mother and father and their grandfather come from. They all think that they're just from one, like their mother side or father side. But they got two different grandmothers like for their father side and their mother side. They can go to their father country or to their mother country. From their grandmother and grandfather side. Maybe they don't, see none of them fellas not like showing them what part of the country where they're from and where them story places and what the name of them places. Some of these places thinking now got some English, some of them got bit of a language, Lardil language name.

Among persons of this man's generation – those born from about the 1960s to the early 1980s[15] – authority depended less on their knowledge of country or association with a particular 'tribal identity' and more on their exhibition of leadership qualities similar to those identified by Anderson (1988). These qualities, primarily exuberance for political manoeuvring, were exemplified in their capacity to orate in public contexts. Their willingness to 'speak up', particularly in the presence of government representatives, demonstrated their ability to interpret and represent the opinions of the community with confidence and tenacity.[16] Their identification by outsiders as a 'leader' went some way to similar recognition among Aboriginal people. Likewise, their ability to successfully intervene in social conflicts among similarly aged kin garnered them support that they also relied on to bolster their claims to particular country identities. These traits were often clustered in particular sibling groups, perhaps indicating the role of parental socialization in leadership building. For example, in one sibling group of three brothers (of one mother and one father) born in the 1970s, one was the Chairperson of the local Aboriginal land council and another was the Mayor of the local shire council.

Figure 5.6. Cyril Moon talks to the Wellesley Islands Rangers about country, September 2007 (photograph by the author).

It was because of both the breadth and depth of their knowledge that particular people in Cyril Moon's generation (born in the 1930s and 1940s) were deferred to on matters relating to country, particularly when disputes arose. In such disputes, younger people would often evoke the name of an older person when contextualizing their own position on a matter: 'X told me', and 'he/she would know'. Conversely, in asserting their own knowledge, an older person might similarly say, 'He/she only little boy/girl longside me', referring to their age in terms of size as a factor of their knowledge of cultural information. One example of this was during a journey out bush in 2007 with the Wellesley Islands Rangers and Cyril Moon, as shown in Figure 5.6.

On the trip, Cyril talked at length about the historical complexities of individuals' associations with countries, as well as the complex genealogical relationships between people. His position facing the men, and his upright posture, demonstrated his confidence and authority in the situation. In other subsequent situations when I was present, the Rangers referred to the occasion and the kinds of information that had been imparted. Thus, exchanges such as this formed a part of an individual's structural understanding of the transmission of country, to be drawn upon and recounted in future exchanges. Equally important were the connections formed and re-formed through trips out on country, a practice often described as 'going bush'.

Creating Knowledge and Asserting Ownership of Country by 'Going Bush'

Mornington Islanders' most immersive experiences of country were when they 'went bush', travelling out to various parts of the Wellesley Islands by four-wheel-drive vehicle, boat or on foot, on weekends, after work or when there was little else to do in town. Going bush was important in establishing what Myers (1986: 128) described as a 'dialectical' relationship between land use and ownership, in which using country reinforced one's connection with it. During the 2000s, I made over eighty separate trips out bush with Aboriginal families and the Wellesley Islands Rangers, travelling by four-wheel-drive vehicle to almost every individual country on Mornington Island. This also included travel further afield to Sydney, Denham, Forsyth, Andrew, Bentinck, Fowler, Sweers and Douglas Islands by small charter plane and boat.

Weekend trips were often undertaken in convoy, a number of four-wheel-drive vehicles or boats travelling together with a range of kin, or a family group. Trips such as these often included a *dulmada* and their immediate kin, partner and children, while other cars might include close peripheral kin such as aunts, uncles and cousins who were 'following' the owners. Thus, a typical discussion between two people arranging a trip 'out bush' might proceed as follows:

Where you f'la going?

Mekigian [name of a country], beach side [identifying the part of the country to be visited].

Oh well, we might follow then?

Yeah, well go on then [i.e. yes, you may].

The request to 'follow' was both a form of asking permission,[17] with the implicit recognition of a person's position as a primary owner of the place, and a logistical arrangement. Thus, the accompanying kin were both literally 'following' the *dulmada* and his family in their car, as well as 'following' in a metaphorical sense of deferring to their knowledge of and connection to the country. In 2009, I recorded a typical setting for a day out bush with Tom, a *dulmada* for a country at the top end of Mornington Island, and members of his extended family (shown in Figure 5.7).

> Tom told me a few good fishing tips and we had a good old yarn while we pulled up fish – rock cod, parrot fish, snappers. The middle sized kids [aged] 8+ were running around the rocks cracking oysters and spearing crabs in the shallows. After a couple hours we all retreated up to the shade where all the women and kids had set up camp. There were three fires going … a main one used by Jean [Tom's wife], Jean's father, Jean's younger brother and his wife and all their children. Then Anne had a small one up behind that for her and Zack [her de facto] and Louise [their daughter] and then Angie had one for their whole car further along from that. Each fire had its own billy and most were cooking their fish they'd caught.

Although the emphasis of these excursions was for people to be in country together, as was the case in this example, kin did not necessarily share the same activity space. As in the example above, when a number of families travelled to a country together, separate cooking fires would often be lit in proximity, usually along a beach.[18] The establishment of different fires allowed kin to cook and consume their own food and be 'together but separate' (Austin-Broos 2010: 155). Separate fires also facilitated more selective sharing of food with others (Memmott 1979: 149), as to produce food in the immediate presence of kin or others, especially children, created an expectation that sharing would

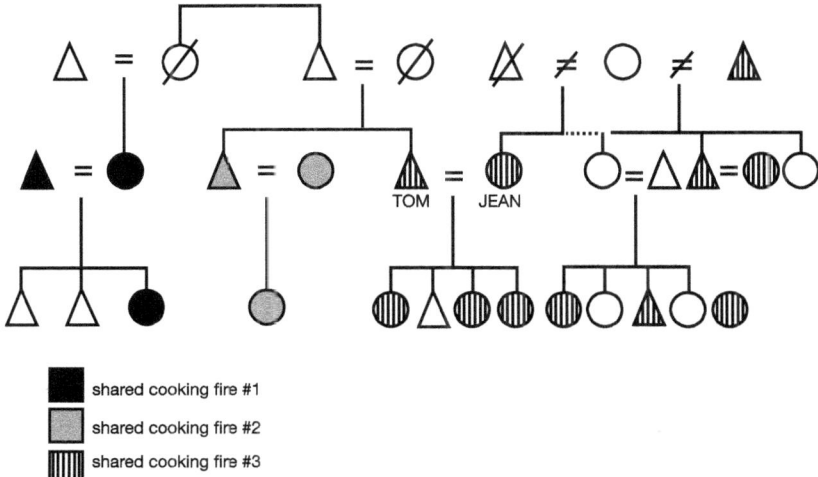

Figure 5.7. Genealogy of a typical day out bush, identifying which kin shared cooking fires (figure created by the author).

occur.[19] This was not necessarily a case of trying to maliciously obscure food consumption from others, but more to avoid awkward situations where particular individuals had access to a food while others did not. These situations particularly related to food that had been caught or collected out bush, which was more highly prized than store-bought food.[20] For the same reason, fishing was often undertaken quietly, with large or favoured fish quickly placed into a bag or bucket to evade the requests of kin demanding a share (see also Myers 1988: 59 for another example of hiding food). Peterson's (1993) writing on 'demand sharing' similarly illustrates these points across a variety of other Australian contexts.

The establishment of separate fires in some cases also reflected the observance of avoidance relationships, described for Lardil culture in the pre-contact period as those 'essentially affinal relationships' (McKnight 1999: 38). Historically, these relationships were affines of the opposite sex; for a man, for example, this included his wife's mother, wife's sister and son's wife, while for a woman, her husband's father, husband's brother and daughter's husband would all be classed as avoidance relations. Brothers and sisters were also in an avoidance relationship, particularly once they had reached adulthood (ibid.: 34). In the more recent period, however, such rules were selectively observed, and I only witnessed avoidance among some kin of the opposite sex, notably mother-in-law/son-in-law and some brother/sister relationships. As was previously the case, such affines 'avoid physical contact and eye contact, conversation is kept to a minimum ... communication is mainly through the children or is feigned to be through the children' (ibid.: 41). One way for those in avoidance relationships to communicate was to speak an observation or request loudly such that anyone nearby could hear. When 'out bush', these kin often sat apart, facing away from one another, or at different fires, and rarely shared food. A man aged in his late thirties once described to me how he had 'kicked out' the fire where he and his de facto partner were sitting when his partner's mother (mother-in-law) had joined them at the fire.

Although often using separate fires, kin, and women especially, would share utensils and basic food staples: a wire rack for cooking fish, salt for seasoning fish, hot water from a boiling billy to make tea, sugar and so on. Instrumental in these exchanges were children, especially girls, who acted as go-betweens, ferrying items between adults. Large numbers of children were a mainstay of trips out bush, usually outnumbering adults by a factor of at least two to one. In a single trip out bush in 2007, my Toyota 'Troop Carrier' (with a usual maximum capacity of eleven) contained a total of five adults and nine children.

Figure 5.8. Children cooking and eating mud shells that they had helped to collect during a trip out bush, June 2009 (photograph by the author).

This ratio partly reflected the fact that parents often sent their children out with other families going bush in order to give themselves a 'rest'. Sometimes non-drinkers, or adults who had not consumed alcohol on a previous evening, would take out the children of kin who were 'grog sick' (i.e. hungover) in order to let the parents recover. The participation of children in trips out bush enabled them to be socialized into behaviours at a young age, so that many were proficient at fishing and collecting their own bush foods by the time they were eight or nine years old.

These trips were also an opportunity for adults to show children particular places in country, as Tom explained: 'Ah yeah I show them [his children] where the sacred sites are. Show them the burial sites'. These physical places were sometimes imbued in some way with the essence of mythic beings, often animals but also humans, who had traversed the landscape during the mythic past. The stories associated with these places varied in complexity, from the relatively one-dimensional, for example a Dugong story place with the name being the extent of the story, to elaborate narratives involving multiple creatures interacting to create a range of features across a landscape. For example, at *Neyithalan* on the north-eastern side of Mornington Island, there was a creek lined with stones said to be the scales of the Rainbow Serpent *Thuwathu*, which he shed as he writhed in pain after having been set on fire by his sister (McKnight 1999: 87). It was said that *Thuwathu* then travelled to *Bukakan* where he died, leaving a freshwater spring (ibid.). *Neyithalan* and *Bukakan* were connected to a much broader landscape of story places associated with *Thuwathu*, which tracked through the sea and around the Wellesley Islands and Mornington Island in particular.

Knowledge of story places (and the accompanying narratives) varied between generations, but also between those who regularly travelled out into different countries and those who stayed predominantly in the community. Older people in general had more intricate bodies of knowledge about story places and of the language names associated with them, knowledge acquired over long periods of time. This complexity was matched by very few younger people, who tended only to retain the one-dimensional elements of stories and who lacked the self-confidence in storytelling of older people. Partly, this may reflect the intergenerational loss of Aboriginal languages, and also the increasing orientation of younger people towards community life and away from life 'out bush'. Even without the detailed knowledge of more senior people, though, younger people were well aware of a number of aspects of behaviour that were important while being out bush. Swearing, whistling and 'makin noise' were seen as inappropriate, and women who were breastfeeding or pregnant were often said to cause bad luck for those fishing. Aboriginal people believed that showing children sites in country and modelling appropriate behaviour maintained a connection to Aboriginal law; as one man put it, 'cause it's our law, not to break those rules'.

The most commonly known law related to *markirii* (also spelled *malkri*), the belief that eating certain types of food, ostensibly 'land foods' but particularly meat and animal fats,[21] before touching saltwater could cause stomach complaints, bloating and constipation (as discussed extensively by McKnight 1999: Chapter 11; Memmott 1979: 213–26, 1982).[22] The cause of this discomfort was the spirit being *Thuwathu*, the Rainbow Serpent, whose essence patrolled the seas and could be angered by strangers polluting the water. In order to avoid *markirii*, a person washed their hands and mouth with freshwater before going fishing or touching the saltwater. As noted earlier, when a person claimed a country, their essence was said to be intimately tied to that country, thus protecting them from *markirii*. As an Aboriginal man aged in his late thirties explained: 'I can do anything, I can walk, well we got a way that saying *markirii* and stuff, but I can get a butter or something and go in the water and I'll never get *markirii* because I'm from that land. If a stranger do that yeah he'll be shitting feathers[23] for the rest of his week. He'll have a very bad experience you know'.

The concentration of settlement in Gununa resulted in a reduction in the amount of time spent in particular parts of Mornington Island and the other Wellesley Islands. Places that were not regularly visited were often thought of as being particularly 'dangerous', partly because a person could upset mythic beings by unknowingly disturbing story places that lay dormant in the landscape. There was also a sense in which the failure to transmit knowledge about a story place and to visit it regularly was a lapse in obligations to country and a failure to treat it with an appropriate level of respect.

Most of the South Wellesley Islands, including parts of Bentinck Island, were considered in this category of place, particularly by Lardil and Yangkaal people, owing to their depopulation in the 1940s when the Kaiadilt people were relocated to the Mornington Island Mission (Evans 2008: 57). Following this relocation, Bentinck Island remained devoid of permanent occupants until the outstation movement returned Kaiadilt people there during the mid-1980s (ibid.: 58). In 2007, during a trip with the Wellesley Islands Rangers, the Lardil and Yangkaal Rangers often objected to visiting particular places on Bentinck Island because as they put it, 'I don know the story for this place'. During the same trip, late one evening while sitting around a campfire at the outstation settlement at Nyinyilki, a red light (later found to be emanating from a small barge) became visible on the horizon. Interpreting the light as a (potentially malevolent) spirit being, all of the eight Rangers ran inside a nearby house and locked the front door.

This contrasted with people's connections to their own country, as one of the Rangers explained, discussing how he felt when he went to his own country on Mornington Island: 'First time I went up there I felt a presence ay, you know, your home. Heard lot of people say "one scary country" but when I went there I just felt so at home'. At the same time, however, Aboriginal people were actively creating new histories and stories for places in country, often based on unusual or humorous events. For example, new stories were created around a place where a family spent the night out under the stars after bogging their car. Going 'out bush' was a way of generating experience and creating knowledge, thus reinforcing a relationship with country beyond that which was transmitted through descent. While a person might claim a particular country, it was the expression of connection through visitation that strengthened others' perceptions of that ownership.

Access to Country, Access to Cars and Boats

In other parts of Australia, colonial settlement and the extension of private land tenure have contributed to the dislocation of Aboriginal people from their traditional lands (Babidge 2010: 2–3; Trigger 1992). In those parts of Australia, Aboriginal people's experiences with country are often limited to access via more formalized engagements with private land holders, such as through cultural heritage surveys, or through employment on pastoral properties or with mining companies. This formalization has impacted on the types of activities carried out, the knowledge of country and the potential for rights and ownership to be formally recognized. In contrast, and as I have already described, Aboriginal rights have been recognized over the vast majority of the Wellesley Islands, through the Wellesley Sea Claim and subsequent land claim (NNTT 2004, 2009). Although the restrictions of private ownership that operate in other parts of Australia did not exist in the Wellesley Islands, other factors impacted on individuals' ability to access their country, the most significant being the availability of transport.

In other parts of Australia, anthropologists have explored the ways in which Aboriginal people engage with 'things' or resources which connect them in particular ways to their country (Austin-Broos 2003; Myers 1988; Redmond 2006). One facet of these studies has been discussion of the role of 'trucks' (usually four-wheel-drive vehicles), purchased by the state and used by Aboriginal people to access land to which they derived particular affiliations (Myers 1988; Redmond 2006). The importance of transport in remote parts of Australia, and the degree to which such resources were communally owned, converged in negotiations between Aboriginal people about their use and control of transportation. Unlike in some of these locations, such as with the Arrernte in Central Australia, who used lease payments derived from mining activities (Austin-Broos 2010: 193–95) to fund outstations, Aboriginal people on Mornington Island and the surrounding North Wellesley Islands had no ongoing funding to assist with upkeep or transportation. In 2006 and 2007 particularly,[24] the high cost of purchase, barge transport[25] to the Island and operating costs limited the number of privately owned four-wheel-drives and boats. At the 2006 Census, 117 of the total 214 private dwellings on Mornington Island did not have a vehicle (ABS 2006: Table B29). Of the 97 private dwellings which did have a vehicle, a proportion of these (I would estimate approximately half) were Whitefella residences, which almost always had their own vehicles. While living there in 2007, I was able to identify all of the cars on the Island and their owners, and some I could even identify by the sound of the engine alone (when indoors for example).

One way in which Mornington Islanders could afford the purchase of cars and boats was through the use of one-off government payments such as tax returns, the 'baby bonus' (a government payment to new mothers) and amounts paid as restitution and compensation. Between 1995 and 2009, one examples of these cash payments was criminal injury compensation, payments made under the *Criminal Offence Victims Act (Qld) 1995*.[26] Under the Act, victims of serious crimes against the person[27] such as assault, grievous bodily harm and attempted manslaughter were sometimes eligible for one-off payouts to a maximum of AUD 75,000. In one publicized case, a Mornington Island woman shot twice in the back by her husband was awarded AUD 25,000 (Forster 1999: 13). In another example, a Mornington Island woman was ordered to pay her mother criminal compensation of AUD 21,000 after stabbing her in the back in 2007 (Flatley 2011). In at least two other instances that I was aware of, both involving young women, these large one-off payments were reportedly used to purchase four-wheel-drive vehicles.

Another type of restitution was 'Stolen Wages' payouts made by the Queensland Government to Aboriginal people born on or before 1951 who had worked as government employees and for whom the government had retained a percentage of their wages (Queensland Government Department of Communities 2010b). The first payment, of AUD 4,000 in 2007, was followed by a secondary payment of AUD 3,000 in 2008 (ibid.). One elderly couple used their payments to buy a utility vehicle and another man used the money to buy an aluminium dinghy and outboard motor. The most well-known and commercially successful art painter on the Island, whose works were sold for between AUD 9,000 and AUD 60,000, sometimes bought vehicles for her children and grandchildren.

Money gained as a windfall was also used in the same way. Neil and Clare (a couple discussed in Chapter 3) described their car ownership since the birth of their eldest child in 2004: 'When we first moved back here when [my eldest son] was small, we had a Subaru and bought it for [AUD] 1,500 but … it broke. We didn't have a car for four years. We went to Mount Isa for a meeting and went to the pokies and I ended up winning [AUD]12,490 … We ended up going to Brisbane and buying a car'. Other young couples, including three couples aged in their thirties, purchased four-wheel-drive vehicles on finance and paid it off over subsequent years. The remoteness of many countries on Mornington Island and the quality of the roads meant that most were only accessible by four-wheel-drive vehicle or boat.

In spite of the centrality of transport in visiting areas outside the town, some asserted their determination in maintaining connection. Tom described his country as 'one of the places that is rarely touched from outsiders, or even locals, yeah. Kinda winding little road. No one wants to go there with their flash car'. However, when questioned if that had made it difficult for his family to access their country he replied: 'Nah. Ah mate, if I make my mind up to go there, I'm going there, no matter what it takes'. Mornington Islanders were indeed extremely resourceful in mobilizing the resources of kin to access country. For example, two women, both aged in their fifties, both explained how they sought out lifts to country with their close kin, especially their children, often rotating such requests across different weekends.

For Aboriginal people who identified their country as being in the South Wellesley Islands, visiting was more onerous owing to the distance, about three hours by boat or 15 minutes in a small charter plane, from Mornington Island. A Kaiadilt man aged in his fifties noted how the journey impacted on his ability to spend time in his country: 'Yeah it make it hard to look after it ... I find it hard to go across sometimes. I haven't got a [outboard] motor yet. We borrow the one belong to [my mother-in-law]. It's hard, even by plane, gotta use opportunities to get over there'. The opportunities the man referred to were the boats and small planes sometimes chartered by government agencies (and researchers) to visit Bentinck Island. Government agencies provided essential services, such as health care, to a small number of Kaiadilt people residing semi-permanently on the Island, and spare seats were sometimes offered to others wishing to visit. During the wet season, access around all of the Wellesley Islands was considerably reduced, as most of the roads, especially on Mornington Island, were cut off, the airstrip on Bentinck Island became unusable because of the heavy rains and the seas in the Gulf of Carpentaria were often too rough for boat travel.

In understanding the factors that contributed to Aboriginal people's access to country, Austin-Broos (2003: 119), following on from Myers (1988: 65–68), argued that for the Arrernte, 'their objectifications of self, or their "identities", come not only from engagements with places but also through an engagement with things'. These 'things' included 'cars, nondurables, and cash', which were used to 'make places interesting' (Austin-Broos 2003: 119). Following from Austin-Broos, the Mornington Island case demonstrates how country can also be mediated by the access that people have to it. As a consequence, cars and boats, i.e. forms of transport used to access country, were highly valued by Aboriginal people primarily because of their scarcity. Nevertheless, going out bush was a vital part of maintaining an interest in a country, and also allowed the owners of country to check on any unapproved visits made by others – or as McKnight (2002: 169) explained, it 'established people's claim on their Country and checked interlopers'. Sometimes the activities of these 'interlopers', those who visited country without permission, precipitated disputes with those who considered themselves to be the legitimate owners.

Asserting Ownership, Restricting Access and Contestations in Country

Shared experiences of country, and the generosity of allowing others to visit when requests were made, were an important ethic among Mornington Islanders. This principle was based at least in part on the historical movements of people through different countries to visit family, or to access particular resources (Memmott 1979: 466). During an interview in 2007, Cyril Moon remembered these travels during the 1940s when he was a child. He began by telling me:

> When they go visit from different camp-to-camp, travel the bush, they used to go visit countrymen, people, families.
>
> *You remember that from when you were a small boy?*
>
> Yeah.
>
> *They used to take you?*
>
> Yeah. I used to be la [on] my father's shoulder. My father used to carry me la shoulder before.
>
> *When you were a small boy?*
>
> Yeah.
>
> *And you used to travel round and see different families?*
>
> Oh yeah. Different family, our families.

Despite this generalized ethic of sharing country and of visiting others, Mornington Islanders also emphasized the importance of seeking permission to access country. During the Wellesley Sea Claim of the late 1990s, evidence in the form of affidavits from Aboriginal witnesses illustrated the potential for conflict to arise when those visiting country, both Aboriginal people and Whitefellas, failed to adequately seek permission from those that asserted primary interests (e.g. Jacob 1999: paragraphs 71, 72). One instance reportedly resulted in rounds of gunfire being discharged in the air by Aboriginal persons when a group of Whitefellas in a fishing boat ventured close to Bentinck Island without obtaining permission (Yarrak 2000: paragraph 28).

In 2006 and 2007, there was rarely such intense disputes relating to country. From time to time, Mornington Islanders would grumble privately about others, both Aboriginal people and Whitefellas, accessing their country without permission, although such complaints were seldom aired publicly (see also McKnight 2002: 56). However, in the years following the closure of the Pub in 2008, Mornington Islanders themselves commented on the larger numbers of people purchasing four-wheel-drive vehicles.[28] One outcome of this was an increase in on-country activities, particularly on weekends and also on weekday afternoons when many had previously been drinking at the Pub. As I described in Chapter 4, country had also become a preferred place for drinking illicit alcohol, away from the demands of kin and the scrutiny of the police. The increased time being spent on country resulted in more decisive management, which sometimes led to contestation. These decisions were often the attempt of one claiming group of people to restrict others' access to their country (see example in McKnight 2002: 174). In one example, a man aged in his thirties who was affiliated with an area in proximity to the town erected a barricade across the main access road into his country.

The sign spray-painted on a piece of wood read 'NO PERMISSION NO ACCESS', alerting people that they should not enter unless they had sought permission from the country's owners. In an interview, the man explained that he had put up the barricade because on a number of trips out to his country, he had found rubbish 'at his family's camp' left by 'outsiders' (Whitefellas) and 'locals too' (Aboriginal people). The man had also found it difficult to get his 'own feed' of fish and crabs (usually abundant) because of what he described as overfishing by others. In contextualizing his actions, the man referred to the authority bestowed in him by his late father to manage the country. As he explained:

> I put a gate across the road. The other family members I told them, 'I'm going to put a gate across', because this that and the other thing happening

when I'm not out there. Yeah, I put a gate up there cause when Dad was alive he said that us boys, we had to maintain the river system. There's still a bit of friction about it. I don't care, that's my father's birth country. He was born there, was given that country by his old mother-in-laws, they gave him that country.

Thus, the establishment of the barrier was both a performative expression of ownership and a judgement about the use of the country by others.

In another example later in 2008, an older man, who was also the *dulmada* of a different country on the north-eastern side of Mornington Island, attempted to restrict access by declaring the country 'CLOSED to the community' on a sign posted outside the Mornington Shire Council offices in town. The sign went on to explain: 'If you have NO ties this Land or are NOT part of the Family Clan Group, you have NO authorisation to enter the ROADS to ACCESS this LAND and AREA'.

In 2010, a more divisive situation occurred on the southern side of Mornington Island when an access track to a favourite drinking spot was fenced off. As in the previous example, those who put the fence up were reportedly concerned about the 'mess being left' there by drinkers. As in the other examples, the fence did not actually prevent access as it was possible to drive around it, but served as a distinct reminder of the ownership of country. When another man, who also claimed the same country, went to visit, he reportedly tore down the fence using heavy machinery. The dispute escalated into threats of violence between two families, with each disputing the legitimacy of the other to make decisions about country, and was eventually referred to mediation at the police station. A woman from one of the families involved expressed relief at the mediated outcome, noting that it could have become much more serious with 'proper' fighting (in this instance meaning physical) among the young men from opposing families. During this time, a number of Aboriginal people from Mornington Island contacted me seeking recorded information that identified the 'real owners' of the particular country.[29]

Putting up non-restricting fencing and signs was an assertion of the exclusivity of country ownership and was often associated with overt expressions of autonomy; 'I don't care [what others think]'. These contestations also highlighted the ways in which the ethic of 'caring for country' was socially mediated and inextricably linked to questions of ownership and claim. That is to say that Aboriginal people used discourses about caring for country as justification for the exclusion of others.

Outstations, Infrastructure and Aspirational Statements

> I really want to go up there and stay one day.

Country was the focus of many aspirational comments by Mornington Islanders. The ability of people to realize these aspirations was linked to the presence or otherwise of housing and infrastructure on their country, often referred to as 'homelands' and 'outstations'. The building of outstations for and by Aboriginal people across Australia began in the Northern Territory in the 1960s, and was linked to the realization of self-determining forms of governance through which Aboriginal people could achieve social and economic autonomy by living off their land (Altman 2006: 1; B.R. Smith 2005: 228). In 1987, a review by the Standing Committee on Aboriginal Affairs recommended that 'the Commonwealth Government continue to provide "seeding" funding for the establishment of new homeland centres' (Commonwealth of Australia 1987: xvii). In the early 1990s, the Mornington Shire Council and the Federal Government (through ATSIC) funded outstations at about eight locations around Mornington Island, as well as another three on Bentinck, Denham and Forsyth Islands (Memmott 1998: 130). A valuable development associated with the construction of outstations was the cutting of roads across Mornington Island and to a lesser extent Bentinck Island, which dramatically improved accessibility. Using existing infrastructure, other outstations were subsequently established by Aboriginal people themselves, using materials salvaged from around the community and from the Mornington Shire Council stores (ibid.: 130–31).

The number of people living in outstations across Australia has varied widely, but for the Wellesley Islands, at the 'peak circa 1995 there were about 130 people living in 29 outstations' (McKnight 2002: 170).[30] From 1995 to the late 1990s, there was a gradual decrease in the number of people residing permanently at outstations (ibid.: 171) and by 2006, I was only aware of four (three on Mornington Island and one on Bentinck Island) occupied with any regularity. During the 2000s I visited twenty-four outstations, of a total of twenty-seven across the Wellesley Islands, each equipped with infrastructure ranging from a single tin shed to small-scale settlements with a number of separate prefabricated dwellings. Most consisted of a single steel-framed shed clad in colourbond steel and raised slightly off the ground with a wood floor deck and interior, without electricity or running water.

By 2010, the number of people living with any regularity in outstations had again decreased, as two couples and their dependants, who had been living in two of the outstations, were granted new and renovated houses in the Gununa community (see Chapter 3 for a discussion of the allocation of housing). For one of the couples, aged in their thirties, this decision was precipitated by one of their young sons being bitten by a snake, prompting an emergency dash to the hospital in the community and out on a Royal Flying Doctor Service (RFDS) plane to Mount Isa. The incident meant that the couple were given priority on the housing waiting list and they relocated to the community shortly thereafter. The move into the community gave both couples better access to basic services, such as the hospital, store and school, the latter being especially important as both couples cared for school-aged children.

By 2010 most of the outstation infrastructure around the Wellesley Islands that I visited had fallen into disrepair, ravaged by white ants, fire and cyclones, overgrown with weeds, corroded by salty air and sometimes vandalized. There were also some instances in which outstations that were seldom visited, or had been owned or occupied by an absent or deceased person, were subsequently unfit for occupation.[31] Unsurprisingly, Mornington Islanders who slept out bush on weekends or holidays usually preferred to camp on the beach in the cool breeze or around a fire rather than in the outstation buildings. This suggests a somewhat different perspective on outstations to what was described by Altman as follows: 'Infrastructure, of course, is more concerned with places than people … because infrastructure, once constructed, exists in places irrespective of whether people are there or not' (Altman 2006: 9). In the case of the Wellesley Islands, however, the remote and harsh environmental conditions meant that 'once constructed', infrastructure required ongoing maintenance to preserve it as suitable or desirable for occupation.

Aboriginal people often contextualized their reason for not living in country or spending more time there as being due to insufficient infrastructure, specifically housing. A man aged in his late thirties, whose country was located at the furthest end of Mornington Island from the community, described his living situation during a visit on his country: 'I don't really like town [Gununa] much but you gotta live there. If I can live out here somewhere I'd be the happiest man on earth. I'm waiting on some other money, just [to] put me a decent house up there. Yeah ah one day I'll have a house. One day my dream will come true, but it's all "one day". At the moment I'm just taking things day by day'.

Similarly, in 2008, I interviewed a Kaiadilt man aged in his fifties about the construction of outstations on Bentinck Island. The man recalled how in the mid-1980s, seven houses were built at *Nyinyilki*, or 'Main Base' as it became known, on the southern side of Bentinck Island. Another house and a radio tower were also established at other parts of the island (Evans 1998: 50). Each of the outstations was built for a specific person or persons at their request, and thus my first question (as indicated in italics) had been:

Did you ask for a house?

No.

How come you didn't ask for a house?

Cause really I wanted a house up at Oak Tree Point [on his country].

So you were holding out?

Yeah.

You've been holding out for a long time!

Until something happens.

You think they will build houses there?

Probably.

When the man visited Bentinck Island in the meantime, he stayed with one of his sisters who lived at the main outstation at *Nyinyilki*.

In the more than 20 years since outstations first began to be built in the Wellesley Islands, no new outstations have been established. However, works have been undertaken by government-funded organizations to provide labour, tools and materials to assist in the redevelopment of existing outstations. In 2005 and 2006, for example, an organization called Bushlight installed three energy systems each valued at over AUD 100,000 at outstations on Mornington Island. In information about the projects, Bushlight (2005, 2006a, 2006b) stressed how the provision of the energy systems was connected to Aboriginal people's aspirations to live in their 'homelands'. One of these outstations was described as being '29kms from the main township of Gununa', and a place where the family often 'live a quiet and traditional lifestyle on their homelands' (Bushlight 2006a: 1).

In another project, an affiliated organization, the Centre for Appropriate Technology (CAT), in collaboration with the not-for-profit group Engineers Without Borders (EWB), undertook a development project on Bentinck Island in 2008 (Grant 2008: 7). Using salvaged materials, vol-

Figure 5.9. Plaque on Bentinck Island commemorating the establishment of Stage One Outstation at Main Base, *Nyinyilki* (photograph by the author).

unteers and Aboriginal workers built an amenities block and repaired damage to a single men's quarters which had become overgrown and had been vandalized (ibid.). The CAT/EWB project involved complex logistics in getting volunteer students and Kaiadilt people to Bentinck Island to assist with the building. The small settlement on Bentinck Island had been one of the first outstations in the Wellesley Islands, a project described on a plaque commemorating its partial completion as: 'Fulfilling a dream of the Kaiadilt people to return to their homeland' (see Figure 5.9).

Also in 2008, the Queensland Government built a new health centre on Bentinck Island at a reported cost (including construction) of AUD 3,000,000. Despite the outlay on infrastructure, the health centre was never staffed, though health workers visiting from Mount Isa reportedly used it intermittently. Between 2006 and 2010, Bentinck Island had a population of between four and eight elderly Kaiadilt women who lived on the island for between six and nine months of the year, generally in the dry seasons, with younger kin intermittently visiting from Mornington Island. An elderly Papua New Guinean couple also lived on the island as caretakers and were responsible for basic maintenance and the operation of generators that provided electricity for some hours of the day. The ability to secure ongoing funding for the costs associated with this maintenance was an ongoing concern for the elderly women between 2006 and 2010, after which time they settled more permanently on Mornington Island.

During a group interview in 2008, the women contrasted the time that they spent on Mornington with that on Bentinck Island, and were unequivocal in their dislike for life on Mornington Island, describing it as 'awful'. One of the women noted that on Mornington Island: 'As we getting older, it's getting hard, can't get decent feed, get cursed at when our children are drunk and it very hard to go out fishing' (see similar sentiments in Evans 1998: 50). This was contrasted to their feelings of relief each time they returned to Bentinck Island:

> Woman A: Sometimes when we stay away too long on Mornington, we get home sick.
>
> Woman B: Homesick. We try to get back [to Bentinck Island].
>
> Woman C: When we first get on the beach we sit on the floor [ground]. Or just sit and cry [with relief].

A contributor to the women's financial capacity to continue travelling to and from Bentinck Island was their successful participation in the art economy on Mornington Island (Evans 2008: 59). Some of the women are among Queensland and Australia's most celebrated contemporary Indigenous artists (Martin-Chew 2009: 95).

The situation on Bentinck Island, and to a lesser extent the use of outstations on Mornington Island, typified the description by Kowal (2010: 181) of outstations in Aboriginal Australia as: 'classical Indigeneity; small family groups occupying their traditional country and subsisting on the products of hunting with limited contact with the outside world except as a market for their artistic production'. Life on Bentinck Island, perhaps more than other outstations in the region, was idealized in the way that Ben Smith (2005: 228) described for central Cape York, where 'tradition resonates'. For this reason, outstations take on particular resonance in cultural politics and hold as much conceptual appeal for Aboriginal people as they do for the government and non-government organizations that strive to support them. The romanticization of outstation living 'stressed Aboriginality' and facilitated a sense of autonomy 'both figuratively and actually from White people' (McKnight 2002: 169). This autonomy was not only from Whitefellas, who ran the majority of services in Gununa, but also from other Mornington Islanders.

At the same time, however, it seemed that it was the separation from the Aboriginal social world that posed the biggest barrier to the realization of continuous outstation living. During a trip to Bentinck Island with the Wellesley Islands Rangers in 2007, each of the men (including the Kaiadilt Rangers) eagerly anticipated news from Mornington Island, not just from their families but emanating from the broader social milieu. To be away from the intensity of this milieu, and therefore from the embeddedness of social interaction, posed challenges for Mornington Islanders and their senses of identity as based in their relationships with others.

Conclusion

In this chapter I have explored the ways in which Mornington Islanders are connected to country across the Wellesley Islands. I have examined systems of country identification and the changes to these systems over time. Country was the site of affective connections for Mornington Islanders, linking them to kin, both alive and deceased, and with bodies of practice and knowledge. The density of these relations and their production contributed to the intense politicking of country between generations of Mornington Islanders. While descent played a major role in the establishment of authority and legitimacy in claims to country, there were other factors that mediated the success of these claims. These factors included the capacity of the individual to assert their own authority in country. At the same time, however, these connections are interpolated by the practicalities and logistics associated with remote contemporary life. Access to four-wheel-drive vehicles and boats, for example, determined the frequency with which people could go 'out bush' and visit their country. These visits had an iterative effect on ownership, as they demonstrated Aboriginal people's connections to country to others.

At times, country was the focus of intense tensions and disputes, specifically about the ways in which it was being used, and the authority of particular individuals to make decisions about that use. The aspirational statements of wanting to 'return to country' exemplified the fact that country had strong associations for most Mornington Islanders, even if the practical realization of these statements remained elusive. Ultimately, country was seen as connected to forms of Aboriginal identity deeply rooted in 'culture'.

Notes

1. McKnight (1999: 77) refers to *dulmada* broadly as 'members of a particular Country', although his subsequent listing of *dulmada*s for each country suggests that his usage was the same as Memmott's (1979), that is, a more exclusive group being the most senior owners of country.
2. Kmart is the name of a major affordable department store in Australia.
3. Lardil territory also included offshore islands Sydney Island and Wallaby Island, and further offshore islands Rocky, Manowar and the Bountiful Islands.
4. In total, fifty-five Aboriginal people provided witness affidavits for the Wellesley Islands Sea Claim, including residents of Mornington Island, Doomadgee and Burketown. Approximately twenty-seven of the total fifty-five were deceased in September 2017.
5. While 'estate' was the term of choice for McKnight and Memmott, in the Mornington Island vernacular estates were referred to as 'a country'. This is not to be confused with Mornington Islanders referring to 'country' as a means of identifying the particular social and cultural ways in which Aboriginal people relate to land.
6. When Memmott (1979) and McKnight (1999: 77,81) were undertaking fieldwork on Mornington Island during the 1960s and 1970s, individuals in a shared descent group to land affectionately referred to one another as 'countrymen', though the term is now in less common use.
7. I use this term advisedly. There is no evidence to suggest that the Lardil and Yangkaal systems for the descent of rights to country were what Sutton (1998: 54) critiqued as 'fluid', 'indeterminate' or 'ambiguous'.
8. The relocation of mainland children to Mornington Island, especially during the 1920s and 1930s, and the movement of young Lardil, Yangkaal and Kaiadilt women as domestics on the mainland during the 1950s and 1960s were key periods from which children of ambiguous paternity were born. In the more recent period, the mobility of young Mornington Islanders for boarding school, health care and drinking also contributed to the number of children with a parent from outside the known Mornington Island social realm (see also Dalley 2018).
9. It is unclear whether the practice of considering women as *dulmarra dangka* occurred pre-contact for the Kaiadilt (c.1947); however, Evans (1998: 64) does refer to elderly women who were alive during the 1990s (i.e. born in pre-contact times) in this way. The linguist Dr Erich Round, at the University of Queensland (pers. comm., 2011) also reports a senior Kaiadilt woman born in 1935 (i.e. pre-contact) as referring to herself as *dulmarra dangka* for a particular country in 2005.
10. Mornington Islanders and anthropologists have commented previously that many of those involved in the Wellesley Sea Claim could be described as 'forceful individuals', obviously a deciding factor in their selection to give evidence as part of the native title proceedings.
11. Anderson (1988: 518) suggested that it was important that leaders also 'take responsibility for those decisions'. On Mornington Island, however, there seldom seemed to be instances where leaders were actually judged on the efficacy of their decisions or on the realization of particular outcomes. Thus, the emphasis was very much in demonstrating leadership qualities during decision-making (consultation) processes.
12. These people were aged in their sixties, seventies and eighties during the 2000s.
13. The position of 'Mainlanders', that is, people of mainland descent born on the mainland and raised in the dormitory on Mornington Island, is complex. There has been some suggestion that Mainlanders of this generation were not associated to the same

degree as others with legitimate cultural identities (Memmott 1979: 295). The high degree of intermarriage between groups and the number of mixed-descent children, however, has made it difficult to assess the continuing relevance of 'Mainlanders' as an identity category.

14. Where available, I have used the spellings for these places in McKnight (1999) to allow for easy comparison.
15. These people were aged in their twenties, thirties and forties in the 2000s.
16. In other parts of Australia, these skills assisted a person's ability to generate and maintain a cache of resources for outstations (Austin-Broos 2003; B. R. Smith 2005: 229). However, as I will explore later in this chapter, use of outstations in the Wellesley Islands was insufficient for them to be associated with sources of power in this way.
17. There were other, more formal examples of 'asking permission', especially to visit a country without the presence of a person designated as an 'owner'.
18. When I used the fires of others to cook fish or boil water on trips out bush, I was often told, perhaps only partly in jest, 'you wanna [should] learn how to make ya own fire!'
19. Mothers often complained that when they attempted to hold birthday parties for their children, others who lived nearby would come and 'hang round looking for feed'. Invariably, the hangers-on would be invited into the party and fed, even becoming involved in party games and similar. In her justification for allowing uninvited children into her daughter's fourth birthday party, one mother explained that she did not refuse because of the guilt she felt at denying them food, or in her words, 'they make you [feel] sorry [for them]'.
20. Fish, crabs, oysters and other bush foods such as bush blackberries, which were in a different category, however, to the two *most* prized foods among Wellesley Islanders: dugong and turtle, historically the subject of particular rules relating to butchering and distribution (Dalley 2012). That dugong and turtle were so highly prized also demonstrates that the degree to which an item is prized is not always proportionate to its availability, as dugong and turtle meat were relatively available during my period of fieldwork.
21. McKnight (1999: 212) recorded that *markirii* applied to any land food, including plants. During my period of research the emphasis was very much on greasy or fatty foods, particularly meat and especially 'tin meat', but also butter, cheese, chocolate and so on.
22. McKnight (1999: 213) suggested that the opposite was also true, i.e. to enter freshwater with seafood could cause *markirii*. While this may have been true in the past, I never experienced the observance of this aspect of *markirii* during my fieldwork.
23. Feathers and stones had particular ritual associations among Mornington Islanders.
24. As I discuss later in this chapter, the number of four-wheel-drive vehicles owned by Mornington Islanders dramatically increased in the year following the closure of the Pub.
25. Between 2007 and 2011, to barge a single vehicle one-way from Karumba (on the mainland) to Mornington Island cost between AUD 750.00 and AUD 1,100.
26. The *Criminal Offence Victims Act (Qld) 1995* was repealed in late 2009. Since 2009, however, victims of crime have been able to pursue civil restitution from an offender.
27. When the legislation was first implemented, it did not include provisions for rape or sexually based assaults. However, some judges began to award damages in these instances, and eventually the law was amended (Forster 1999).
28. This was supported by the observation that during visits to Mornington Island in 2008 and 2009, I was unable to recognize the majority of cars on the Island. Anecdot-

ally, the fact that Mornington Islanders were able to do this reflected the retention of revenue formerly spent at the Pub, but possibly also that there was additionally a slight increase in the numbers of people engaged in full-time work.
29. This was one of the only occasions on which I received a request for written information about Mornington Island (although I was asked countless times for photographs). In general terms, this was probably because the knowledge of older living Aboriginal people was seen as more authoritative than written accounts by anthropologists, but also because levels of literacy were low.
30. Memmott (1998: 130–31) recorded twenty-five outstations around the North Wellesley Islands in 1998.
31. In 2007, an Aboriginal man and the anthropologist Paul Memmott conducted a smoking ceremony at an outstation on the western side of Mornington Island which had formerly been 'owned' and occupied by a deceased man. The ceremony allowed an archaeology PhD student to use the outstation as a base for his fieldwork in 2007. During the period the student paid rent to the family of the deceased man.

Conclusion

Many Returns

Over the last fifteen years I have returned to Mornington Island regularly, drawn back to the treasured friendships that I formed there but also to the place itself and its consuming sociality. As the duration of my connection to Mornington Island extends, it sometimes feels as though time moves differently. Some aspects of life stay the same while others change dramatically as I dip in and out of social life. Often familiar faces greet me and I probe my memory for a name, sometimes managing to pluck one from the recesses, careful not to confuse siblings, cousins and relatives. I cannot believe how different people look. I look different too. Young girls are now mothers; many of the older people that I met early on, as well as some younger people, have died. Others have moved to the mainland, seeking out different lives. There is a generation of Mornington Islanders whose names I am yet to learn. New hospital staff, school teachers and police arrive and depart, each attempting to engage the community, while replicating many of the programs and projects that came before them. At a distance, news stories about Mornington portray the extremes: 'good news' stories of emerging artists or sporting heroes alongside 'bad news' stories of alcohol-fuelled violence and the novelty of crocodile sightings in a region not known for its apex predators. These narratives give an exoticized sense of the spectacular but say little of the daily life that ultimately characterizes the place.

In this book, I have tried to give a sense of what propels Mornington Islanders, and in doing so provide an account of contemporary Aboriginal life in remote Australia. The portrayal intentionally leaves unanswered the perennial question asked about remote Aboriginal communities in Australia: 'what now?' Instead, this book becomes part of a dialogue about how such communities endure, and how their marginality is continuously reproduced. Throughout the book, I have purposefully engaged with the works of my anthropological forebear David McKnight, whose pronouncements were so stark as to leave little hope for anything but the most diminished of future lives for Mornington Islanders. In my own distress at the situations of loss, trauma, and poverty, I have often found myself wondering how persistence is possible under such conditions. It has been both the longevity and intimate nature of my experiences with Mornington Islanders that have enabled me to appreciate the permanence of this gritty persistence. Yet appreciating this endurance also requires the shedding of expectations. In their place is an imagination for the continuation of a kind of life unbounded by simplistic notions of progress or the kinds of improvement in life circumstances that so consume the broader society. This approach is attentive to history and colonialism but does not foretell the end of these societies, at least not in the way that McKnight did, or to see them as steeped in a kind of unrecoverable misery. What emerge then are mundane accounts of of getting by and making do, the results of the particular form of polity that I have detailed in this book.

As a framing for contemporary life in remote Australia, I remain convinced that anthropology, with its attention to fine-grained ethnography, has something to offer in detailing contexts of this kind. In particular, I highlight the value of characterizing the complexity of a social whole and the ways in which various components of daily life inform one another. This distinguishes this work from those developed over shorter time frames or studies which isolate particular aspects of life.

It is the case that many Aboriginal people now argue against ethnographic accounts, suspicious of the role that anthropologists play in writing about Aboriginal lives, or seeking to limit the purview to constrained aspects of identity. Increasingly, Aboriginal people are positioned as the only ones legitimately able to comment on issues impacting their communities. In Australia at least, the stickiness of these representational debates means that the empirical underpinnings of anthropology are unpalatable in the political present. In many ways, this path opens up the way for less nuanced, more politically reified constructions of Aboriginal identity that evade critical analysis, as the anthropologically trained Aboriginal academic Marcia Langton argued in a 2009 lecture. According to Langton, essentialism is not only foundational to Aboriginal activism, but actually emerged out of the 'strategic use of vast knowledge of the Aboriginal past contained within the anthropological literature'. At stake in the reproduction of such essentialism, Langton argues, is the future of Aboriginal lives and what she describes as: 'the bad habit of proceeding with programs and policies in Indigenous affairs in the absence of sound evidence' (Langton 2011: 2). In highlighting the limitations of political ideology, Langton's (ibid.: 20) speech critiqued anthropologists, not for their research but for their 'relative absence' in 'critical public debates'.

Anthropologists are still sometimes drawn into public debates in particular ways, asked to use their knowledge and structural agency to advance the causes of those that they work with. However, the necessity of anthropology's role in informing public policy is increasingly difficult to realize, and not only because of representational politics. Policy is a product of governments who are driven by the salability of ideas to the broader public, which, if current trajectories are indicative, entails increasingly punitive modes of engaging with marginal people and communities. Punitive policies do not seek evidence as justification because their rationale comes from ideology, not from a considered, evaluative approach to outcomes.

Endurance and the Perpetuation of Social Intensity

A particular aspect of this study has been the emphasis on the remote and contained nature of the community in its island setting. While across much of Australia, including remote mainland communities, movement and travel is part of an expectation generated by widespread motor-vehicle ownership, island life presents an altogether more contained and particularized sense of spatiality. Arising out of this spatial containment, and constituting it, is intensity in social relations among Aboriginal people, where virtually everyone is considered to be kin. On Mornington Island the reproduction of these relationships absorbed and contained the Aboriginal residents, and the desire to remain connected to known persons significantly limited the porousness of the local sociality. A specific outcome of this intensity was the difficulty with which people moved between different locales, but more specifically in interacting with those from outside known interpersonal spheres.

It is this tension, between remaining in situ or becoming integrated as part of the broader society, which concerns a great deal of policy-making and political discussion about Aboriginal people in the current era. Understanding this sense of direction for policymaking in Aboriginal affairs gives pause to reflect on the colonial processes and history of policymaking during the twentieth century. In many ways, the legacy of these processes was that they acted to affirm rather than disentangle the intensity of Mornington Islanders' connections to one another. The devastating paternalism of the dormitory system, and the Presbyterian mission's restriction and control of the travel of Aboriginal people, ensured that the local population of Aboriginal people remained on the Island. The coalescing of Kaiadilt and mainland Aboriginal people and gradual integration with Lardil and Yangkaal people has resulted in what I have referred to by the shorthand 'Mornington Islander' identities. What this emphasizes is that the formation of local subjectivities is and will continue to be both intense and internally reproducing. It is with some irony that policymakers more broadly now contemplate ways to leverage remote-living people away from these settings by attempting to transform what Peterson (2010: 249) has described as 'everyday practices, values and beliefs'.

While Mornington Islanders have mostly lived apart from the broader society, they have been heavily implicated in it and their lives continue to be impacted by the decisions of government. Nevertheless, the alchemy of policy remains unrealized, at least not in the ways that are hoped for and anticipated. Policies loudly touted by government to bring change create alarm when first announced, scepticism when introduced, and are continually refashioned, some creating long-term detrimental impacts and others being eroded until they become ineffectual. The slow but continuous creep of new policy implementation gives the sense that the status quo is being maintained. When the public's interest shifts from one locus of concern to another, such as to education instead of health or welfare over housing, policies that were once controversial become something akin to cobwebs, intermittently and quietly brushed away, only to be rebuilt anew in another shape by another government. As the policy churn continues, so too does the public's interest in Aboriginal affairs.

What Now?

Public interest in remote Indigenous communities in Australia was probably greatest when the Australian Government mounted its Emergency Intervention into communities in the Northern Territory in 2007. More than ten years later, the interest of the media and of the voting public has largely moved on. New State and Federal Governments every four years pose, and then set out to solve, new problems in relation to Aboriginal people. The cyclical nature of the political landscape and its gaze enables a kind of forgetting, where memory not only of the settler past but also of more recent policy explorations is expunged. Yet for Indigenous Australians, maintaining visibility is vital to the potency of their claim to the care and concern of the settler state.

The current form of this visibility is one in which an analysis of the failures of social policy is eschewed to make way for a national conversation about forms of constitutional recognition and state-based treaty agreements, arguably the predilection of a different Indigenous populace to those in remote Australia. Of particular focus now are various kinds of recognition, including, for example, embedding recognition of Indigenous Australians within the Constitution. In 2017, the Australian Referendum Council began consultation with Indigenous people around Australia about this process, culminating in a meeting at Yulara in Central Australia and the production of a statement written by a collective of 250 Aboriginal and Torres Strait Islander delegates, including well-known Indigenous leaders. The document that emerged, the *Uluru Statement from the Heart*, refers to the rates of Indigenous incarceration and the numbers of children in care and youth in detention centres, and calls for an Indigenous voice to be enshrined in the Australian Constitution. In calling for 'structural reform', the Statement asserts that such a voice could be the basis of a new conversation between Indigenous people and the Government about policies made for and about Indigenous Australians.

Alongside conversations about constitutional recognition, some state governments are undertaking consultations about the possibility of entering into treaties with Indigenous residents. Responding to a widely held perception that such agreements have benefitted Indigenous peoples in New Zealand and Canada, Indigenous people in Australia seek out agreements with the aspiration that they will restructure their relations with the state and non-Aboriginal people more broadly. What material resources might be made available and how treaties would explicitly address the issue of sovereignty remains unclear, but the involvement of Indigenous people in policy formation has already emerged as a central issue requiring further discussion.

In has been the elaboration of the everyday that has characterized this book, where sometimes messy and chaotic ways of being are nonetheless underpinned by a pervasive attentiveness to social forms. It is the gritty persistence of Mornington Islanders which propels them forward. It seems evident that part of this endurance may involve substantial leakages away from what at any point can be thought of as the core, or the establishment of more permanent and substantial spatial and conceptual peripheries. Departures from the cultural forms of old do not necessarily entail change solely equated with loss, or, as Mc-

Knight (2002: 6) would have it, that Mornington Islanders will become 'bereft of a social identity'. What this does mean is that people, culture and lives will continue to move forward in ways that are not yet imagined. These flows will invariably create tensions of push and pull that will redefine what it means to be Aboriginal in remote Australia. Of utmost importance is that Mornington Islanders can continue to ask 'what now?'

Appendix

Residential Survey 2010

In February 2010, I undertook a census of all Aboriginal houses on Mornington Island using two interviews with two Aboriginal women. The data collected were the names of all of the house residents and the relationships between each of the residents. The identification of house residents was aided by an aerial photograph of the town overlain with the house number system used by the local council.

The first participant was a woman aged in her late twenties who had lived in a number of parts of the town over her lifetime. The woman was particularly knowledgeable about the residences of her Kaiadilt and Mainland Aboriginal family, particularly at the bottom (north-east) end of the town. The second interviewee was a woman also aged in her late twenties who had lived in the same area of town for the majority of her lifetime. The women were interviewed alone and on separate days. At the conclusion of the second interview, I conducted a joint interview with both women, working through discrepancies or gaps which had arisen in their accounting of residences. In such instances, the women deferred to one another if they believed that the other's information was more likely to be correct.

A summary of the recorded information is provided here.

Basic Demographics

The total number of houses identified as being part of the social housing system (known in local parlance as 'Council housing') and being occupied at the time of the interviews was 180, with a total of 886 residents.

Summary of Data

- 33.0 per cent (n=59) of houses were occupied by three or more generations of the same family.

- 39.4 per cent (n=71) of houses were occupied by two generations of the same family.

- 23.3 per cent (n=42) of houses were comprised solely of a nuclear family, i.e. mother, father and their biological or socially adopted children.

- 1.0 per cent (n=19) of the houses were sole occupancy.

- 0.6 per cent (n=11) of houses had ten or more residents.

- There was an average of 4.92 residents per house.

Discussion of Results

The census did not include houses where only Whitefellas lived, such as housing occupied by employees of the Queensland Police Service, Education Queensland, Queensland Health or those of Mornington Shire Council staff. However, houses where an Aboriginal woman lived with a Whitefella were numerated in the same way as other houses and the Whitefella partner was included in the count. There were seventeen of these Whitefellas.

It is likely that the count of 886 is an undernumeration of the population, partly as a result of the high degree of mobility. The Queensland Government Department of Communities (2010b: 45) estimated that Mornington Island had a population of 1,103 as of 30 June 2009. There is a section of the community, particularly men and women aged between 15 and 25 years, who are highly mobile both within Gununa town and off the island. As a result of their high mobility, these individuals, especially those without children, are often not associated with one particular residence.

In addition, the Aged Persons Hostel (APH) was not included in the census as it represents an atypical residence. In 2010, the APH had approximately seven full-time Aboriginal residents. Similarly, the six usual residents of Bentinck Island were not numerated as part of the survey, although they often spent a significant portion of their time on Mornington Island during the wet season and for important community events such as funerals. On these visits, the women often stayed with one of their daughters.

References

Altman, J. 2006. *In Search of an Outstations Policy for Indigenous Australians.* Centre for Aboriginal Economic Policy Research Working Paper 34. Canberra: Australian National University.

Altman, J. and M. Hinkson (eds). 2007. *Coercive Reconciliation: Stabilise, Normalise, Exit Aboriginal Australia.* North Carlton, Victoria: Arena Publications Association.

———. 2010. *Culture Crisis: Anthropology and Politics in Aboriginal Australia.* Sydney: University of New South Wales Press.

Andersen, J. 2010. 'Woman Faces Isa Murder Charge'. *Townsville Bulletin.* 7 August 2010: 9.

Anderson, C. 1988. 'All Bosses Are Not Created Equal'. *Anthropological Forum* 5(4): 507–23.

Australian Broadcasting Corporation. 2008. 'Police Criticised for Searching under 14's Bags for Grog' [online]. *Australian Broadcasting Corporation News.* 1 February 2008. Available from: https://www.abc.net.au/news/2008-02-01/police-criticised-for-searching-under-14s-bags-for/1030186 [accessed 21 April 2020].

Australian Bureau of Meteorology. 2010. *Monthly Mean Maximum Temperature: Mornington Island* [online]. Available from: http://www.bom.gov.au/jsp/ncc/cdio/weatherData/av?p_nccObsCode=36&p_display_type=dataFile&p_startYear=&p_c=&p_stn_num=029039 [accessed 25 October 2010].

Australian Bureau of Statistics [ABS]. 2006. *Basic Community Profile (BCP) – Gununa (L) (Urban Centre/Locality)* [online]. Canberra: Australian Bureau of Statistics.

———. 2010. *Remoteness Structure* [online] Canberra: Australian Bureau of Statistics. Available from: http://www.abs.gov.au/websitedbs/D3310114.nsf/home/remoteness+structure [accessed 5 November 2011].

———. 2011. *Basic Community Profile (BCP) – Gununa (L) (Urban Centre/Locality)* [online]. Canberra: Australian Bureau of Statistics.

———. 2016. *General Community Profile – Mornington (S) (LGA35250)* [online]. Canberra: Australian Bureau of Statistics.

Australian Government. 2020. *Office of the Registrar of Indigenous Corporations* [online]. Available from: https://www.oric.gov.au [accessed 17 April 2020].

Austin-Broos, D. 2003. 'Places, Practices, and Things: The Articulation of Arrernte Kinship with Welfare and Work'. *American Ethnologist* 30(1): 118–35.

———. 2009. *Arrernte Present, Arrernte Past: Invasion, Violence, and Imagination in Indigenous Central Australia*. Chicago: University of Chicago Press.

———. 2010. 'Quarantining Violence: How Anthropology Does It', in J. Altman and M. Hinkson (eds), *Culture Crisis: Anthropology and Politics in Aboriginal Australia*. Sydney: University of New South Wales Press, pp. 136–49.

———. 2011. *A Different Inequality: The Politics of Debate about Remote Aboriginal Australia*. Crows Nest, New South Wales: Allen & Unwin.

Babidge, S. 2010. *Aboriginal Family and the State: The Conditions of History*. Surrey, England: Ashgate.

Bain, M.S. 1972. 'Alcohol Use and Traditional Social Control in Aboriginal Society', in B.S. Hetzel, M. Dobbin, L. Lippmann and E. Eggleston (eds), *Better Health for Aborigines? Report of a National Seminar at Monash University*. St Lucia: University of Queensland Press, pp. 42–52.

Batty, P. 2005. 'Private Politics, Public Strategies: White Advisers and Their Aboriginal Subjects'. *Oceania* 75(3): 209–21.

Beckett, J. 1964. 'Aborigines, Alcohol and Assimilation', in M. Reay (ed.), *Aborigines Now: New Perspectives in the Study of Aboriginal Communities*. Sydney: Angus & Robertson pp. 32–47.

Bentinck, P. 1999. Affidavit of Pluto Bentinck, 2 August 1999. Filed in the Federal Court, Queensland District Registry, QG 207 of 1997, The Lardil, Kaiadilt, Yangkaal and Gangalidda Peoples and State of Queensland and Ors.

Bessire, L. 2014. *Behold the Black Caiman: A Chronicle of Ayoreo Life*. Chicago: University of Chicago Press.

Birdsall, C. 1988. 'All One Family', in I. Keen (ed.), *Being Black in 'Settled' Australia*. Canberra: Aboriginal Studies Press for the Australian Institute of Aboriginal Studies, pp. 137–58.

Birrell, B. and J. Hirst. 2002. 'Aboriginal Couples at the 2001 Census'. *People and Place* 10(3): 23–28.

Blake, T. 1998. 'Historical Report Wellesley Islands Sea Claim'. Unpublished report prepared for the Carpentaria Land Council and the Claimants.

Bradley, J., with Yanyuwa families. 2010. *Singing Saltwater Country: Journey to the Songlines of Carpentaria*. Crows Nest, New South Wales: Allen & Unwin.

Brady, M. 1988. *Where the Beer Truck Stopped: Drinking in a Northern Australian Town*. Research Report for the Drug and Alcohol Bureau, Northern Territory Department of Health. Canberra: Australian National University North Australia Research Unit.

———. 1990. 'Indigenous and Government Attempts to Control Alcohol Use among Australian Aborigines'. *Contemporary Drug Problems* 17(2): 195–220.

———. 1992. 'Ethnography and Understandings of Aboriginal Drinking'. *The Journal of Drug Issues* 22(3): 699–712.

———. 2007. 'Out from the Shadow of Prohibition', in J. Altman and M. Hinkson (eds), *Coercive Reconciliation: Stabilise, Normalise, Exit Aboriginal Australia*. North Carlton, Victoria: Arena Publications Association, pp. 185–94.

Brady, M. and K. Palmer. 1984. *Alcohol in the Outback: Two Studies of Drinking*. Canberra: Australian National University North Australia Research Unit.
Brigg, M., P. Memmott, P. Venables and B. Zondag. 2018. 'Gununa Peacemaking: Informalism, Cultural Difference and Contemporary Indigenous Conflict Management'. *Social & Legal Studies* 27(3): 345–66.
Brine, J. 1980. 'After Cyclone Ted on Mornington Island: The Accumulation of Physical and Social Impacts on a Remote Australian Aboriginal Community'. *Disasters* 4(1): 3–10.
Brown, T. 2005. *Trolling for Sharks: Adventures of a Teacher in a Remote Aboriginal Community*. Southport, Queensland: Keeaira Press.
Bushlight. 2005. *Case Study 10: Birri Williams* [online]. December 2005. Available from: https://cfat.org.au/bushlight-archive [accessed 21 April 2020].
———. 2006a. *Case Study 15: Gunun Woonun* [online]. March 2006. Available from: https://cfat.org.au/bushlight-archive [accessed 21 April 2020].
———. 2006b. *Case Study 18: Gunbah* [online]. June 2006. Available from: https://cfat.org.au/bushlight-archive [accessed 21 April 2020].
Cairns Post. 2007 'Island Death'. *The Cairns Post*, 7 May 2007: 9.
Carruthers, R.D. 2000. Affidavit of Robert David Carruthers. Lardil, Kaiadilt, Yangkaal and Gangalidda Peoples v State of Queensland & Ors [1997]. Federal Court of Australia QG207, volume 3, Federal Court of Australia, Queensland District Registry, Brisbane, pp. 410–15.
Carsten, J. 2011. 'Substance and Relationality: Blood in Contexts'. *Annual Review of Anthropology* 40: 19–35.
Cawte, J. 1972. *Cruel, Poor and Brutal Nations: The Assessment of Mental Health of an Australian Aboriginal Community by Short-Stay Psychiatric Field Team Methods*. Honolulu: University Press of Hawaii.
Channells, G. 2000. Affidavit of Graeme Channells. Lardil, Kaiadilt, Yangkaal and Gangalidda Peoples v State of Queensland & Ors, [1997] Federal Court of Australia QG207, volume 3, Federal Court of Australia, Queensland District Registry, Brisbane, pp. 404–9.
Christen, K. 2009. *Aboriginal Business: Alliances in a Remote Australian Town*. Canberra: Aboriginal Studies Press.
Clough, A.R., S.A Margolis, A. Miller, A. Shakeshaft, C.M. Doran, R. McDermott, R. Sanson-Fisher, S. Towle, D. Martin, V. Ypinazar, J.A. Robertson, M.S. Fitts, K. Bird, B. Honorato and C. West. 2016. 'Alcohol Control Policies in Indigenous Communities: A Qualitative Study of the Perceptions of Their Effectiveness among Service Providers and Community Leaders in Queensland (Australia)'. *International Journal of Drug Policy* 36: 67–75.
———. 2017. 'Alcohol Management Plans in Aboriginal and Torres Strait Islander (Indigenous) Australian Communities in Queensland: Community Residents Have Experienced Favourable Impacts but Also Suffered Unfavourable Ones' *BMC Public Health* 17(55): 1–14.
Collmann, J. 1979. 'Social Order and the Exchange of Liquor: A Theory of Drinking among Australian Aborigines'. *Journal of Anthropological Research* 35(2): 208–24.

Commonwealth of Australia (C.A. Blanchard, Chairman). 1987. *Return to Country: The Aboriginal Homelands Movement in Australia*. Report of the House of Representatives Standing Committee on Aboriginal Affairs, March 1987. Canberra: Australian Government Publishing Service.

Corbert, L. 2010. 'Bondi Vet: Island-Style'. *North-West Star*. 6 January 2010.

Council of Australian Governments [COAG]. 2010. *Working Together Towards A Better Future on Mornington Island: Local Implementation Plan 2010–2014*. Canberra: Commonwealth of Australia.

Cowlishaw, G. 1988. *Black, White or Brindle: Race in Rural Australia*. Cambridge: Cambridge University Press.

———. 2003. 'Euphemism, Banality, Propaganda: Anthropology, Public Debate and Indigenous Communities'. *Australian Aboriginal Studies* 1: 2–18.

———. 2004. *Blackfellas, Whitefellas and the Hidden Injuries of Race*. Carlton, Victoria: Blackwell Publishing.

———. 2010. 'Helping Anthropologists, Still', in J. Altman and M. Hinkson (eds), *Culture Crisis: Anthropology and Politics in Aboriginal Australia*. Sydney: University of New South Wales Press, pp. 45–60.

Crime and Misconduct Commission (CMC). 2009. *Restoring Order: Crime Prevention, Policing and Local Justice in Queensland's Indigenous Communities*. Brisbane: Crime and Misconduct Commission.

Dalley, C. 2012. 'Dugong Hunting as Changing Practice: Economic Engagement and an Aboriginal Ranger Program on Mornington Island, Southern Gulf of Carpentaria', in N. Fijn (ed.), *Indigenous Participation in Australian Economies II*. Canberra: Australian National University Press, pp. 261–86.

———. 2018. 'Mobility and the Education of Indigenous Youth Away from Remote Home Communities', in D. Austin-Broos and F. Merlan (eds), *People and Change in Indigenous Australia*. Honolulu: University of Hawai'i Press, pp. 130–45.

Dalley, C. and P. Memmott. 2010. 'Domains and the Intercultural: Understanding Aboriginal and Missionary Engagement at the Mornington Island Mission, Gulf of Carpentaria, Australia from 1914 to 1942'. *International Journal of Historical Archaeology* 14(1): 112–35.

Dalley, C. and R. Martin. 2015. 'Dichotomous Identities? Indigenous and Non-Indigenous People and the Intercultural in Australia'. *The Australian Journal of Anthropology* 26: 1–23.

Department of Education, Employment and Workplace Relations (Australian Government). 2014. *Improving School Enrolment and Attendance through Welfare Reform Measure (SEAM) Trial (2009 – 2012): Final Evaluation Report* [online]. Available from: https://www.niaa.gov.au/sites/default/files/publications/Improving_School_Enrolment_Attendance_through_Welfare_Reform_Measure_trial.pdf [accessed 21 April 2020].

Dominy, M.D. 2001. *Calling the Station Home: Place and Identity in New Zealand's High Country*. Lanham: Rowman & Littlefield Publishers.

Education Queensland. 2009. *Gallery – Teacher Housing* [online]. Available from: http://mornislass.eq.edu.au/wcms/index.php?option=com_phoca

gallery&view=category&id=5:teacher-housing&Itemid=54 [accessed 6 October 2011].

Eickelkamp, U. 2011. 'Changing Selves in Remote Australia? Observations on Aboriginal Family Life, Childhood and "Modernization"'. *Anthropological Forum* 21(2): 131–51.

Electoral Commission Queensland. 2010. *2008 Mornington Shire – Councillor Election – Mornington Shire Council* [online]. Available from: https://results.ecq.qld.gov.au/elections/local/lg2008%5CMorningtonShireCouncil/results/Councillor/district1.html [accessed 17 April 2020].

———. 2012. *2012 Mornington Shire – Mayoral Election – Election Summary* [online]. Available from: http://results.ecq.qld.gov.au/elections/local/LG2012/MorningtonShireCouncil/results/mayoral/summary.html [accessed 8 January 2018].

———. 2016. *2016 Mornington Shire – Mayoral Election – Election Summary* [online]. Available from: http://results.ecq.qld.gov.au/elections/local/LG2016/MorningtonShireCouncil/results/mayoral/summary.html [accessed 8 January 2018].

Elks, S. 2011. 'Family of Speared Man Claim Police Not Coping'. *The Australian*, 4 October 2011: 7.

Evans, N. 1992. *Kaiadilt Dictionary and Thesaurus: A Vocabulary of the Language of the Bentinck Islanders, North-West Queensland*. Melbourne: University of Melbourne, Department of Linguistics and Language Studies.

———. 1998. 'Wellesley Islands Sea Claim: The Kaiadilt Group'. Expert report to the Carpentaria Land Council.

———. 2008. 'People of the Strand: The Kaiadilt of Bentinck Island', in N. Evans, L. Martin-Chew and P. Memmott (eds), *The Heart of Everything: The Art and Artists of Mornington & Bentinck Islands*. Fitzroy, Victoria: McCullock & McCullock Art Books, pp. 54–59.

———. 2016. 'Born, Signed and Named: Naming, Country and Social Change among the Bentinck Islanders', in J.C. Verstraete and D. Hafner (eds), *Land and Language in Cape York Peninsula and the Gulf Country*. Amsterdam: John Benjamin Publishing Company, pp. 305–35.

Ferguson, J. 2015. *Give a Man a Fish: Reflections on the New Politics of Distribution*. Durham, NC: Duke University Press.

Finlayson, J. 1991. 'Don't Depend on Me: Autonomy and Dependence in an Aboriginal Community in North Queensland', unpublished PhD thesis. Australian National University, Canberra.

———. 1997. 'Aboriginal Tradition and Native Title Representative Bodies', in D.E. Smith and J. Finlayson (eds), *Fighting Over Country: Anthropological Perspectives*. Research Monograph 12. Canberra: Centre for Aboriginal Economic Policy Research, Australian National University, pp. 141–52.

Flatley, C. 2011. 'Daughter to Pay Mum $21k for Stab Attack'. *Australian Associated Press* General News, 24 February 2011.

Forster, C. 1999. 'Old Scheme, Old Stories: Chong V Chong'. *Indigenous Law Bulletin* 4(25): 13–15.

Francis, C. 2010. 'Indigenous Economic Development: Challenges for Traditional Owners, Council and Community'. Paper presented at the Aligning Indigenous Land Management and Economic Development Conference, 24 March 2010, Darwin.

Geertz, C. 1988. *Works and Lives: The Anthropologist as Author*. Stanford: Stanford University Press.

Gerritsen, R. 1982. 'Blackfellas and Whitefellas: The Politics of Service Delivery to Remote Aboriginal Communities in the Katherine Region', in P. Loveday (ed.), *Service Delivery to Remote Communities*. Darwin: The Australian National University North Australia Research Unit, pp. 16–31.

Grant, A. 2008. 'Bentinck Bathroom Blitz'. *Our Place* 33: 7–9. Alice Springs: Centre for Appropriate Technology.

Grant, K. 2011. 'Island Business' [video recording]. *Living Black*, Special Broadcasting Service. 22 May 2011. Available from: https://www.sbs.com.au/ondemand/video/11769923675 [accessed 17 April 2020].

Hall, R.I. 1986. *Missionary Pioneer: Insights from Diaries, Letters and Articles by Robert Hall, Mornington Island, North Queensland, Australia*. Wiahola, Otago, New Zealand: Self-published.

Healy, S. 2013. 'Killer Handed 10 Year Term'. *Townsville Bulletin*, 6 December 2013: 17.

Hearn, T. 2007. *Mornington Island Leaders* [video recording online]. Rockhampton, Queensland: BushTV. 30 June 2011. Available from: http://www.youtube.com/watch?v=-umIVOtk7wk [accessed 10 September 2011].

Hinkson, M. 2009. 'The Trouble with Suffering'. Review of P. Sutton (2009), *The Politics of Suffering: Indigenous Australia and the End of the Liberal Consensus* (Melbourne: Melbourne University Press), *Arena Magazine* 101: 54–57.

Holcombe, S. 2005. 'Luritja Management of the State'. *Oceania* 75(3): 222–33.

Huffer, V. (with collaboration from Elsie Roughsey and other women from Mornington Island). 1980. *The Sweetness of the Fig: Aboriginal Women in Transition*. Sydney: New South Wales University Press.

Hunt, J. 2008. 'Between a Rock and a Hard Place: Self-Determination, Mainstreaming and Indigenous Community Governance', in J. Hunt, D. Smith, S. Garling and W. Sanders (eds), *Contested Governance: Culture, Power and Institutions in Indigenous Australia*. Canberra: Centre for Aboriginal Economic Policy Research, Australian National University, pp. 27–54.

Jacob, K. 1999. Affidavit of Kenneth Jacob, 4 August 1999. Filed in the Federal Court, Queensland District Registry, QG 207 of 1997, The Lardil, Kaiadilt, Yangkaal and Gangalidda Peoples and State of Queensland & Ors.

Johnson, R. 2010. 'Teen "Bled to Death" Woman's Injuries Detailed as Man Faces Murder Charge'. *Townsville Bulletin*. 20 July 2010: 6.

Jordan, M.E. 2005. *Balanda: My Year in Arnhem Land*. Crows Nest, New South Wales: Allen & Unwin.

Kapferer, B. 1995. 'Bureaucratic Erasure, Identity, Resistance and Violence – Aborigines and a Discourse of Autonomy in a North Queensland Town', in D. Miller (ed.), *Worlds Apart: Modernity Through the Prism of the Local*. London: Routledge, pp. 69–90.

Karvelas, P. 2011. 'Parents' Welfare Cut as Kids Miss School'. *The Australian*, 21 May 2011: 9.
Koch, T. 2003. 'A Sobering Assessment of Gulf Life'. *The Courier Mail*, 13 December 2003: 27.
———. 2007. 'Teenagers Bashed into Having "Bonus Babies"'. *The Australian*, 13 October 2007: 13.
———. 2008. 'Danger to Nurses Ignored'. *The Australian*, 24 March 2008: 4
Kowal, E. 2008. 'The Politics of the Gap: Indigenous Australians, Liberal Multiculturalism, and the End of the Self-Determination Era'. *American Anthropologist* 110(3): 338–48.
———. 2010. 'Is Culture the Problem or the Solution? Outstation Health and the Politics of Remoteness', in J. Altman and M. Hinkson (eds), *Culture Crisis: Anthropology and Politics in Aboriginal Australia*. Sydney: University of New South Wales Press, pp. 179–94.
———. 2011. 'The Stigma of White Privilege'. *Cultural Studies* 25(3): 313–33.
———. 2015a. *Trapped in the Gap: Doing Good in Indigenous Australia*. Oxford and New York: Berghahn Books.
———. 2015b. 'Time, Indigeneity and White Anti-Racism in Australia'. *The Australian Journal of Anthropology* 26: 94–111.
Langton, M. 1993. 'Rum, Seduction and Death: "Aboriginality" and Alcohol'. *Oceania* 63(3): 195–206.
———. 2010. 'The Shock of the New: A Postcolonial Dilemma for Australianist Anthropology', in J. Altman and M. Hinkson (eds), *Culture Crisis: Anthropology and Politics in Aboriginal Australia*. Sydney: University of New South Wales Press, pp. 91–115.
———. 2011. 'Anthropology, Politics and the Changing World of Aboriginal Australians'. *Anthropological Forum* 21(1): 1–22.
Lattas, A. and B. Morris. 2010. 'The Politics of Suffering and the Politics of Anthropology', in J. Altman and M. Hinkson (eds), *Culture Crisis: Anthropology and Politics in Aboriginal Australia*. Sydney: University of New South Wales Press, pp. 61–87.
Lea, T. 2008. *Bureaucrats & Bleeding Hearts: Indigenous Health in Northern Australia*. Sydney: University of New South Wales Press.
———. 2012. 'When Looking for Anarchy, Look to the State: Fantasies of Regulation in Forcing Disorder Within the Australian Indigenous Estate'. *Critique of Anthropology* 32(2): 109–24.
Lex, B.W. 1986. 'Measurement of Alcohol Consumption in Fieldwork Settings'. *Medical Anthropology Quarterly* 17(4): 95–98.
Local Government Reform Commission (LGRC, State of Queensland). 2007. *Report of the Local Government Reform Commission* [online]. Brisbane: State of Queensland. Available from: https://www.parliament.qld.gov.au/documents/TableOffice/TabledPapers/2007/TP1809-2007.pdf [accessed 20 April 2020].
Loogatha, N. 1999. Affidavit of Netta Loogatha, August 1999. Filed in the Federal Court, Queensland District Registry, QG 207 of 1997, The Lardil, Kaiadilt, Yangkaal and Gangalidda Peoples and State of Queensland & Ors.

Loogatha, O. 1999. Affidavit of Olive Loogatha, August 1999. Filed in the Federal Court, Queensland District Registry, QG 207 of 1997, The Lardil, Kaiadilt, Yangkaal and Gangalidda Peoples and State of Queensland & Ors.

Maat, M. 2007. 'Discussion Regarding Issues and Proposed Projects on Mornington Island'. Unpublished report summary of projects as of 2007, written by the Federal Government Coordinator of services on Mornington Island.

———. 2008. 'Current Situation'. Unpublished memo written by the Federal Government Coordinator of services on Mornington Island.

MacAndrew, C. and R.B. Edgerton. 1969. *Drunken Comportment: A Social Explanation*. Melbourne: Thomas Nelson.

Macdonald, G. 2000. 'Economies and Personhood: Demand Sharing among the Wiradjuri of New South Wales', in G.W. Wenzel, G. Hovelsrud-Broda and N. Kishigami (eds), *The Social Economy of Sharing: Resource Allocation and Modern Hunter-Gatherers*. Osaka: National Museum of Ethnology, pp. 87–112.

———. 2013. 'Autonomous Selves in a Bureaucratised World: Challenges for Mardu and Wiradjuri'. *Anthropological Forum* 23(4): 399–413.

Mahood, K. 2012. 'Kartiya Are Like Toyotas: White Workers on Australia's Cultural Frontier'. *Griffith Review* 36: 43–59.

Martin, D.F. 1993. 'Autonomy and Relatedness: An Ethnography of Wik People of Aurukun, Western Cape York Peninsula', unpublished PhD thesis. Canberra: Australian National University.

———. 1996. 'Case Studies'. Unpublished consultancy report to the Review of the Aboriginal Councils and Associations Act, Australian Institute of Aboriginal and Torres Strait Islander Studies and Centre for Aboriginal Economic Policy Research, Australian National University, Canberra.

———. 1998. 'Deal of the Century? A Case Study from the Pasminco Century Project'. *Indigenous Law Bulletin* 4(11): 4–7, 18.

———. 2003. *Rethinking the Design of Indigenous Organisations: The Need for Strategic Engagement*. Discussion Paper No. 248. Canberra: Centre for Aboriginal Economic Policy Research, Australian National University.

———. 2005. 'Governance, Cultural Appropriateness and Accountability', in D. Austin-Broos and G. Macdonald (eds), *Culture, Economy and Governance in Aboriginal Australia: Proceedings of a Workshop Held at the University of Sydney, 30 November to 1 December 2004*. Sydney: University of Sydney Press, pp. 187–99.

———. 2009. *Domesticating Violence: Homicide among Remote-Dwelling Australian Aboriginal People*. AIC Reports, Research and Public Policy Series 104. Canberra: Australian Government, Australian Institute of Criminology.

Martin, D., F. Morphy, W. Sanders and J. Taylor (eds). 2002. *Making Sense of the Census: Observations of the 2001 Enumeration in Remote Aboriginal Australia*. Canberra: Australian National University Press.

Martin, D. and J. Finlayson. 1996. *Linking Accountability and Self-Determination in Aboriginal Organisations*. Discussion Paper No. 116. Canberra: Centre for Aboriginal Economic Policy Research, Australian National University.

Martin, D. and M. Brady. 2004. 'Human Rights, Drinking Rights? Alcohol Policy and Indigenous Australians'. *The Lancet* 364 (October 2–October 8): 1282–83.

Martin, R. 2015. 'Reconfiguring Indigeneity in the Mainland Gulf Country: Mimicry, Mimesis, and the Colonial Exchange of Difference'. *The Australian Journal of Anthropology* 26: 55–73.

Martin-Chew, L. 2009. 'Paula Paul'. *Australian Aboriginal Art* 2: 86–95.

McDonnell, S. and D.F. Martin. 2002. *Indigenous Community Stores in the 'Frontier Economy': Some Competition and Consumer Issues*. Discussion Paper No. 234. Canberra: Centre for Aboriginal Economic Policy Research, Australian National University.

McKnight, D. 1999. *People, Countries, and the Rainbow Serpent*, Oxford: Oxford University Press.

———. 2002. *From Hunting to Drinking: The Devastating Effects of Alcohol on an Australian Aboriginal Community*. London: Routledge.

———. 2004. *Going the Whiteman's Way: Kinship and Marriage among Australian Aborigines*. Aldershot: Ashgate.

———. 2005. *Of Marriage, Violence and Sorcery: The Quest for Power in Northern Queensland*. Aldershot: Ashgate.

Meade, K. 1999. 'Lost Pilot Ran from Weather'. *The Australian*, 26 November 1999: 3.

Memmott, P. 1979. 'Lardil Properties of Place: An Ethnological Study of Man-Environment Relations', unpublished PhD thesis. St Lucia: School of Architecture, University of Queensland.

———. 1982. 'Rainbows, Story Places, and *Malkri* Sickness in the North Wellesley Islands'. *Oceania* 53: 163–182.

———. 1998. 'Expert Witness Report on the Lardil and Yangkaal Sea Claim in the Wellesley Islands'. Unpublished report prepared for Andrew Chalk and Associates on behalf of the Carpentaria Land Council and the Claimants.

———. 2008. 'Origins of the Contemporary Art Movement', in N. Evans, L. Martin-Chew and P. Memmott (eds), *The Heart of Everything: The Art and Artists of Mornington & Bentinck Islands*. Fitzroy, Victoria: McCullock & McCullock Art Books, pp. 16–30.

Memmott, P. and R. Horsman. 1991. *A Changing Culture: The Lardil Aborigines of Mornington Island, Student Text*. Wentworth Falls, New South Wales: Social Science Press.

Memmott, P., R. Stacey, C. Chambers and C. Keys. 2001. *Violence in Indigenous Communities: Full Report*. Report to Crime Prevention Branch, Attorney-General's Department. Canberra: Attorney-General's Department, Commonwealth of Australia.

Memmott, P., S. Long and L. Thomson. 2006. *Indigenous Mobility in Rural and Remote Australia*. Report for the Australian Housing and Urban Research Institute, Queensland Research Centre, Brisbane.

Memmott, P. and D. Trigger. 1998. 'Marine Tenure in the Wellesley Islands Region, Gulf of Carpentaria', in N. Peterson and B. Rigsby (eds), *Customary*

Marine Tenure in Australia. Oceania Monograph 48. Sydney: University of Sydney Press, pp. 109–124.

Merlan, F. 1998. *Caging the Rainbow: Place, Politics and Agency in a North Australian Town*. Honolulu: University of Hawaii Press.

———. 2009. 'Black Sorrows Left, Right and Centre'. Review of P. Sutton (2009), *The Politics of Suffering: Indigenous Australia and the End of the Liberal Consensus* (Melbourne: Melbourne University Press), *The Canberra Times*, 15 August 2009: 17.

Michael, P. 2008. 'Mt Isa Mayor Wants Curfew for Drunk Kids Who Run Wild'. *The Courier Mail*, 26 November 2008: 3.

———. 2010. 'Tragedy of Girl's Death – Homebrew Mix Blamed'. *The Courier Mail*, 15 July 2010: 10.

Mirndiyan Gununa Aboriginal Corporation. 2009. *Mirndiyan Gununa Aboriginal Corporation Annual Report 2009* [online]. Gununa, Queensland: Mirndiyan Gununa Aboriginal Corporation. Available from: http://www.morningtonisland.com.au/index.php?id=403 [accessed 21 September 2011].

———. 2010. *Mirndiyan Gununa Aboriginal Corporation Financial Statement 2010* [online]. Gununa, Queensland: Mirndiyan Gununa Aboriginal Corporation. Available from: https://register.oric.gov.au/document.aspx?concernID=100217 [accessed 21 September 2011].

Morgan, G. 2006. 'Aboriginal Politics, Self-Determination and the Rhetoric of Community'. *Dialogue* 25(1): 19–29.

Morphy, F. 2006. 'Lost in Translation? Remote Indigenous Households and Definitions of the Family'. *Family Matters* 73: 23–31.

———. 2007. 'Uncontained Subjects: "Population" and "Household" in Remote Aboriginal Australia'. *Journal of Population Research* 24(2): 163–84.

Morris, B. 1989. *Domesticating Resistance: The Dhan-Gadi Aborigines and the Australian State*. Oxford: Berg.

Morton, J. 1998. 'Essentially Black, Essentially Australian, Essentially Opposed: Australian Anthropology and Its Uses of Aboriginal Identity', in J. Wassmann (ed.), *Pacific Answers to Western Hegemony: Cultural Practices of Identity Construction*. Oxford: Berg, pp. 355–85.

Moss, R. 2010. *The Hard Light of Day: An Artist's Story of Friendships in Arrernte Country*. St Lucia: University of Queensland Press.

Musharbash, Y. 2000. 'The Yuendumu Community Case Study', in D. Smith (ed.), *Indigenous Families and the Welfare System: Two Community Case Studies*. Research Monograph 17. Canberra: Centre for Aboriginal Economic Policy Research, Australian National University, pp. 53–82.

———. 2001. *Indigenous Families and the Welfare System: The Yuendumu Community Case Study, Stage Two*. Discussion Paper 217. Canberra: Centre for Aboriginal Economic Policy Research, Australian National University.

———. 2007. 'Boredom, Time, and Modernity: An Example from Aboriginal Australia'. *American Anthropologist* 109(2): 307–17.

———. 2008. *Yuendumu Everyday: Contemporary Life in Remote Aboriginal Australia*. Canberra: Aboriginal Studies Press.

———. 2010. '"Only Whitefella Take That Road": Culture Seen through the Intervention at Yuendumu', in J. Altman and M. Hinkson (eds), *Culture Crisis: Anthropology and Politics in Aboriginal Australia*. Sydney: University of New South Wales Press, pp. 212–25.

Myers, F.R. 1986. *Pintupi Country, Pintupi Self: Sentiment, Place and Politics among Western Desert Aborigines*. Canberra: Australian Institute of Aboriginal Studies.

———. 1988. 'Burning the Truck and Holding the Country: Property, Time, and the Negotiation of Identity among Pintupi Aborigines', in T. Ingold, D. Riches and J. Woodburn (eds), *Hunters and Gatherers (Vol. 2): Property, Power and Ideology*. Oxford: Berg, pp. 52–74.

National Native Title Tribunal [NNTT]. 2004. 'Determination of Native Title: The Lardil Peoples v State of Queensland [2004] FCA 298'. *Native Title Hot Spots* 9: 19–29.

———. 2005. *Native Title Determination: QC96/2 – QG207/97 (Wellesley Islands Sea Claim)*. Map created by Geospatial Services, National Native Title Tribunal. Canberra: NNTT.

———. 2009. 'Determination Recognised Gulf Islanders' Home'. *Talking Native Title* 30: 1, 5.

Nelson, N.F. 1936. 'Record of Visits to Mission Stations 1936', unpublished manuscript and original photographs held at Fryer Library, University of Queensland, Brisbane.

Ngakulmungan Kangka Leman (Language Projects Steering Committee). 1997. *Lardil Dictionary*. Gununa, Queensland: Mornington Shire Council.

O'Connor, R. 1984. 'Alcohol and Contingent Drunkenness in Central Australia'. *Australian Journal of Social Issues* 19(3): 173–83.

Ortner, S. 1995. 'Resistance and the Problem of Ethnographic Refusal'. *Comparative Studies in Society and History* 37(1): 173–93.

Paradies, Y. 2006. 'Beyond Black and White: Essentialism, Hybridity and Indigeneity'. *Journal of Sociology* 42(4): 355–67.

Pearson, N. 2000. *Our Right to Take Responsibility*. Cairns, Queensland: Noel Pearson and Associates.

———. 2009. *Up From the Mission: Selected Writings*. Melbourne: Black Inc.

Peters-Little, F. 2000. *The Community Game: Aboriginal Self-Definition at the Local Level*. Australian Institute of Aboriginal and Torres Strait Islander Studies (AIATSIS) Research Discussion Paper 10. Canberra: AIATSIS.

Peterson, N. 1991. 'Cash, Commoditization and Authenticity: When Do Aboriginal People Stop Being Hunter-Gatherers'. *Senri Ethnological Studies* 30: 67–90.

———. 1993. 'Demand Sharing: Reciprocity and the Pressure for Generosity among Foragers'. *American Anthropologist* 95(4): 860–74.

———. 2010. 'Other People's Lives: Secular Assimilation, Culture and Ungovernability', in J. Altman and M. Hinkson (eds), *Culture Crisis: Anthropology and Politics in Aboriginal Australia*. Sydney: University of New South Wales Press, pp. 248–58.

———. 2013. 'On the Persistence of Sharing: Personhood, Asymmetrical Reciprocity, and Demand Sharing in the Indigenous Australian Domestic Moral Economy'. *The Australian Journal of Anthropology* 24: 166–76.

Peterson, N. and J. Taylor. 2002. 'Aboriginal Intermarriage and Economic Status in Western New South Wales'. *People and Place* 10(4): 11–16.

———. 2003. 'The Modernizing of the Indigenous Domestic Moral Economy: Kinship, Accumulation and Household Composition'. *The Asia Pacific Journal of Anthropology* 4(1&2): 105–122.

Povinelli, E. 2011. *Economies of Abandonment: Social Belonging and Endurance in Late Liberalism*. Durham, NC: Duke University Press.

Probyn-Rapsey, F. 2007. 'Paternalism and Complicity: Or How Not to Atone for the "Sins of the Father"'. *Australian Literary Studies* 23(1): 92–103.

Purtill, T. 2017. *The Dystopia in the Desert: The Silent Culture of Australia's Remotest Aboriginal Communities*. Kew, Victoria: Australian Scholarly Publishing.

Queensland Government. 2003. 'Mornington Shire Alcohol Restrictions from Tomorrow' [online]. Ministerial Media Statement by Minister Judy Spence. Published 27 November 2003. Available from: http://www.cabinet.qld.gov.au/MMS/StatementDisplaySingle.aspx?id=22737 [accessed 20 January 2011].

———. 2008a. 'Alcohol Related Violence Forces Closure of Mornington Island Hotel' [online]. Ministerial Media Statement by Premier Anna Bligh. Published 24 January 2008. Available from: http://www.cabinet.qld.gov.au/MMS/StatementDisplaySingle.aspx?id=56214 [accessed 20 January 2011].

———. 2008b. *Alcohol Reforms Fact Sheet 2: Summary of Legislative Changes* [online]. Available from: http://www.atsip.qld.gov.au/government/programs-initiatives/alcohol-reforms/about-alcohol-reforms/ [accessed 20 January 2011].

Queensland Government Department of Aboriginal and Torres Strait Islander Partnerships. 2014. *Annual Bulletin for Queensland's Discrete Indigenous Communities 2014–2015* [online]. Available from: https://www.datsip.qld.gov.au/resources/datsima/publications/key-reports/annual-bulletin-jul13-jun14.pdf [accessed 23 January 2018].

———. 2015. *Annual Bulletin for Queensland's Discrete Indigenous Communities 2014–2015* [online]. Available from: https://www.datsip.qld.gov.au/resources/datsima/publications/key-reports/annual-bulletin-2014-15.pdf [accessed 23 January 2018].

———. 2016. *Annual Bulletin for Queensland's Discrete Indigenous Communities 2015–2016* [online]. Available from: https://www.datsip.qld.gov.au/resources/datsima/publications/key-reports/2015-16-annual-bulletin-qld-discrete-indigenous-communities.pdf [accessed 23 January 2018].

Queensland Government Department of Communities. 2010a. *Quarterly Report on Key Indicators in Queensland's Discrete Indigenous Communities January–March 2010* [online]. Published 2 September 2010. Available from: http://www.atsip.qld.gov.au/government/programs-initiatives/partnerships/quarterly-reports/report-jan-march-2010.asp [accessed 18 November 2010].

———. 2010b. *History of Stolen Wages and Savings in Queensland* [online]. Available from: http://www.atsip.qld.gov.au/people/claims-entitlements/wages-savings/wages-history/ [accessed 20 February 2011].

———. 2011. *Mid-Year Update on Key Indicators in Queensland's Discrete Indigenous Communities: Incorporating the October–December 2010 Quarter* [online]. Published 24 August 2011. Available from: http://www.communities.qld.gov.au/atsis/government/programs-and-initiatives/reports/mid-year-report-incorporating-the-october-december-quarter [accessed 10 October 2011].

Queensland Government Department of Housing. 2008. *Mornington Island Shire Council Housing Improvement Plan, 25 June 2008*. Brisbane: Queensland Department of Housing, Brisbane/Mornington Island: Mornington Island Shire Council.

Redmond, A. 2005. 'Strange Relatives: Mutualities and Dependencies between Aborigines and Pastoralists in the Northern Kimberley'. *Oceania* 75(3): 234–46.

———. 2006. 'Further on up the Road: Community Trucks and the Moving Settlement', in T. Lea, E Kowal and G. Cowlishaw (eds), *Moving Anthropology: Critical Indigenous Studies*. Darwin: Charles Darwin University Press, pp. 95–114.

Reed, L. 2005. 'Out of Place'. Review of M.E. Jordan (2005), *Balanda, My Year in Arnhem Land* (Crows Nest, New South Wales: Allen & Unwin), *Australian Women's Book Review* 17(2): 4–7.

Room, R. 1984. 'Alcohol and Ethnography: A Case of Problem Deflation?' [with comments by M. Agar, J. Beckett, L.A. Bennett, S. Casswell, D.B. Heath, J. Leland, J.E. Ley, W. Madsen, M. Marshall, J. Woskalewicz, J.C. Negrete, M.B. Rodin, L. Sackett, M. Sargent, D. Stru and J.O. Waddell]. *Current Anthropology* 25(2): 169–91.

Rosendahl, D., S. Ulm, H. Tonkins and P. Memmott. 2014. 'Late Holocene Changes in Shellfishing Behaviors from the Gulf of Carpentaria, Northern Australia'. *Journal of Island & Coastal Archaeology* 9: 253–67.

Roughsey, D. (Goobalathaldin). 1971. *Moon and Rainbow: The Autobiography of an Aboriginal*. Brisbane: Rigby Books.

Roughsey, L. 1999. Affidavit of Lindsay Roughsey, 7 August 1999. Filed in the Federal Court, Queensland District Registry, QG 207 of 1997, The Lardil, Kaiadilt, Yangkaal and Gangalidda Peoples and State of Queensland & Ors.

Rowling, T. 2010. 'Business Plan'. *North-West Star*, 7 January 2010.

Rowse, T. 1990. 'Are We All Blow-Ins?' Review of G. Cowlishaw (1988), *Black, White or Brindle: Race in Rural Australia* (Cambridge: Cambridge University Press), *Oceania* 61(2): 185–91.

———. 1992. *Remote Possibilities: The Aboriginal Domain and the Administrative Imagination*. Darwin: North Australia Research Unit, Australian National University.

———. 1993. 'The Relevance of Ethnographic Understandings to Aboriginal Anti-Grog Initiatives'. *Drug and Alcohol Review* 12: 393–99.

———. 2000. 'Culturally Appropriate Indigenous Accountability'. *American Behavioural Scientist* 43(9): 1514–32.

———. 2005. 'The Indigenous Sector', in D. Austin-Broos and G. MacDonald (eds), *Culture, Economy and Governance in Aboriginal Australia: Proceedings of a Workshop Held at the University of Sydney, 30 November to 1 December 2004*. Sydney: University of Sydney Press, pp. 213–29.

———. 2007. 'Family and Nation: The Indigenous/Non-Indigenous Relationship', in J. Jupp and J. Nieuwenhuysen (eds), *Social Cohesion in Australia*. Cambridge: Cambridge University Press, pp. 90–102.

———. 2011. 'Debating the Categories of Remote Indigenous Sociality'. *Alternatives: Global, Local, Political* 36(1): 39–47.

———. 2012. *Rethinking Social Justice: From 'Peoples' to 'Populations'*. Canberra: Aboriginal Studies Press.

Sackett, L. 1977. 'Liquor and the Law: Wiluna, Western Australia', in R.M. Berndt (ed.), *Aborigines and Change: Australia in the '70s*. Social Anthropology Series No. 11. Canberra: Australian Institute of Aboriginal Studies, pp. 90–99.

———. 1988. 'Resisting Arrests: Drinking, Development and Discipline in a Desert Context'. *Social Analysis* 24: 66–77.

———. 2004. Review of D. McKnight (2002), *From Hunting to Drinking: The Devastating Effects of Alcohol on an Australian Aboriginal Community* (London: Routledge), *The Australian Journal of Anthropology* 15(2): 240–41.

Saggers, S. and D. Gray. 1998. *Dealing with Alcohol: Indigenous Usage in Australia, New Zealand and Canada*. Cambridge: Cambridge University Press.

Sanders, W. 2002. *Towards an Indigenous Order of Australian Government: Rethinking Self-Determination as Indigenous Affairs Policy*. Discussion Paper No. 230. Canberra: Centre for Aboriginal Economic Policy Research, Australian National University.

———. 2007. 'The Political Economy of Self-Government', in J. Altman and M. Hinkson (eds), *Coercive Reconciliation: Stabilize, Normalize, Exit Aboriginal Australia*. North Carlton, Victoria: Arena Publications Association, pp. 63–72.

Sansom, B. 1980. *The Camp at Wallaby Cross: Aboriginal Fringe Dwellers in Darwin*. Canberra: Australian Institute of Aboriginal Studies.

———. 1988. 'A Grammar of Exchange', in I. Keen (ed.), *Being Black in 'Settled' Australia*. Canberra: Aboriginal Studies Press for the Australian Institute of Aboriginal Studies, pp. 159–77.

Sewter, W. 1999. Affidavit of William Sewter, 6 August 1999. Filed in the Federal Court, Queensland District Registry, QG 207 of 1997, The Lardil, Kaiadilt, Yangkaal and Gangalidda Peoples and State of Queensland & Ors.

Sharp, L. 1935. 'Semi-Moieties in North-Western Queensland'. *Oceania* 6(2): 158–174.

Sharp, N. 2002. *Saltwater People: The Waves of Memory*. Crows Nest, New South Wales: Allen & Unwin.

Shaw, P. 2009. *Seven Seasons in Aurukun: My Unforgettable Time at a Remote Aboriginal School*. Crows Nest, New South Wales: Allen & Unwin.

Simpson, A. 2014. *Mohawk Interruptus: Political Life across the Borders of Settler States*. Durham, NC: Duke University Press.

Smith, B.R. 2003. 'Whither "Certainty"? Coexistence, Change and Land Rights in Northern Queensland'. *Anthropological Forum* 13(1): 27–48.

———. 2005. 'Culture, Change and the Ambiguous Resonance of Tradition in Central Cape York Peninsula', in L. Taylor, G.K. Ward, G. Henderson, R. Davis and L.A. Wallis (eds), *The Power of Knowledge and the Resonance of Tradition*. Canberra: Aboriginal Studies Press, pp. 223–35.

———. 2008. 'Still under the Act? Subjectivity and the State in Aboriginal North Queensland'. *Oceania* 78(2): 199–216.

Smith, D. 2005. 'Indigenous Families, Households and Governance', in D. Austin-Broos and G. MacDonald (eds), *Culture, Economy and Governance in Aboriginal Australia: Proceedings of a Workshop Held at the University of Sydney, 30 November to 1 December 2004*. Sydney: University of Sydney Press, pp. 175–87.

Smith, D. (ed.). 2000. *Indigenous Families and the Welfare System: Two Community Case Studies*. Research Monograph 17. Canberra: Centre for Aboriginal Economic Policy Research, Australian National University.

Strutton, A. 2009. '"Intervention Refugees": Mayor's Plea for Temporary Accommodation for the Isa'. *Townsville Bulletin*, 2 May 2009: 5.

Sullivan, P. 2011. *Belonging Together: Dealing with the Politics of Disenchantment in Australian Indigenous Policy*. Canberra: Aboriginal Studies Press.

Sutton, P. 1998. *Native Title and the Descent of Rights*. Perth: National Native Title Tribunal.

———. 2001a. 'The Politics of Suffering: Indigenous Policy in Australia since the 1970s'. *Anthropological Forum* 11(2): 125–73.

———. 2001b. *Kinds of Rights in Country: Recognising Customary Rights as Incidents of Native Title*. Occasional Paper Series No. 2. Perth: National Native Title Tribunal.

———. 2005. 'Rage, Reason and the Honourable Cause: A Reply to Cowlishaw'. *Australian Aboriginal Studies* 2: 35–42.

———. 2007. 'The Unwavering Eye: David McKnight's Ethnographic-Historical Legacy'. Review of D. McKnight (2004), *Going the Whiteman's Way: Kinship and Marriage among Australian Aborigines* (London: Routledge), *The Australian Journal of Anthropology* 18(2): 227–30.

———. 2009. *The Politics of Suffering: Indigenous Australians and the End of the Liberal Consensus*. Melbourne: Melbourne University Press.

Tamisari, F. 1998. 'Body, Vision and Movement: In the Footprints of the Ancestors'. *Oceania* 68: 249–70.

Tapim, F. 2010. 'Qld Mayor in Court on Fraud Charges' [online]. *Australian Broadcasting Corporation News*, Australian Broadcasting Corporation. 12 January 2010. Available from: https://www.abc.net.au/news/2010-01-12/qld-mayor-in-court-on-fraud-charges/1205498 [accessed 21 April 2020].

Tonkinson, M. 1994. 'Thinking in Colour', in D. Graham (ed.), *Being Whitefella*. Freemantle: Freemantle Arts Centre Press, pp. 162–76.

Toohey, P. 2009. 'Move over Mary Concepta, Bquinda's on the Scene'. *The Australian*, 16 May 2009: 3.

Townley, G.M. 2001. 'Missionaries, Mercenaries and Misfits: Service Relations in the Administration of Remote Aboriginal Communities in the Western Desert Region of Australia', unpublished PhD thesis. Perth: Department of Anthropology, University of Western Australia.

Townsville Bulletin. 2010. 'Police Believe Dead Teen Drank Home Brew'. *Townsville Bulletin*, 19 July 2010: 4.

———. 2011. 'Manslaughter Charge'. *Townsville Bulletin*, 9 June 2011: 7.

Trigger, D.S. 1986. 'Blackfellas and Whitefellas: The Concepts of Domain and Social Closure in the Analysis of Race-Relations'. *Mankind* 16(20): 99–117.

———. 1992. *Whitefella Comin': Aboriginal Responses to Colonialism in Northern Australia*. Sydney: Cambridge University Press.

———. 1997a. 'Land Rights and the Reproduction of Aboriginal Culture in Australia's Gulf Country'. *Social Analysis* 41(3): 84–106.

———. 1997b. 'Reflections on Century Mine: Preliminary Thoughts on the Politics of Indigenous Responses', in D.E. Smith and J. Finlayson (eds), *Fighting Over Country: Anthropological Perspectives*. Research Monograph 12. Canberra: Centre for Aboriginal Economic Policy Research, Australian National University, pp. 110–28.

———. 1998. 'Citizenship and Indigenous Responses to Mining in the Gulf Country', in N. Peterson and W. Sanders (eds), *Citizenship and Indigenous Australians: Changing Concepts and Possibilities*. Cambridge: Cambridge University Press, pp. 154–66.

———. 2005. 'Mining Projects in Remote Aboriginal Australia: Sites for the Articulation and Contesting of Economic and Cultural Futures', in D. Austin-Broos and G. MacDonald (eds), *Culture, Economy and Governance in Aboriginal Australia: Proceedings of a Workshop Held at the University of Sydney, 30 November to 1 December 2004*. Sydney: University of Sydney Press, pp. 41–62.

———. 2009. 'Whitefellas Hanging from the Learning Cliff'. Review of P. Shaw (2009), *Seven Seasons in Aurukun: My Unforgettable Time at a Remote Aboriginal School* (Crows Nest, New South Wales: Allen & Unwin) and Y. Musharbash (2008), *Yuendumu Everyday: Contemporary Life in Remote Aboriginal Australia* (Canberra: Aboriginal Studies Press), *Australian Literary Review*, 3 June 2009: 14.

———. 2011. 'Anthropology Pure and Profane: The Politics of Applied Research in Aboriginal Australia'. *Anthropological Forum* 21(3): 233–55.

Trigger, D. and R.J. Martin. 2016. 'Place, Indigeneity, and Identity in Australia's Gulf Country'. *American Anthropologist* 118(4): 824–37.

Turner, D.H. 2003. Review of D. McKnight (2002), *From Hunting to Drinking: The Devastating Effects of Alcohol on an Australian Aboriginal Community* (London: Routledge), *Australian Aboriginal Studies* 1: 81–83.

Vincent, E. 2017. *'Against Native Title': Conflict and Creativity in Outback Australia*. Canberra: Aboriginal Studies Press.

von Sturmer, J. 1984. 'The Different Domains', in *Aborigines and Uranium: Consolidated Report on the Social Impact of Uranium Mining on the Aborigines of the Northern Territory*. Canberra: Australian Institute of Aboriginal Studies, pp. 218–37.

Watson, T. 2011. 'Time to Address the Big Issue'. *North-West Star*, 23 March 2011.

Wenham, M. 2008. 'Health Accommodation Deemed Safe after Audit'. *The Courier Mail*, 27 May 2008: 8.

Wharton, G.S. 2000. *'Mission Time': A Guide to Queensland Presbyterian Church Records Relating to the Gulf Missions at Aurukun, Mapoon, Mornington Island, Weipa and Thursday Island Mission Agency 1891 to 1978*. Fortitude Valley, Brisbane: Presbyterian Church Press.

Wray, M. 2008. 'Island Sex Danger Ignored by Health'. *The Courier Mail*, 17 March 2008: 8.

Wright, A. 1997. *Grog War*. Broome: Magabala Books.

———. 2016. 'What Happens When You Tell Somebody Else's Story?' *Meanjin* 4: 58–76.

Yanagisako, S.J. 1979. 'Family and Household: The Analysis of Domestic Groups'. *Annual Review of Anthropology* 8: 161–205.

Yarrak, V. 2000. Affidavit of Valmae Yarrak, 1 August 2000. Filed in the Federal Court, Queensland District Registry, QG 207 of 1997, The Lardil, Kaiadilt, Yangkaal and Gangalidda Peoples and State of Queensland & Ors.

Index

Page numbers in italics refer to figures and tables.

A
alcohol: Alcohol Management Plan, 131–3; and drinking, 9–10, 128–31; homebrew, 149–50; and off-Island mobility, 152–5; sly grog, 149–52; and violence, 126–8, 145–7, 155–9. *See also* Pub, the
Altman, Jon, 197
anthropology. *See* ethnography
Appel Channel, 66, 136
Aurukun: mediators in, 181; and mining, 30; and missions, 50n2; and off-Island mobility, 153; and space, 132, 138
Austin-Broos, Diane, 94–5, 156, 192–3

B
Babidge, Sally, 93–4, 139, 163–9
beche-de-mer, 5, 26
Belcher, Reverend Douglas, 7, 88n13, 134
Bentinck Island: and Kaiadilt people, 7, 28, 140, 175–8; outstations on, 8–9, 196–201, *199*; and permission to enter, 194; and plane crash, 169; and story places, 189; and transport, 192
Birri Fishing Lodge, 68, 148–9
boats, 59, 151, 184, 190–3
boredom, 14
Borroloola, 98
Brady, Maggie, 129, 150

bureaucracy, 24–5, 43–4, 78
bureaucrats, 55, 57
Burketown: and sly grog, 151; and off-Island mobility, *153*

C
Cairns, 73, 87n8, 111–12, 151, 152–3
cannabis, 14, 150–1
cars, 125n12, 190–3, 204n28
Cawte, John, 8, 28
Century Lead and Zinc Mine, 45–6, 49, 111, *153*
Channells, Graeme, 31–2
children, *6*, *26*, 26–8, 202n8; childcare, 119–23; child support, 125n14; mixed race, 83–4; out bush, 186–8, *187*; Save the Children (NGO), 44–5; stolen ones, 103–5. *See also* descent (genealogy); family; kinship
Church, the. *See* missionaries; Mornington Island Mission
Closing the Gap, 11, 23, 39, 78
Community Development Employment Projects (CDEP), 9, 155
community engagement, 43. *See also* mediators
corporations, Aboriginal, 34–8
council. *See* Mornington Shire Council
country, 164–7, 202n5, 202n6, 202n7; and authority, 180–2; and *dulmada*s, 202n1, 202n9; and 'going bush', 184–9, *185*, *187*; and Moon, Cyril, 181, 182,

183; and outstations, 196–9, *199*; permission to access, 194–5, 203n17; and Pub groupings, 139–41; and story places, 187–9; and transport, 190–3. *See also* descent (genealogy); family; kinship; marriage; native title
Cowlishaw, Gillian, 17, 24; on racial boundaries, 71, 85; on Whitefellas, 54–5, 57
crisis, 2, 17, 19
cyclones, 8, 21n3, 29, 197
Cyclone Ted, 8

D

dispossession, 16, 27, 50
democracy, 32–3
descent (genealogy), 178–9, *179*; North Wellesley Islands, 170–5, *173–4*; South Wellesley Islands, 175–7, *177*
Doomadgee: and country, 165; and democracy, 32; and housing, 62; and hunting, 162n15; and kinship, 98; and off-Island mobility, *153*; and school attendance, 40–1; and Sea Claim, 202n4; and sly grog, 151; and Whitefellas, 72
dormitories, 5–7, 25, 28, 50, 202n13
Dreaming. *See* story places
dugong, 116–17, 151, 162n15, 187, 203n20
dulmadas, 171–2, 176, 180, 202n1
dulmarra dangka, 176, 202n9

E

economy: frontier economy, 47–8; and sharing, 90–2, 94–5, 116–19, 142–3; and small business, 45–9
education. *See* schools
Eickelkamp, Ute, 17–18
Elders, 43–4
employment, 13–14, 44–5, 125n13; bureaucrats, 55, 57; health workers, 66–7; teachers, 6, 40–1, 68, 75, 79
endurance, 2–3, 6, 18–19, 206

ethnography, 14–18, 206; and alcohol consumption, 130; of bureaucracy, 14; and endurance, 3–4; and family, 107; and violence, 156; and Whitefellas, 54
Evans, Nicholas, 8, 28, 175–6, 202n9

F

family, 89–95, 106–7; and childcare, 119–23; families of polity, 93; and household, 90–3; and housing, 107–16, *109–10*; and the Pub, 138–41; and sharing, 94–5, 116–19, 142–3, 146–7. *See also* children; descent (genealogy); kinship; marriage; Middle families
Finlayson, Julie, 91–2, 170
fighting. *See* violence
four-wheel-drives (trucks), 184, 190–2, 194, 203n24
From Hunting to Drinking, 9–10, 130–1, 161n1
funerals, 22–3, 34

G

Gabori, Sally, 37
gambling, 14, 62, 110; and alcohol, 129
Garawa, people, 27, 98
Geertz, Clifford, 16
gender, 120, 138, 175, 180
genealogy. *See* descent (genealogy)
Gerritsen, Rolf, 79–80
Gulf Communities Agreement, 45–6
Gulf of Carpentaria, 1, 9, 27
Gununa, 4–5; Birri Loge, 68; and housing, 8, 62; and marriage, 99; and Middle families, 90; and social life, 12; and Whitefellas, 66
Gununamanda Limited, 35, 48

H

Hall, Reverend Robert, 5, 88n13
health: and hospital compound, *63*, 63–4; workers, 66–7
Hinkson, Melinda, 156
homebrew, 133, 138–9, 146–52, 160

homelands. *See* outstations
household, 90–3
housing, 8–9, 29, 51n8, 87n2; and family, 107–16, *109–10*; and outstations, 196–8; and spatial divisions, 62–7, *63, 65*, 69–70, 82–3, 85; waitlist, 113
Huffer, Virginia, 8, 120
hunting, 14, 98, 116–17, 162n15, 200; *From Hunting to Drinking*, 9–10, 21n6, 130–1, 161n1

I

identity. *See* personhood
income, 13–4
Intervention, the. *See* Northern Territory Intervention

J

Justice Group, Junkuri Laka, 44, 73, 131–2, 161
Justice Project, Mornington Island Restorative, 41

K

Kaiadilt people, 7, 28–9; and country, 175–7
Kanba, 140, 182
Karumba, 7, 203n25
kinship, 89–91, 94, 95–9; and children, 103–5, 119–23; and *dulmadas*, 171–2, 180, 202n1, 202n9; and housing, 107–16, *109–10*; and Mainlanders, 27–2; and marriage, 99–103, *101–2*, 125n4; out bush, 185–7, *185, 187*; and the Pub, 139–41; and relational density, 13; and relational ontology, 18; and sharing, 94–5, 116–19, 142–3; and Whitefellas, 75–8. *See also* country; descent (genealogy); family
Kowal, Emma, 55–6, 58, 200

L

Langton, Marcia, 17, 206–7
Lardil people, 5, 29, 125n3, 181; and avoidance relationships, 186, and descent, 170–5, 178, 202n7; kin terms, 96–7; language, 181–2; and McKnight, David, 10; and Mainlanders, 27–8; and Mornington Island Mission, 25; and native title, 167, 202n3; and Roughsey, Dick, 7
Lea, Tess, 55, 57
Lelka Murrin Tavern. *See* Pub, the
localism, 34, 170

M

McCarthy, Reverend James, 28
McKnight, David, 3–5, 8–10, 21n4, 206; on Aboriginal groups, 28–9; on alcohol, 130–1; on democracy, 32; and gender, 120; on kinship, 13, 95, 99; on Whitefellas, 56, 80, 82
Mainlanders, 27–8, 178, 202n13
markirii, 188–9, 203n21, 203n22
marndagi. *See* Whitefellas
marriage, 95, 99–103, *101–2*; intermarriage, 12–3; and Mainlanders, 202n13; and stolen children, 104; straight, 97, 125n4; and Whitefellas, 79–80
Martin, David, 31, 46, 132
Martin, Richard, 77, 86
mediators, 41–2; and Aboriginal Police Liaison Officers, 42–3; Elders, 43–4, 77
Memmott, Paul, 29–30, 62, 134, 159
men: and descent, patrilineal, 171–5; and initiation, 97–8, 125n5; Men's Group, 35–6
Middle families, 90; and children, 121; and housing, 108–10, *109–10*, 115; and sharing, 116
mining, 30, 36, 169, 190; and Gulf Communities Agreement, 45–6, 49
Mirndiyan Gununa Aboriginal Corporation, 36–7, 44
missionaries, 28–9, 50n2, 56; Belcher, Reverend Douglas, 7, 88n13, 134; and family structure, 89, 91–2;

Hall, Reverend Robert, 5, 88n13; and kinship structure, 95, 98; McCarthy, Reverend James, 28; Wilson, Reverend Robert, 5, 27, 177. *See also* Mornington Island Mission
Mission Australia (NGO), 45
missions. *See* Mornington Island Mission
Moon, Cyril, 3, 116, 181, 183, *183*, 193
Mornington Island Mission, 5–8, *6*, 25–30, *26–7*, 50n1
Mornington Shire Council, 30–4; and alcohol, 39, 133; and housing, 51n8, 82–3, 113–15, 125n11; and outstation, 196; and small business, 49
Morphy, Frances, 93
Morton, John, 24
Mount Isa, 11–13, 134, 154
Musharbash, Yasmine, 65–6, 92
Myers, Fred, 90–1, 179–80, 184, 192

N
naming, 75–7, 124n1; of children, 122; and country, 139–40, 176–7; place names, 182
native title: and family, 93–4; *Native Title Act 1993 (Cwth)*, 35, 167; Sea Claim, 9, 167–71, *168*, 202n4, 202n10
NGOs. *See* non-government organizations
non-government organizations, 44–5
Normanton, 153–4
Northern Territory Intervention, 11, 38, 57
North Wellesley Islands, 170–5, *173–4*, 202n4
Nyinyilki, 8, 189, 198

O
Oak Tree Point, 140, 198
Ortner, Sherry, 15
outstations, 8–9, 196–201, *199*, 203n16, 204n30; and alcohol, 150–2; at Bentinck Island, 189
Oxfam (NGO), 45

P
Paradies, Yin, 60, 86
Pearson, Noel, 39–40
personhood, 4, 13, 18, 24, 165–6
Peterson, Nicolas: and sharing, 94–5, 142, 186; and Taylor, 81–2
planes, 151, 192
police: Aboriginal Police Liaison Officers, 42–3; community, 68; Police Service House, 65, *65*; raids, 151–2, 162n13, 162n16
Povinelli, Elizabeth, 2–3
protection, 5, 25–6. *See also* Mornington Island Mission
Pub, the, 132–3, 134–8, *135*, *137*; and 'barred off' patrons, 147–9, *148*; and family, 138–41; and sharing, 142–3; and violence, 145–7; and Whitefellas, 143–5. *See also* alcohol

Q
Queensland Government, 66; and Alcohol Management Plan, 126–8, 131–3, 156–7; and Mornington Shire Council, 30; Stolen Wages compensation, 191

R
Redmond, Anthony, 76–7, 83, 86
responsibility, 38–9, 144
rights, 31–3; and descent, 171–6, 202n7; and native title, 9, 167–9
Roughsey, Dick, 7
Round, Erich, 96, 202n9
Rowse, Tim, 23, 53, 84–5, 86

S
Sackett, Lee, 131, 146, 159, 160
Sanders, Will, 30, 56
Sansom, Basil, 74, 94, 129
Save the Children (NGO), 44–5
schools: attendance, 40–1, 127–8; boarding schools, 84, 112, 153, 202n8; and Save the Children, 45; teachers, *6*, 40–1, 68, 75, 79
Sea Claim, 9, 167–71, *168*, 202n4, 202n10

self-determination, 29–30, 34
sharing, 90–2, 94–5, 116–19, 142–3
Simpson, Audra, 15
sly grog, 133, 138–9, 146–52, 160
Smith, Ben, 168, 200
Smith, Diane, 90, 116
South Wellesley Islands, 175–7, 177
space: Birri Lodge, 68, 148–9; Gununa, hospital compound, 63, 63–4; Gununa, spatial divisions, 125n10; Police Service house, 65, 65; and spatial divisions, 61–7, 63, 65, 69–70, 85. *See also* Pub, the
state, 23–5, 50, 209. *See also* Queensland Government
story places, 13, 165–6, 181–2, 187–9
suffering: politics of, 16–18
Sutton, Peter: on alcohol, 130, 157; on family, 93, 107, 202n7; and politics of suffering, 16–17
Sweers Island: and Mornington Island Mission, 7, 28

T
teachers, 6, 40–1, 68, 75, 79
time: and Aboriginal culture, 11–12; Wild Time, 26
Tonkinson, Myrna, 58–9
transport, 12, 73, 190–3; boats, 151, 184, 190–3; cars, 125n12, 190–3, 204n28; planes, 151, 192; trucks (four-wheel-drives), 184, 190–2, 203n24
trauma, 7, 9
Trezise, Percy, 7
Trigger, David: on Doomadgee, 32, 62, 72, 165; on Mainlanders, 20n2, 26–7; on native title, 169–70
trucks (four-wheel drives), 184, 190–2, 203n24
turtle (sea turtle), 116–17, 151, 162, 203n20

U
Uluru Statement from the Heart, 209

V
Vincent, Eve, 169
violence: and alcohol, 126–8, 145–7, 155–9; colonial, 50; Cowlishaw on, 17

W
welfare, 13, 40, 48–9
Wellesley Islands. *See* North Wellesley Islands; South Wellesley Islands
Wellesley Islands Rangers, 183–4, 183, 189, 201
Wellesley Sea Claim. *See* Sea Claim
Whitefellas, 52–87; bureaucrats, 55, 57; in ethnography, 54–6; and friendship, 74–5; health workers, 66–7; and intermarriage, 79–84, 87n10; and kinship, 75–9; police, 65, 65, 68; and 'the Pub', 143–5; and racial segregation, 61–7, 63, 65, 69–70, 85; as social category, 58–60; and social interaction, 71–4, 86–7; teachers, 6, 40–1, 68, 75, 79; and unfamiliarity, 60–1
Wild Time, 26
Wilson, Reverend Robert, 5, 27, 177
women: and children, 103–5, 119–21, 125n14; and *dulmada*s, 180, 202n9; and employment, 125n13; and intermarriage, 79, 81, 83–4, 87n10; women's camps (*jilimi*), 92
work. *See* employment

Y
Yangkaal people, 27–29; and country, 170–5; and kin terms, 96–7; and Mornington Island Mission, 5, 25; and native title, 167
Yanyuwa, people, 27, 98

www.ingramcontent.com/pod-product-compliance
Lightning Source LLC
Chambersburg PA
CBHW051537020426
42333CB00016B/1963